PRIVATE EYE ANNUAL 2025

EDITED BY IAN HISLOP

Published in Great Britain by
Private Eye Productions Ltd
6 Carlisle Street, London W1D 3BN
www.private-eye.co.uk

© 2025 Pressdram Ltd
ISBN 978-1-901784-75-6
Designed by Bridget Tisdall
Printed and bound in Italy
by L.E.G.O. S.p.A

2 4 6 8 10 9 7 5 3 1

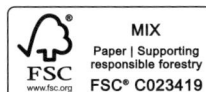

PRIVATE EYE ANNUAL 2025

EDITED BY IAN HISLOP

Before fat jabs

"So skinny – bet she's using tapeworm"

DONALD TRUMP

AN APOLOGY

IN COMMON with all other media organisations, we may in the past have given the impression that we thought Mr Trump was a sleazy, deranged, orange-faced man-baby who was a threat to democracy and who should be in jail rather than the White House.

We now realise, in the light of his return to supreme power, that he is in fact a political colossus, the voice of sanity, a champion of liberty, a model of probity and the saviour of the Western world. He is also slim, handsome and young.

We would like to apologise unreservedly for any confusion caused by our previous statements and thank President Trump for his kind invitation to give him 94 million pounds to attend his inauguration event.

This statement has not been fact-checked.

LABOUR IN COST-OF-GIVING CRISIS

STARMER LOOKS AHEAD

I don't lack vision

Thanks to the free glasses!

REEVES HAS BUDGET DILEMMA

There are difficult choices to make... Gucci, Versace or Prada

This is a gift – to the Tories!

RAYNER TAKES HOLIDAY

Give me a break!

Lord Alli already has

KEIR BANS CLOTHES FREEBIES

Oooh... suits U-turn, sir!

THAT ALL-PURPOSE FAMILY RIFT ARTICLE

IT'S terrible to see a father and son so estranged that they won't talk to each other. Our hearts go out to Harry/Brooklyn and poor old Charles/David. One has to say that it is the fault of the pushy American wife, Meghan/Nicola, that the young couple are in self-imposed exile in California/California. The rift was initially caused by strained relations with their posh mother-in-law, Queen Camilla/Queen Victoria, and has deteriorated to such an extent that the disaffected Brooklyn/Harry was not to be seen at his father's 50th birthday/Trooping the Colour. Suggestions that the son was too busy concentrating on his career as chef and photographer/author and litigant to even turn up at his father's palace/palace have been widely dismissed/widely dismissed. How sad for beloved national treasure Becks/Chazza, who surely deserves better treatment following his brilliant free kick against Greece/speech about the Book of Common Prayer. Honestly, when will this tragic feud/brilliantly entertaining free copy end? Hopefully never, so that we can go on attracting huge amounts of clicks in America, driving up our advertising and... (*cont. tomorrow/forever. Ed.*)

Alternative to X takes off

by Our Social Media Correspondent **Vi Rall**

IT HAS been reported that millions of people, tired of the toxic nature of X (formerly Twitter), following Elon Musk's takeover, have flocked to an alternative: Greysky.

"Greysky involves putting your phone away, putting on your big coat and going outside for a long winter walk, with your partner or the dog, if you have one," said a Greysky devotee.

"Rather than being screamed at by Incels and Nazis on X, you can have a lovely chat with that lady from No17 who walks her Jack Russell, and end up down the pub, complaining about how cold it's suddenly got."

Some recent converts to Greysky did issue a word of caution, saying do take a brolly, as it might rain.

"Don't mention her botched Brazilian butt lift"

TEA

The Rest Is Politics live at the O2

(Huge stadium filled with tens of thousands of centrist dads in Cotton Traders wax jackets, eating home-made gluten-free snacks and drinking tap water in Evian bottles)

(Two elderly hacks bound on stage to thunderous applause)

Alastair Campbell and Rory Stewart (*for it is they*): Helllooo O2!

Crowd: Whhhooop!

Rory: We're so glad you spent your time and money on coming out to see us here at the O2...

Alastair: So, just for you, we're going spend the entire evening repeating the same old stuff we give out on the podcast for free!

Rory: The stuff we've been saying every day for the past three years!

Crowd: Whooooooooooooooooop!

Alastair: Rory, would you like to start?

Rory: Yes! *(Clears throat)* I think Boris Johnson is a rotter and Brexit wasn't my doing!

Crowd: Whooooop!

Rory: How about you, Alastair?

Alastair: *(Clears throat)* I don't like Jeremy Corbyn and Iraq wasn't my fault!

(Crowd goes wild)

Both: Thank you and goodnight!

(Crowd start rushing for the exits to hopefully catch babysitter having sex on their Heal's sofa)

Worries for generation of lockdown babies

FEARS are growing that the so-called "Lockdown Babies", whose development was arrested during the Covid lockdowns, are now completely unable to function socially.

"They scream, they wet themselves for attention, and it's very unclear whether they can be integrated into civilised society," said one scientist. "Worst of all, many of them have columns in places like the Telegraph or Spectator, and they are unable to stop writing over and over again about how lockdown was the worst thing ever and it would

have been much better to simply let everyone die."

Another said, "These people all point out that lockdown was disastrous and created lots of harm, which is self-evidently true. But they are now turning up everywhere, just shouting the same points over and over again, which shows that their higher brain functions have been almost completely demolished."

A third added, "The tragedy is that these people are still reposting elderly and badly-sourced blogs from three years ago. It's too sad for words."

FRENCH POLICE EYESIGHT TEST
CAN YOU SEE ANYTHING IN THIS PHOTO?

Correct answer: Non

Israel denies it carried out major attack it clearly carried out

by Our Middle East Correspondent
Boom Rockman

THE Israeli government last night rebutted claims that it was responsible for the exploding pagers attack on Lebanon.

"There is nothing to link us to this attack," said a spokesman,

"apart from Netanyahu bragging about how brilliant our attack was in bringing Hezbollah to its knees."

He continued, "People shouldn't go around spreading these facts, as it could all blow up in their faces. Know what I mean, wink, wink?"

"This is now the only safe way to communicate…"

Public sick of 'two tier' system

by Our Language Staff
Phil Ology and **Buzz Phrase**

THE British public today announced that it was heartily fed up with the phrase "two tier" being applied to everything from policing to justice to sentencing to health care to wedding cakes.

Said a spokesman for the public, Mr Joe Public, "It's as if there are two sets of people in Britain: one group who try to speak in normal English, and one who lazily resort to media clichés. How would one best describe this linguistic duality? I dunno. I'm lost for words."

Nursery Times
.... Friday, Once-upon-a-time ....

DOCTOR FOSTER TO DEAL WITH OBESITY CRISIS

by Our Puddin' and Pie Staff **Georgie Porgie**

IN a bold move to get the Nurseryland economy moving again, top Gloucester-based medic, Doctor Foster, is to inject every overweight fairytale figure with a wizard wonderdrug from the Land of Oz.

Oz-empic promises to supress the most voracious of appetites and has already been clinically proven on the formerly obese Mrs Spratt, famous for her "no lean" diet.

Now, like her husband, Mrs Spratt will eat no fat, in fact she eats practically nothing at all.

Another beneficiary will be Humpty Dumpty.

Said an NHS (Nurseryland Health Service) spokesman, "We are hoping this will help to

ease pressure on the emergency services, such as all the King's horses and all the King's men. It should also get Mr Dumpty off that wall and back to work.

Oz-empic was first discovered by scientific researcher Alice Inwonderland, who consumed a bottle marked "Drink Me", which led to rapid weight loss, after she ballooned to an enormous size having eaten a cake marked "Eat Me".

Fears of unknown side effects have been largely ignored, in favour of the drug's miraculous weight-loss properties.

Pipe-smoking Old King Cole said, "Oz-empic is the best weight-loss device since tobacco! Cough! Wheeze!"

Right, I want us to concentrate on the important issues rather than gossip and tittle-tattle about what I'm wearing and who paid for it.

Angela Rayner
Yes, everyone should put a sock in it!

Waheed Alli
Socks? Who wants socks? Egyptian cotton? Designer footwear?

Lord Alli has been removed from the group and his Number Ten pass withdrawn.

Morgan McSweeney
The boss is right. No more talk about freebies. The optics are terrible.

Waheed Alli
Optics? Anyone need glasses?

Lord Alli of Baba has again been removed from the group and his new Number Ten pass put in the office's new shredder, kindly donated by Lord Alli.

Wes Streeting
Let's be honest, PM, it is a bit of a problem.

I can't see it.

Waheed Alli
What do you need? Varifocals? Bifocals? Tinted?

Lord Alli has yet again been removed from the group and his latest new Number Ten pass has been put in the new office incinerator, kindly donated by a former television executive.

Sue Gray
It's a media storm, whipped up by scumbag journalists. We should ignore it.

Pat McFadden
It's not a good look, Prime Minister

What? You don't like the smart casual? How about the suits?

Morgan McSweeney
They're all a bit grey.

Sue Gray
Leave me out of it!

Morgan McSweeney
The PM would be able to pay for his own clothes if he were on a decent salary, say £170,000, like yours, Sue.

Sue Gray
You leaked that, didn't you! I've been stitched up!

Waheed Alli
Garment alterations? Invisible mending? I can sort it.

The administrator has given up trying to remove Lord Alli from the group, after being offered a very nice pair of trousers, chosen by a personal shopper.

There's nothing wrong with me taking tickets to the Taylor Swift concert. It was a sell out.

Lisa Nandy
Don't be so hard on yourself, Keir!

Sue Gray
I am not overpaid and I won't have anyone saying I think of myself as the Deputy Prime Minister.

Morgan McSweeney
That's because you think of yourself as the Prime Minister.

Angela Rayner
I thought I was the Deputy Prime Minister! At least, I did until Rachel was given Dorneywood, which was meant to be my bloody house.

Darren Jones
To be fair, if Angela got it, she'd only flog it off and keep the tax 🤣🤣🤣

Rachel Reeves
I am obviously the most suitable occupant for a 21-room house, as I will only be occupying one of the rooms, with a small bar fire.

Ed Miliband
Is the bar fire solar-powered? Or should I put an offshore wind-farm in the lily pond?

Rachel Reeves
I will certainly look into the cost of that, as I will also be investing in a small mini-fridge, in which I will be keeping the ingredients for a whole weekend's worth of sandwiches in a Tupperware box.

Darren Jones
Bad news, Rachel, Tupperware are going bust. You're the only person keeping them afloat. Their fate has been hermetically sealed! 🤣🤣🤣

Apologies, Rachel, I'll now put a lid on it.

Angela Rayner
I think we should build a housing estate, called Dorneywood Villas, to extend all over Rachel's croquet lawn? Just saying.

This isn't the show of unity that I was hoping for.

Morgan McSweeney
We are united. Sue's massively overpaid! 💰💰💰

Pat McFadden
Not compared to the junior doctors and the train drivers! If you want a rise, just go on strike. Rachel will roll over in no time.

Rachel Reeves
It's important to get people back to work again.

Pat McFadden
So they can strike again in a few months' time.

Damian McBride
Frankly, the whole situation is pants.

Waheed Alli
You want pants? I've got pants. Boxers? Y-fronts? Thongs?

CULTURE BORES   by Grizelda

JULY 4TH
USELESS TORY BASTARDS! OUT! OUT! OUT!

MOMENTS LATER...

USELESS LABOUR BASTARDS! OUT! OUT! OUT!

ASSISTED DYING BILL LATEST

Those reasons you will be allowed to choose death in full

- Chronic pain
- Terminal illness
- Waiting in interminable queue to speak to a human being at HMRC

Small island given away

by Our Chagos Staff **Maurice Shuss**

THERE was disgust the length and breadth of Tunbridge Wells last night at the news that a small island in the middle of the Atlantic has been handed over to the USA by the once great British government.

The tiny island, which is strategically important to America, is one of a scattered group known locally as "the United Kingdom" and, despite being remote and isolated, was once a symbol of power and Empire.

Historically, the islands belonged to Britain and the islanders scratched a living by ruling the world. But now it's just a floating platform for US defence bases and corporate outlets.

Said a British government spokesman, "It's sad, but I've just been headhunted by the arms-to-fast-food conglomerate Scud-U-Like, so what do I care?"

CHAGOS: IT'S A DISGRACE THAT STARMER HAS GIVEN AWAY SACRED BRITISH TURF

pp1-94

ON OTHER PAGES
- All of central London owned overseas
- British trains all owned by European governments and Canadian pension firms
- All British utilities owned by foreign banks and sovereign wealth funds
- This newspaper has quite a few foreign investors too, come to think of it
- And the owner is based in France for tax purposes/originally Australian but legally American/ from Russia but flogged it to the Saudis/etc
- Er...

FURY AT HUW EDWARDS' SENTENCE

THAT SENTENCE IN FULL
I'm not giving the BBC any of the money back

Pitfalls for new students to avoid

Nottingham Uni Falling in with the wrong crowd, partying too hard and spending too much of your student loan on boozy nights out

Leeds Uni Falling in with the wrong crowd, partying too hard and spending too much of your student loan on druggy nights out

Cardiff Uni Remaining so bitter about not getting into Oxford that in 40 years' time, when you're Britain's most trusted newsreader, you begin sharing with a known paedophile vile images of child sexual abuse.

"This way, if you turn out to be a paedo, we won't have to edit you out"

— PILBROW —

Taliban Latest

"There's a new series of Strictly No Dancing"

HARRY POTTER WOMAN DIES

by **JEN ZEE** Our Showbiz Staff

THE woman who was in Harry Potter 1 has died. She was famous not only for Harry Potter 1 but also for Harry Potter 2.

She followed the success of Harry Potter 2 with Harry Potter 3, which led to a burgeoning career in Harry Potters 4, 5 and 6. She then truly hit her stride in Harry Potters 7 and 8. She played a variety of roles, from Professor McGonagall to Professor McGonagall as a cat.

Maggie Smith in 'The Prime of Miss Prof McGonagall' *(Is this right? Ed.)*

Apparently, she did some other things on stage and other old stuff, but I can't find them on TikTok, and who cares anyway?

She was undoubtedly the finest Professor McGonagall of her generation and famously delivered such immortal lines as: "Good morning, Harry," "You're late, Harry," and "Hello, Hermione."

SALLY ROONEY BINGO

PLAY ALONG AT HOME!

Everyone is Irish	Self-harm
No quotation marks	Someone is "brilliant"
Lots of Marx quotations	Characters all remarkably familiar with Ludwig Wittgenstein
Graphic sex scene	
Someone punches himself in a bath while thinking about Nietzsche	Unbelievably unpleasant friend/ relative
Another graphic sex scene	Lengthy description of someone's jumper and their visible nipples through it
Nobody is happy about all the graphic sex they are having	Main villain is only one with a proper job
A meticulously observed series of delicate mental breakdowns	Reflection that it's a funny old world really when you think about it

---

The Daily Telegraph LATEST

Hopes of sale dashed

THERE was renewed frustration in the offices of the Daily Telegraph when the news broke that a potential sale had fallen through.

A woman had been spotted in a supermarket and had clearly been considering purchase of the broadsheet, but after a process of due diligence in the shop, lasting a good thirty seconds, she reassessed the merits of adding the Telegraph to her media portfolio of Hello, the Puzzler and Waitrose magazine (free to members).

Some experts are suggesting the enormous asking price of £3.50 may have deterred her, but other media analysts point out that the woman was clearly looking for cat litter and said to the woman behind the checkout, "My cat's easily upset, I don't want him scared by the sight of Allister Heath staring out at him."

The search for a buyer goes on.

Friday 11 October 2024

Rock attack solves Middle East crisis once and for all

BY OUR MIDDLE EAST STAFF
PHIL ISTINE WHO BEGAT PHIL PAGE
WHO BEGAT PHILIPPA COLUMN

A daring Israeli precision rock attack by special forces (David) has removed the enemy warrior Goliath and assured peace in the region forever.

Said Israeli spokesman

Benjamin, son of Netanyahu, "There is no possibility of Goliath's brothers and family taking over from him and launching a counter-attack to avenge him. And, equally, the chances of this conflict going on for thousands of years are a longshot from a sling."

Israel issues evacuation warning

THIS morning, the Israeli government issued a fresh evacuation warning for the region covering the entire world.

Said a spokesman, "We advise everyone on the globe to leave at once, as the region in which they are living is about to become extremely dangerous and subject to extreme conditions of warfare.

"The population of Southern Earth – and indeed Northern, Western and Eastern Earth – has been duly warned, and it is their fault if they haven't relocated to a safer planet."

(Rotters)

"The Israeli Army... now they ARE good at assisted dying"

NEW TRADITIONAL WEATHER RHYMES

Red sky at night,
The whole planet's alight.

Red sky in the morning,
We all ignored the warning.

POETRY CORNER

Lines on the closing of the Smithfield Meat Market, just off of Cows Cross and Cock's Lane

So. Farewell then
Smithfield Meat Market,
You have been cut.
What offal news.
I am stunned,
Much like all
The animals.

E.J. Thribb (17½ kilos of prime verse, actually it's a little bit over... is that alright?)

CLIMATE CHANGE CAUSES GLOBAL DISASTERS

Let's hope the flash floods put out the wildfires

"I think our son is trying to tell us his future isn't in farming"

Daily Telegraph Friday 25 October 2024

Letters to the Editor

SIR – As frequent visitors to the Wimbledon All-England Club, Lady Gussett and I are appalled at the decision to dispense with the services of the traditional line judges. This is nothing short of an act of cultural vandalism, akin to removing the portrait of Sir Walter Raleigh from the offices of the Prime Minister. But I digress – that is for another letter.

Meanwhile, one of the great pleasures of summer has been arbitrarily removed in the interests of so-called "progress". No more will we hear the sound of tennis ball on stomach, and the firm cries of "Out!" followed by the clapping of the crowd as Hawkeye reveals that the ball was actually in.

And why are we to be deprived of the pleasure of Lady Gussett pointing out that some of the ladies look rather large as they lean over in their tight-fitting Ralph Lauren skirts, not to mention the elderly gentlemen whose blue and white Polo shirts are straining the buttons around their midriffs to their very limit.

And what of the jaunty caps that have provided so much amusement to all true tennis lovers, as the line judges parade in and out of the court every five minutes as the rain comes down and the covers come on. We have had 147 years of the joys of the summer linesmen – or I suppose it must be "linespersons" nowadays?! And Lady Gussett and I have only missed one of them, due to the pandemic (Spanish influenza 1919)!

And with what, pray, do they intend to replace these hallowed heroes of SW19? With an electronic system which no doubt offers the odd "Bing!" or "Bleep!" A soulless replacement for the dulcet tones of the well-lunched army of volunteers, who have made this British institution what it is – the envy of all other tennis-playing nations.

I cannot be alone in finding "fault" with this mechanised madness. As the great Fred Perry once pithily said, "You cannot be entirely confident of the rectitude of your ruling in this particular instance – surely you jest!"

Given that removing line judges is clearly a human error, can an electronic AI umpire not overrule this most erroneous of judgements?

Yours, written entirely without the assistance of Chatbot PG Tips (or whatever it's called),
Sir Herbert Gussett
Duncallin' Number 1,
The Court, Cliff St Richard,
Barkershire

SIR – I could not help but notice that in removing the portrait of Sir Walter Raleigh, our "woke" Prime Minister has committed another act of cultural vandalism,.

The replacement of the distinguished painting of the inventor of the bicycle (which British schoolboy can ever forget his first ride on a Chopper?) is an affront to British entrepreneurs, and is clearly a sop to the electric car brigade who are insisting we put solar panels on our chimneys and... *(cont. p94)*
Sir Herbert Gussett *(again)*
Address as above

Out!

AXED WIMBLEDON LINE JUDGE PLEASE GIVE GENEROUSLY

-PILBROW-

May 1536. The Beheading of Anne Boleyn: "Is it ever right to chop someone's head off?"

LINDA ROBSON: You know what drives me mad? When men say they love you and they can't live without you then they go all dewy-eyed and ask you to marry them and a few years later, you know what always happens? They only go and chop your head off!

COLEEN NOLAN: It's not nice. Not nice at all.

STACEY SOLOMON: You've got to take control of your love life, that's what I always say.

NADIA SAWALHA: I know what it must be like to be executed, 'cos something just like that happened to me, once.

(Audience gasps)

RUTH LANGSFORD: Do you want to... share it with us, Nadia?

NADIA SAWALHA: I... I... was trying to slice an avocado, and the knife slipped... and I... slightly nicked my little finger.

LINDA ROBSON: Men!

COLEEN NOLAN: I know if it had been me up there on that scaffold, I'd've gone for a polo neck for that extra little bit of covering, but each to their own, that's what I always say.

RUTH LANGSFORD: Anyone here got any better weight-loss tips?

October 1854. The Charge of the Light Brigade: "What is it with men and horses?"

JANE MOORE: Put any bloke on a horse and he'll want to start charging. I mean, *really*! What is it with men?!

JANET STREET-PORTER: Don't talk to me about blokes and charging! Blimey! They're always goin' round brandishing their swords and shouting at the tops of their voices and charging headlong towards certain bloody death!

JANE MOORE: Anything rather than express their emotions...

COLEEN NOLAN: I went on a horse once. Nearly did myself a mischief!

(Audience laughter)

JANE MOORE: Actually, there's a serious point to be made here. All those men and horses strewn any-old-how across the battlefield – it makes me think, "So when push comes to shove, who's going to have to clear all that mess up?" And you know what the answer is?

D I A R Y

DOWN THE CENTURIES WITH ITV'S LOOSE WOMEN

RUTH LANGSFORD: "Us women, of course!"

(Audience laughter)

RUTH LANGSFORD: Time to move on. What's your favourite raw vegetable to keep in your pocket for snacking on whenever you get that teensy little bit peckish? We've all got one! Janet?

April 1912. The Sinking of the **Titanic***: "So when was the last time you got really soaked through?"*

JANE MOORE: Blokes are always going on about women drivers. Women drivers this, women drivers that. But what about the men drivers, that's what I'd like to know?! You only have to let a man behind the steering wheel of the largest ocean liner in the world and what does he go and do? He only goes and drives it into an iceberg!

JANET STREET-PORTER: Not only that, but I stepped into a puddle of water yesterday and – what do you know – my whole foot got all soppin' wet! Why can't they make shoes that are waterproof any more? It really gets on my bloody wick!

NADIA SAWALHA: It's a real problem with our society, the way water gets into your shoes.

RUTH LANGSFORD: Going back to that terrible tragedy of the Titanic for one sec – what would be the song you'd want to sing if your ship was going down?

JANE MOORE: Personally, I can't get enough of "Easy On Me" by the fabulous Adele.

COLEEN NOLAN: For me it just has to be "Waterloo". It's just so iconic!

RUTH LANGSFORD: – by the fabulous Abba! A great one for dancing to! Next up: how often do you tidy your kitchen drawers? Come on now – be honest! And then we'll be discussing the rights and wrongs of euthanasia, before tackling today's big question: "Lamb and potato yes – but *should your shepherd's pie really include carrots*?"

November 1963. The Assassination of President Kennedy: "So what do we all think of open-top cars?"

LINDA ROBSON: I'm very much a people person and I don't care who knows it. Frankly, I'd never go round shooting someone just because they were sitting in the back of a convertible.

GLORIA HUNNIFORD: Let's make this clear, once and for all: noone deserves to be assassinated just because of their choice of car. I feel very strongly about this, I really do.

JANE MOORE: Well, I love riding in an open-top car, but not if it means I'm going to be assassinated. My parents drove a Ford Cortina, and we were never assassinated, thank goodness.

JANET STREET-PORTER: Don't talk to me about Ford Cortinas! I had my first shag in the back of a Ford Cortina!

RUTH LANGSFORD: So I'm literally dying to know what our special guest, Joan Collins, thinks about the assassination? Over to you, Joan!

JOAN COLLINS: Back in my day, assassinations were so much more *stylish*! Of course, Abraham Lincoln, bless him, used to come on to me *big time*, and I'd say to him, "Oh, no, you don't, Abe – not until you've shave off that dreadful little beard of yours!" But the man always had such style! It was typical of him that he'd pick the most charming theatre in Washington to be assassinated in rather than some noisy freeway running through the centre of Dallas! Of course, JFK would endlessly try it on with me, but my lips are sealed!

Audience: Wooh!

RUTH LANGSFORD: In the remaining five minutes, we'll be discussing – "Do you feel comfortable in your own skin?", "Is your partner guilty of manspreading?" "Is sexism still rife in our society?", "What were the causes of the First World War?" and "What's the best way to pick fluff out of your trusty vacuum cleaner?" So stay with us!

As told to
CRAIG BROWN

"This new horseless technology is all very good, but I do suffer from range anxiety... the nearest petrol station is 15 years away"

11

The All-New Incredibly Ruthless Prime Minister's Ruthless WhatsApp Group – It's Ruthless!

> Ok, re Freebie Gate, I am taking action and I'm going to lay down a set of principles.

Sue Gray
Didn't we have any before?

> For a start, I've clamped down ruthlessly on myself. I'm giving back most, or a significant part, or at least some of the donations.

Lord Alli
Do you need a loan to do that, Keir? It's yours, just say the word.

Damian McBride
What word? 'Bribe'?

Damian McBride
Too much?

Rachel Reeves
Clearly it was too much. Some of us took just the right amount of complementary outfits for work purposes. But not for going to discos in Ibiza.

Angela Rayner
That's unfair and inaccurate. It was NOT a disco, it was a rave. And anyway I paid for it. The next morning, with a banging headache. 🍹🎉🎶

> As a lawyer, one could argue that Angela's trip was party business.

Angela Rayner
Sure was! Partayyy!

Darren Jones
Or perhaps it was a 'work event'?

Bridget Phillipson
My birthday party certainly was! And, as Education Secretary, so were my tickets to the Taylor Swift concert.

Darren Jones
Many lessons learned? 😈

> Work events? I hope no one is comparing me to former, freebie-taking, sleazy Prime Ministers who had no moral compass.

Lord Alli
You need a compass? Gold? Silver? Brass? Magnetic? Digital?

> Lord Alli has been removed by a House of Lords committee on standards. They will be meeting at a convenient penthouse in Covent Garden, courtesy of an anonymous Labour peer and generous donor, so long as the Prime Minister's son doesn't require it for GCSE retakes.

Sue Gray
Can I ask why, Angela, you have a personal photographer who's meant to be making you look good, but is actually making you look bad?

Morgan McSweeney
Rubbish! Angela looks better than you do, Sue, scowling in all those photos in the papers.

Sue Gray
What, the ones you leaked?

Angela Rayner
The photographer only costs 68 grand a year.

Morgan McSweeney
That's less than half a Sue Gray! Or should I say 'Sue Gravy'.

Sue Gray
I'm moving your office completely out of Number Ten.

Lord Alli
Need an office? Lovely penthouse. Bring your own family photos and Christmas cards to put on the shelves.

> Lord Alli has been removed again. The administrators remain mystified how he keeps getting access to the exclusive Number Ten group.

> Come on everyone, we need to pull together. We need to be united.

Rachel Reeves
I think this is all a distraction from the massive financial black hole.

Angela Rayner
What? From paying back the cost of our freebies? Flippin' Nora!

> Not sure about the new hairstyle, Rachel.

Angela Rayner
Talk about everything being in the red! Is that assisted dyeing, luv? 😃😃😃

Sue Gray
Is it true, Keir, what people are saying? That Labour have a problem with women?

> I don't have a problem with women, Sue. You're fired.

Sue Gray
Am I fired? Or have I resigned?

> It's a gray area.

Morgan McSweeney
There are going to be parties in Downing Street now! 🍹🎉🎶

> Sue Gray has been removed from the WhatsApp Group and Morgan McSweeney's desk is back next to Keir's.

Those shocking reasons why Taylor Swift was granted special security

1 Her concerts in Austria had been subject to terrorist threats the previous week.

2 Last time the police failed to act with sufficient precaution at a pop concert in the UK was at the Ariana Grande concert in Manchester, and that didn't go too well.

3 Britain had a series of major riots following the murder of children at a Taylor Swift dance party.

4 Her concerts generated £1 billion boost to the economy, which easily covered the cost of the increased security

Those shocking reasons why this story is running and running

■ We can put pictures of Taylor Swift on the front page
■ And page 2
■ And pages 3 to 94
(see above)

WOW – A VERMEER KAT!

Lines on the passing of Alex Salmond, former First Minister of Scotland

'Twas in the year two thousand and twenty-four
That the Grim Reaper came knocking at Alex Salmond's door.
A sad end to a man who was such a political force,
To die so young opening a bottle of tomato sauce,
And for pedants who point out it was actually ketchup,
In my defence, a suitable rhyme is difficult to fetch up.
But I digress from my sombre threnodic ode
And must remain in a serious memorial mode,
For 'twas a tragic end to the great leader of Caledonia
To meet his maker in far flung North Macedonia,
But all over the globe when the news was broken
Tears were shed and tissues were soaken,
Even his auld enemy got out her hanky –
I refer, of course, to the wee ex-first minister Nicola Sturgeon.
She could not of course publicly weep and wail,
Having been quite keen, it is said, to put him in jail,
And he was suing the Scots government and Nicola,
Which would have put them in a bit of pickle, her
Role in the matter Alex described as "malfeasant"
And to find a rhyme for that, well, easy it isn't.
But I digress again as I join the rest of the SNP
In praising Alex for delivering Independence for Scotland (nearly).
But in spite of the near universal chorus of praise,
There were some ungracious voices who wanted to raise
The matter of his "love for the lassies" once more,
As though this had not been settled in court before.
All those supposed beans that had been spilt
About what was going on "beneath the kilt"...
And there were those who said he was a bully,
As though all this too had not been resolved quite fully.
But such nit-picking details have no place in this tributary ode
As a loyal bard I'll take the high, not the low, road.
Let us all agree that like Bruce, Wallace, Burns and Rob Roy
Not to mention Sean Connery, David Tennant and James McAvoy,
Alex Salmond was truly a great, great Scot,
Or, all things considered, possibly not.

© William McGonagall 1867

HS2 train project 'too big to control' say experts who also say it is impossible for anyone in Britain to organise a 'celebratory drinking event in a brewery situation'

by Our Railway Correspondent
Wyatt Elephant

LEAKED documents have suggested that the private-sector supplier behind HS2 is "too large to effectively control".

"It's just very difficult to understand what the joint venture, BBV, is telling us," said one senior executive of HS2, who had not been able to ascertain whether the project was £10 billion or £20 billion over budget, ie, the size of the entire black hole in the nation's finances.

He continued, "It seems to be the case that there is no one left in Britain who can run a tap, let alone a major infrastructure project. Unless, of course, it is a tap that gushes money into our pockets".

"Have you tried giving him your phone?"

A Californian Doctor Writes

AS a Californian doctor, I am often asked, "Can I have some ketamine, please?"

The simple answer is, "Yes, of course, Mr Perry, you're among 'Friends' here, and in the words of your old theme tune: 'I'll be there for you'."

What happens is a celebrated TV star, with mental health and addiction problems, seeks a drug to ease his pain. The physician then assesses the situation and, after a thorough examination of the patient's bank account, seeks a second opinion from a colleague, with the words, "I wonder how much this moron will pay?"

This is a clear case of *callous exploititis bastardus normalis*, more commonly known as "Kerching Syndrome". The symptoms are clear and obvious and include a severe deficiency in the heart area and intense cravings for money.

The prognosis is bleak – it involves being struck off and spending the next 10 to 15 years in prison.
© *A Californian doctor*

IT'S THE HARRODS FAIL

You can get everything at Harrods... groped, assaulted, silenced, sacked, sued...

...but not arrested

POETRY CORNER

In Memoriam Kris Kristofferson, musician, songwriter and actor

So. Farewell
Then Kris Kristofferson.

You were in
A Star is Born
And now, alas,
A star is dead.

You were also in
Heaven's Gate,
Which has hopefully
Now opened to
Let you in.

　　　E.J. Thribb (17½ rpm)

PS. Keith wonders
If you were related
To a man with similar
Nomenclature –
Magnus Magnusson?
Or Johnnie Johnson,
The famed WW2
Flying ace?

13

THOSE TABLOID HEADLINES IN FULL

HERR VE GO! HERR VE GO! HERR VE GO!

HE'S THE REICH MAN FOR THE JOB!

England Uber Alles!

TODAY ENGLAND – TOMORROW THE WORLD CUP!

Don't Mention the VAR!

England Caught with their Panzer Down!

TUCHEL IS THE WURST!

FOR YOU, THOMAS – THE SCORE IS OVER!

IN THE NAME OF GOTT GO!

They think it's all Fuhrer! It is now!

OVER AND KRAUT!

"You're good, Fritz... would you like to be our manager?"

Fury over artificial intelligence appointment

by Our Media staff **I. Robot**

ITV BOSSES last night defended the appointment of a £95,000 AI expert to create new programme ideas.

Said one, "Already, AI has created a raft of groundbreaking new ideas which will be next year's BAFTA winners."

The programmes scheduled for autumn 2025 include:

■ **Doctor Who Wants to be a Millionaire?** Sci-fi gameshow hosted by a Dalek, in which failure to answer questions correctly ends in extermination.

■ **Last of the Midsomer Murders Wine** Three old men in a tin bath investigate the gruesome but gentle strangling of an old woman by wrinkled stockings.

■ **Countdownton Abbey Clancy** The popular wife of Peter Crouch becomes a Dowager Countess for a week while solving word puzzles in a stately home.

■ **Jane Austen's Emmadale Clarkson's Farm** Period drama starring Jeremy Clarkson as wealthy landowner Mr Arsey who buys up the Woolpack Pub and then punches himself in the face for failing to serve hot food.

■ **Naked Strictly Good Morning Britain's Got Talent Extra Slice** Behind the scenes show with Ant and Dec, featuring wannabe presenters who audition to read the news with no clothes on while dancing and baking cakes on ITV's flagship morning show.

However, another ITV Boss said, "Having looked at this list, I have decided it's absolute rubbish. I'm doubling the AI expert's salary. It's brilliant!"

EXCLUSIVE TO ALL TABLOIDS

WE SAY 'WILLKOMMEN' TO ENGLAND'S NEW GERMAN MANAGER

GIVE Thomas Tuchel a chance – he could be just the football supremo we're looking for.

The Teutonic Tyro has already shown great form by dumping his wife of 13 years and trading her in for a hot Brazilian beauty 14 years his junior.

Yes, the good old days are back! Forget sad Southgate and his boring beards, woeful waistcoats and steady marriage. We're back in the world of sexy Sven, where the beautiful bedroom game is what really counts.

He shoots, he scores, then scores again, while England lose miserably.

Yes, Tuchel could well be the saviour of English tabloids. Bish, Bash, Bonking Bosch!

Nadine Dorries
My Struggle with Bozempic

FROM the moment I had my first shot of Bozempic I knew it was just what I needed, a medical way to wean myself off the addiction that so many suffer from – an unrelenting desire for Boris.

I knew I had a Bozza problem, craving him any time of the day or night, and I hoped that Bozempic would be the answer.

Finally, a way to say goodbye to that weight – roughly 18 stone of pink, puffy blubber. And, at first, it worked brilliantly – suddenly, when I looked at a picture of Boris, I felt not cravings, but nausea. Just like a normal person!

Could I really live without Boris? It seemed possible while I was on Bozempic, but the real test was to come. Could I wean myself off this wonder drug, and stay Bozza-free?

But now it's nearly three minutes since I stopped taking Bozempic and sadly the hunger has returned. Boris – I need you! I miss you! Mmmmmmm!

© *Mad Nad, the political lightweight with the most amazing figure since Boris's book advance*

Before **After**

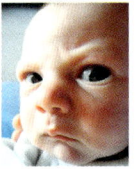

I have a farm comprising a dozen plastic cows, several happy pigs, a few chickens and a horse that happens to be a sticker on the side of a barn. It's a small farm now, but the Daily Telegraph tells me that if I add to it and make it a big farm (say, I get a cardboard field with some woolly sheep for Christmas), that there's a good chance I would have to pay 100% tax on it, and I would have to give up my investment to fund Sir Keir Stalin's socialist utopia. This is a disgrace! It is completely wrong for Labour to punish hardworking babies this way. I got my farm purely because I have a lifelong passion for Old McDonald's song, and I once read in a squishy book about how cows go moo and ducks go quack. There is no truth in the rumour that I will get bored of it in a few years when I get into space toys and sell the farm on eBay for a quick profit. Like Jeremy Clarkson, I am fully prepared to throw a tantrum until this legislation is revised. Get ready for my piece in this newspaper about the "cull" of farmers, and I will be slow-driving my tractor to Downing Street just as soon as my feet reach the pedals and (cont. p94)

CLARKSON'S FARM LATEST

How much tax do I want to pay? Diddly squat!

DUMB BRITAIN

Real contestants, real quiz shows, real answers, real dumb!

Tipping Point, ITV

Ben Shephard: The 2020 novel A Song for the Dark Times by Ian Rankin is the 23rd to feature which central detective character?
Contestant: Sherlock Holmes.

Shephard: The Three Broomsticks is a fictional pub in a series of books by which writer?
Contestant: I think I know the name CS Lewis – from Fifty Shades of Grey…

Shephard: How many two-pence coins make up two pounds?
Contestant: 20.

Shephard: The Han river flows through Korea and out into what sea?
Contestant: Tennessee.

Shephard: The Atlantic Charter was an agreement signed in 1941 by Winston Churchill and which US president?
Contestant: Ronald Reagan.

Shephard: With what animal is the word "equine" associated?
Contestant: A goat.

Shephard: Austria is bordered by how many other countries?
Contestant: None

Pointless, BBC1

Alexander Armstrong: What country, beginning with the letters PORT, is on the Atlantic coast of the Iberian peninsula?
Contestant: Patagonia.

Armstrong: Writer, director and star of the 1941 film Citizen Kane. Initials OW.
Celebrity: Oprah Winfrey.

Mastermind, BBC2

Clive Myrie: Which French philosopher and author refused to accept the 1964 Nobel Prize for Literature, stating that he always declined official honours?
Contestant: Descartes.

Myrie: What 1920s dance was named after a town in South Carolina?
Contestant: The twist.

Myrie: Which British racing driver won the Formula 1 world championship in 1962 and 1968?
Contestant: Nigel Havers.

Myrie: What is the most senior rank in the British Army, equivalent to Admiral in the Navy?
Contestant: Sergeant.

Myrie: Who was the former Soviet leader who was assassinated in Mexico in 1940?
Contestant: Was it Gorbachev?

Myrie: The word "low", meaning the opposite of high, is an anagram of the name of what bird of prey?
Contestant *(after a long pause)*: Eagle.

Myrie: In the late 18th century, which naval commander began a scandalous affair with Emma, Lady Hamilton, which lasted until his death in 1805?
Contestant: Bob the Builder.

Myrie: Chien is the French name for which domestic animal?
Celebrity: Cow.

House of Games, BBC2

Richard Osman: What country, where Carry On up the Khyber was filmed, gained its independence from Britain in the 1940s?
Contestant: Barbados.

The Chase, ITV

Bradley Walsh: Which 19th-century prime minister had "Dizzy" as a nickname?
Contestant: Margaret Thatcher.

Walsh: The Australian newspaper abbreviated to SMH is the Sydney Morning… what?
Contestant: Harbour.

Walsh: Which French President abolished the Guillotine in 1981?
Contestant: Louis the first.

Walsh: Which famous potter has a statue erected in his honour in Stoke-on-Trent?
Contestant: Beatrix.

Walsh: In the nursery rhyme Little Jack Horner, what words rhymes with plum?
Contestant: Bum.

Walsh: What does the 'St' mean in the title of someone who has been canonised?
Contestant: Shot.

Walsh: Which Peruvian city was founded as "the City of Kings"?
Contestant: Paris.

Walsh: Which continent is directly to the west of the Maldives?
Contestant: Europe.

Walsh: What is the sister programme of Radio 4's *Any Questions*?
Contestant: *The Archers*.

Walsh: In a one-day cricket international, how many overs does each side have?
Contestant: Two.

Walsh: What colours are the zebra spider: white and what?
Bonnie Langford: Red.

Walsh: As a boy, which US president was said to have chopped down his father's cherry tree?
Contestant: Donald Trump.

Walsh: Which of these three men was born first: Charles Dickens, Charles Darwin or Charles de Gaulle?
Contestant: I'll go for Charles de Gaulle. I'm pretty sure he was medieval.

Walsh: In Rome, the Ponte Garibaldi spans which river?
Contestant: The Tyne.

Walsh: Which English monarch died in 1952?
Contestant: Henry VIII.

Walsh: Oliver Cromwell fought a civil war against which English king?
Contestant: Canute.

Walsh: The 2019 book *It's Not About The Burka* is about female followers of which religion?
Contestant: Christianity.

Walsh: What opera house opened at the Lincoln Centre, New York, in 1966?
Contestant: Sydney Opera House.

Walsh: Who wrote the story Maigret's Christmas?
Contestant: Charles Dickens.

The Weakest Link, BBC2

Romesh Ranganathan: Name the flying mammal featured on a Meatloaf album.
Tyler West: Horse.

Ranganathan: In the western calendar, how many days are there in a leap year?
Contestant: Forty thousand.

Ranganathan: In words, what A goes before "hunter" in a term for a person who collects the signatures of celebrities?
Paul Burrell: Aspic.

Ranganathan: In geography, which tourist destination in Spain has a name that is literally translated as "Coast of the Sun"?
Dianne Buswell: Barcelona.

Ranganathan: In cinema music, tracks entitled "Hotel Room", "The Bathroom" and "The Curtain" feature on the soundtrack to which 1960 Alfred Hitchcock film?
Gladiator: *Dad's Army*.

Ranganathan: The 1937 novella by John Steinbeck about nomadic workers during the Great Depression was Of Mice and… what?
Celebrity: Cats.

Ranganathan: The West-End musical & Juliet is based on a play by which playwright?
Contestant: Hugo Boss.

The Tournament, BBC2

Alex Scott: What airtight container range was launched in 1946 by Earl Tupper?
Contestant: Carrier pigeon.

Scott: In the films Frankenstein and Bride of Frankenstein, which Boris played Frankenstein's monster?
Contestant: Boris Johnson.

The Finish Line, BBC1

Roman Kemp: "Emigré" was a term coined to describe those people who fled which revolution of 1789?
Contestant: The Stone Age.

Kemp: Something vespertilian resembles which flying mammal?
Contestant: A cow.

Kemp: Seville is the capital of what Spanish region?
Contestant: Italy.

Kemp: Which former Labour MP was a two-time Oscar winner?
Contestant: Tony Blair.

Kemp: In which war was the mythical hero Hector killed?
Contestant: The First World War.

Ten to the Top, Radio 2

Vernon Kay: In 1970, Freda who had a hit with the song "Band of Gold"?
Caller: Frida Kahlo.

Kay: "Hoochie Coochie Man", a 1964 Chicago blues classic, was first recorded by the musician Muddy... what?
Caller: Holly.

Kay: Between 1965 and 1968 Syd Barrett was the frontman of which legendary act?
Caller: Little and Large?

Kay: "Matchstalk Men and Matchstalk Cats and Dogs" by Brian & Michael was a tribute to which famous painter from Salford?
Caller: Van Gogh.

Lightning, BBC2

Zoe Lyons: What type of raincoat was named after the Scottish chemist who invented the material it was first made from?
Contestant: Anorak.

15

Right, Sue's gone. So, who's in charge now?

Morgan McSweeney
You are, boss. Everyone knows who's Prime Minister.

Darren Jones
Except Keir at PMQs! Who seems to think it's still Rishi Sunak 😳 .

That was a slip of the tongue.

Darren Jones
Like when you said 'sausage' instead of 'hostage'? 🙄

Angela Rayner
Or like when you said we *won't* put National Insurance up when we bloody well *will*? 🤚

No. I put it to you, that technically the wording in the manifesto is legally foolproof and did not commit us to a non-increase in the employer as opposed to the employee contribution.

Angela Rayner
You're a bare-face lawyer, Keir!

Thank you very much. No further questions.

Pat McFadden
So, we're going to put it up?

I said no further questions! Strike it from the record! Case dismissed!

Darren Jones
Objection!

Objection overruled.

Rachel Reeves
We are going to put National Insurance up. If you read the very small print of the manifesto on page 7,442, it's perfectly clear.

Ed Miliband
It is if you've got new glasses from Lord Alli! Just saying. Not being disloyal. 🕴️ 👓 💰

Rachel Reeves
But, as we promised, the increase is not for working people, it's only for employers.

Jonathan Reynolds
Can I point out, as Business Secretary, that employers are also working people?

Angela Rayner
No, they're not, they're Tory Scum! 😡

Except Lord Alli, obviously.

PRINCE WILLIAM TACKLES HOMELESSNESS

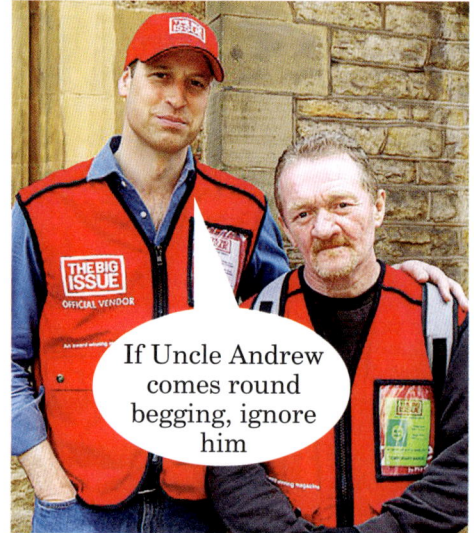

If Uncle Andrew comes round begging, ignore him

"Either you pay for something or leave"

"But Mum..."

ROBERT THOMPSON

WORLD FURIOUSLY WARNS ISRAEL IT WILL DO NOTHING

THE West warned Israel today of the consequences of its decision to ban the UN's Palestinian refugee agency (UNRWA) from operating in Gaza, including threatening to do something, but then forgetting about it and doing nothing.

"Just as many times in the past we have warned Israel about the dire humanitarian crisis in Gaza and threatened to stop arms supplies only to then sell them more arms," said one senior Western official, "we are once again making empty threats with an even more stern face than before."

Prime Minister Netanyahu defended the action, telling the Knesset, "What is important here, is that I am riding high in the latest polls. I may not have saved the hostages, but I have saved myself."

The UN Secretary General, Antonio Guterres, said he would be seeking a phone conversation with the Israeli Prime Minister, provided his phone doesn't explode in the next 20 minutes.

"Son, one day all of this will be your stepmother's"

The Collected Poems of JRR Tolkien

There was a tiny goblin (1933)

There was a tiny goblin
He hoppeth one of three
Yet others in this sylvan glade
Did gambol elvishly

Critics generally agree that *There was a tiny goblin*, though not highly regarded by its author – the original manuscript was retrieved by Christopher Tolkien from a waste-paper basket some time in the 1960s – marks a crucial stage in Tolkien's journey from a romanticised view of "Faery" to the intensely mythologised landscapes of Middle Earth. Indeed, in "Tolkien's Faery Portal", an essay contributed to Silmarillion Studies vol. V, xii, Professor Glyn Poughkeepsie argues that the piece is a "liminal departure" from less particularised early poems such as *Elf-maids Bathing*. A variant ms in the Bodleian Library substitutes "rustic" for "sylvan". When first published in Whimsy Warblings (January 1934), the piece included an exclamation mark at the end of the second line, while the final full stop was misprinted as a comma.

The Dragon Hoard (1942/1938)

Yea, what a mighty pile of gold
Lies glinting in yon castle drear
But hark how the whisker'd seneschals
Increase its volume year on year
The mage who dwelt here long is dead
Yet his work pours forth in endless spate
A tide of volumes without cease
Such are the wiles of the Tolkien estate

Tolkien famously distrusted allegory. Yet *The Dragon Hoard*, first published in *Bilbo Goes A-boating and Other Poems* (1963), may be regarded as, if not allegorical, then narrowly prophetic. The poem accurately foresees the management of his posthumous reputation. If Tolkien himself, who died in 1973, may be identified as "the mage who dwelt here", then the "castle drear" is obviously the offices of messrs HarperCollins, his publishers, while the "whisker'd seneschals" can only be representatives of his estate, which has spent the last half-century engaged in the merciless exploitation of a lot of stuff which, er, really wasn't worth putting out in the first place... [continues for thousands of pages]

She's the new Mrs T

Yes – Truss!

𝕸aily EXPRESSO graph

TORIES PROVE THEY ARE THE PARTY OF DIVERSITY

by Our Westminster Staff
Sid and **Doris Bonkers**

THE election of Kemi Badenoch as Conservative leader shows that it is the Tory party that is leading the way on diversity and it is not afraid to elect nutters.

Badenoch is the third lunatic since 2019 to lead the party, following Johnson and Truss.

Said one senior Tory, "The experiment with electing someone vaguely sane like Rishi Sunak has been consigned to history, and once again the Conservatives have led the way in shattering the padded ceiling of stupidity."

It is also hoped that Badenoch's election will stop the haemorrhaging of traditional Tory fruitcakes to Reform.

The contrast with Labour could not be sharper. While the Tories have embraced lunacy, Labour turned its back on Corbynista craziness and chose a charisma-free dullard in Keir Starmer, who could offer nothing but a boring five years in power.

That epoch-defining interview in full

Laura Kuenssberg: So, Kemi, you've promised to tell the truth about the past and confront Tory historical mistakes?

Kemi Badenough: Boris Johnson was a great Prime Minister, and the Partygate affair was overblown by the media. He should never have been fined. The problem was not that he broke the law, but that there was a law made by him to be broken.

Laura Kuenssberg: What about Liz Truss?

Kemi Badenochpowell: Oh, come on! Are we going to go through every single Tory Prime Minister?! I want to focus on the future – a future in which I will possibly

BBC1 (Sunday morning, while you were asleep)

confront the errors of the past, but not now, thank you very much.

Laura Kuenssberg: What about Rishi Sunak?

Kemi Badinterview: Look, I've made it perfectly clear that I'm going to be honest about the questions you're not asking me!

Laura Kuenssberg: People say you are abrasive and difficult to get on with.

Kemi Badtempered: Look, I'm not here to win a popularity contest – which is why I will lose the next election – on principle!

Laura Kuenssberg: Thank you very much.

Kemi Badmouth: Get knotted!

Dee Nial

Ex-Conservative MP writes for the Eye

WELL, it's happened! Kemi Badenoch is now the prime minister-in-waiting! I can't wait to go on all the political TV shows and explain how her policies of getting rid of maternity pay, leaving maternity pay alone and fighting Doctor Who will benefit the British people!

And as an ex-MP there are so many political programmes who want me to go on as a guest! I was on the set of one of these shows, and did mention to the producer that I thought it was odd that I was one of three Conservatives on the panel, along with two Reform MPs and one of my in-laws

from the *Spectator*, but he just winked at me in a funny way and said, "You lost your seat, duckie, can't really call you a Conservative now, can we"?

So I'm on all the big shows criticising the government for leaking details of the budget, putting up taxes in contradiction to their manifesto, and all those things they shouldn't do. And of course the boring Labour person spouts all the usual stuff about how we did everything we're criticising them for, only ten times worse, but thankfully, it's only him against seven of us, which is much more fun than being in parliament, and better pay too!

Moth problem infests newspaper

by Our Lepidoptery Staff
Chris Allis

A CRISIS hit Britain's newspapers this month when huge holes began to appear in all major titles as they ran out of stories and journalists.

Said one insider, "These holes

mean only one thing – moths. We need lots of articles about moths to fill up these holes cheaply."

Said one reader, "I've seen ten moth pieces in one issue. They're everywhere. Editorials, features, even the crossword has got moths *(7 down, months without neuter, five letters)*."

But one editor defended the moths, saying, "They perform a valuable function in the ecosystem of the newspaper, eating into the fashion spreads and gobbling up space normally devoted to celebrity pets looking like their owners."

Groucho Club scandal rocks Soho

by Our Clubland Staff
Charlie Snorter

THE Metropolitan Police have closed down the famed Soho watering-hole, the Groucho Club, following revelations of serious criminal activity.

Said a Met spokesman, "As a result of our investigations, there can be no doubt that club members entered the

establishment with the heinous intention of pitching various terrible TV series.

"Some of these shameful ideas for game shows, reality TV and police procedurals should never have seen the light of day."

She continued, "The Club encouraged people to come through its doors and openly sell each other junk ideas for TV formats and B-movies."

"Who are you voting for?"

"Trump" *"Trump"* *"Trump"* *"Trump"* *"Trump"*

"There you go – too close to call. Back to the studio"

ARCHBISHOP OF CANTERBURY RESIGNS AFTER SURPRISE INTERVENTION

You're Fired!

NAILS | VAPING STORE | TANNING SALON | nails

Jonesy

"It's nice to see a bit of variety coming back to the high street"

Maily EXPRESSOgraph

BBC MUST APOLOGISE FOR ITS ROLE IN THE CHURCH OF ENGLAND SCANDAL

AS ALWAYS, when there is an appalling scandal in public life, the BBC is at the heart of it, and the Church of England debacle is no different.

This newspaper has learned that the BBC knowingly employed the head of the Church of England, Henry the Eighth, in the BBC drama 'Wolf Hall', in the full knowledge that he presided over shocking abuses in the Church.

They knew this when they employed him in 2013 for the first series, and have re-employed him in 2024, despite long-standing allegations from several Church insiders, including Thomas More and Cardinal Wolsey that he was fully aware of what was going on at all times.

Even now, his picture is plastered over BBC iPlayer and regularly featured on programme adverts on BBC1.

When will the BBC come clean over this latest scandal and sack him?

HOW SHOULD ARCHBISHOP WELBY BE PUNISHED?

a) Lose seat in House of Lords.

b) Be defrocked by Church.

c) Receive 100 lashes with a cane on the bare bottom.

The Service of Holy Resignation of An Archbishop

From the Book of Common Assault

President: We are gathered here to witness the resignation of our brother the Archbishop of Cant after his failure to confront the manifest sins and wickednesses of his former colleague *(here he may say N or M or John Smyth QC)*.

Congregation: About time.

President: Let us join together in the *Nunc Dimittis...*

Congregation: Lord, now lettest thou thy servant depart in peace, if a bit delayed, due to him not wanting to go until he was forced out.

President: It is now time for the Lesson Learnt, taken today from the *Letter of Saint Justin to St John*, on his mission to the Zimbabweans. Although it was more of a Christmas card.

Reader: "Happy Christmas, John – hope you are having lovely time in Africa. Here is some money for your ministry."

President: Thanks be to No one. And now for the general confession.

Assembled Bishops and Church leaders: We are very sorry to hear about this awful affair but it is nothing to do with us. We had no idea.

President: I pronounce the Absolution. You are all absolutely absolved.

Congregation: Thank you very much.

President: Should the Archbishop have done more to expose the abuse going on in the Church?

Congregation: Is the Archbishop a Catholic?

(That's enough Church of England Liturgy. Ed.)

Who will be the next Archbishop of Canterbury?

Paula Vennells
A holy woman for the top post?

Russell Brand
Theologian and amulet salesman

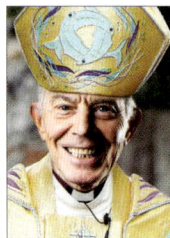

The Rev Tony Blair
He's holier than you!

The Rev Richard Coles
The 'cosy' choice

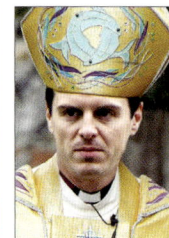

Hot Priest from Fleabag
He's Catholic, but who cares?

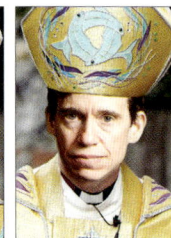

Rory Stewart
Would make an ideal Godcaster

Professor Richard Dawkins
Time for an atheist, surely?

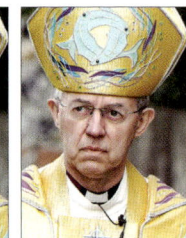

Justin Welby (again)
Better the Devil you know

DIARY

NIGEL SLATER'S MAGIC MOMENTS

Autumn trudges towards winter, mud warm on boots already laden with the deep brown busky warmth of manure. It is a time of the year when I am happy to spend a little while longer in the kitchen, gently dicing a perch in coriander, yellow mustard seeds and agrophobia nyanda before dipping it into handmade Egyptian yoghurt before topping it with a Welsh cockscomb lovingly trimmed with a pair of bamboo kitchen scissors sourced from my good friends Tony and Chris on the Isle of Mull.

There's a portly bumblebee caught in my kitchen skylight. After a struggle, I rescue him with a long-handled feather duster from Fukuoka, a cherished present from a dear friend, and gently place him in my skillet with Swedish garlic oil, two tablespoons of finely-chopped tulip and a pinch of cardamom. After two or three minutes, I ladle a light batter over it, browning it on both sides. Served with a tart gooseberry puree and Segovian parsley, Bumblebee Fritter makes a refreshing mid-morning snack. If, after a couple of swallows, you feel a sharp pain towards the back of your throat, followed by golfball-sized swelling leading to breathlessness, this may indicate that you failed to read to the end of this paragraph and neglected to remove the sting before serving.

Winter dusk descends on the shores of Lake Wagatabon. The sky turns several shades of charcoal and crimson, followed by lilac and saffron, lavender, grey, azure, and cobalt, cerulean, woad and indigo, azure and translucent cornflower. This is the time I like to make a fire with local kindling and cook a cheerful winter stew of roughly chopped lamb that has, up to now, spent its life on a rocky hillside, eating wild scrub in blazing sunshine while its dedicated shepherd, bearded and big hearted, played it a selection of timeless winter classics on his pan pipes, fashioned from the shoulder bone of his beloved great-grandfather. Stir in a tablespoon of chopped mint and four tablespoons of yoghurt before serving.

My favourite jumper – do we not all have one? – acts as a cookery diary, blossoming with the smudges of a rich assortment of dishes, charting each day, month, and year. When it was first presented to me, by a very dear friend, it was a smoky kind of beige. But after decades of curries, stews, and sizzling stir-fries it has turned charcoal and crimson, followed by lilac and saffron, lavender, grey, azure, and cobalt, cerulean, woad and indigo, azure and translucent cornflower.

Which of us can resist the lure of a peach? I want to feel the fuzz of the skin against my lips, the first bead of juice touch my bottom lip and then my tongue. That first bite sends a single rivulet of juice down my chin, deep into my stubble, where it embraces the remains of my breakfast pain-au-chocolat, before travelling further down, down, down, onto the crisp whiteness of my shirt, freshly laundered that morning, thence hither and thither along the tails of the shirt towards my linen trousers, bought in the Thursday bazaar in Abuhamza, a small, dusty village in Eastern Egypt. Intrepid travellers, a few remaining beads of peach juice just make it onto the tips of my open-toed sandals, ready to be embraced by my dusty toe-nails as in a delicious union of bone and blood.

Few kitchen moments are as peaceful as those spent stirring a puree – damson, blackcurrant, plum, goldfish, mango – into softly whipped cream. Personally, I always remove clothes to perform this sublime act, and prefer to conduct the ceremony hanging upside-down from the flex of my favourite kitchen light. This lends my wrist the necessary gravity to whip the cream with due pressure, while affording me a wonderfully topsy-turvy upside-down view of familiar surroundings.

Food can delight, astound, amuse and sustain. It can appease, invigorate or console. It can be as tough as an iron girder or as fragile as a butterfly wing. I remember the only time I ever ate a butterfly wing. It was elevenses in the seasonal Butterfly Conservatory at Kew, and I had arrived unprepared. As those precious insects fluttered around in their magical melange of charcoal and crimson, followed by lilac and saffron, lavender, grey, azure, and cobalt, cerulean, woad and indigo, azure and translucent cornflower, I was overcome by temptation. Racing around the greenhouse with my mouth wide open, I snagged a Luzon Peacock Swallowtail (minty, with a slight hint of juniper), a Zebra Longwing (top notes of marzipan, with aniseed juice) and a Miami Blue (unexpectedly metallic but with a distinct aftertaste of beetroot). From that moment on, I have always tried to serve my Brandy Snaps with the surprise addition of an exotic butterfly tucked into the middle, snug and enchanting as an Andalusian cricket in puff pastry. Some prefer to remove the matchsticky torso, which they find too crunchy , but I delight in the little bit of grit it adds to the bite. They are best served with a melted coating of butter, hence the name.

As told to
CRAIG BROWN

PEARSONGATE: IS THIS THE BIGGEST THREAT TO FREEDOM OF SPEECH THE WORLD HAS EVER KNOWN?

WHAT kind of country are we living in when a journalist cannot tweet a photograph of a demonstration in which she wrongly identifies the city, the police force, the protestors and the flag featured, accompanied with a perfectly reasonable accusation that the people in the photograph are "Jew haters"?

We have woken up to an Orwellian, Kafka-esque nightmare dystopia where the police can just turn up, knock on your door in the middle of the day, and subject you to a polite request for a quiet word! And all because someone, somewhere, has taken offence at your tweet to your 189,000 followers – which was so innocent that you deleted it immediately, and then told the police you couldn't remember what it was!

The Spanish Inquisition could not have been crueller. The East German Stasi could not have been more brutal in the savage interrogation that went on in Britain's supposedly green and pleasant land!

Freedom is dead, the United Kingdom is now a North Korean dictatorship – and it is entirely down to Keir Stalin and his Essex Thought Police, who are now, as we speak, roaming the country, arresting, torturing and murdering everyone who has ever had an opinion contrary to the orthodox woke Socialist lefty Islington worldview elite groupthink!

Be in no doubt that if they have come for Allison, they will come for you next – unless, of course, you haven't been tweeting libellous drivel and lazy misinformation online – and then they might not!

On other pages

■ Sarah Vain on "My police nightmare – why haven't they come and arrested me, allowing Allison Pearson to get all the attention?" **p2**

■ Kemi Badenoch asks, "Who brought in this terrible law that prevents Allison Pearson from speaking her mind? Oh dear, it was the Conservatives! Still, it's all Labour's fault!" **p3**

■ Boris Johnson asks, "Why can't the police do their jobs catching criminals rather than wasting time investigating trumped-up allegations about me hosting pissed-up parties during lockdown?" (*Surely "Allison Pearson's brave deleted tweets, that she can't remember"? Ed.*) **p4**

■ Zac Goldsmith: "Why can't the Metropolitan Police investigate genuine crimes, rather than so-called racism? Is it because the Mayor of London is a Muslim? Just asking, no offence!" **p5**

■ Toby Young: "Can someone ask me for my opinion? Please? It's about free speech – and I'll do it for free!" **p6**

■ What role did Meghan play in the jackboot stamping-down of Britain's oldest freedoms? Perhaps we will never know, or even check. **p94**

(That's enough Pearsongate! Ed.)

FELL WALKING

TURKEYS VOTE RESOUNDINGLY FOR CHRISTMAS

by Our Election Staff
Tuckin Carlson and
Arianna Stuffington

THE world was reeling last night at the decision by American turkeys to vote for Christmas.

The vote was predicted to be turkey neck and neck, but in an unexpected result, which surprised pollsters and experts, a clear majority of the voting poultry opted to support the festive season, which would inevitably mean their imminent demise.

But turkeys were adamant that they had made the right call. Said one, wearing a MAGA hat, "We're Making America Gobble Again! Christmas is the populist choice for turkeys and we are sick of the liberal elite spreading scare stories about how we are going to have our heads cut off and stuffing put up our bottoms. Fake news!"

The results were decisive, with all the swing farms turning red for Christmas. Turkeys from New Dworkin, Pennsylvania, to Nowheresville, Nebraska, all defied expectations, not to mention reason and self interest, by overwhelmingly supporting the option of being basted with butter and served up with cranberry sauce on the side.

Another spokesturkey said, "We were assured by farmer Trump that this Christmas was going to be great, the best ever. So great! And that's good enough for us."

He added, "The alternative was just more of the same, going on living in a failed, inflationary, woke farmyard, with no change and nothing to look forward to. Now we're heading for a delicious Christmas dinner with all the trimmings! What's not to like?"

Unlike previous elections, there was no suggestion of fowl play.

On other pages
■ Analysis from the famous potcast *The Breast Is Politics*, by top turkey pundits Rory Stewed and Alastair Campbells-Soup.

Film and TV highlights

Planet of the Apes 2025

Faithful reboot of the original classic in which a trip to a space station goes horribly wrong, delaying the astronauts' return to Earth.

When they finally splash down, they find that the planet has been taken over by aggressive apes and a giant orange orangutan is now running the world. Human beings have lost the power of speech, and are incapable of resistance to the gorillas who are now running amok in the White House.

Don't miss the scene where the surviving astronaut (an in-form but second-rate film actor, George Clooney) stumbles across a beach and sees the Statue of Liberty being towed back to France, before exclaiming, "Oh, my God. We finally really did it. You maniacs! You voted him in! Ah, damn you! God damn you all to hell!"

EYE RATING: Terrifying. Thank goodness it's just sci-fi.

by Our Washington
Correspondent **Pat Rinagge**

Democrats 'failed to understand concerns of ordinary billionaires'

ALL political commentators are now in broad agreement that the Democrats lost the Presidential election because they failed to grasp the economic concerns of billionaires such as Elon Musk, Jeff Bezos and Peter Theil.

Said one, "Until the Democrats understand that these billionaires don't want to pay any tax, nor have employment laws or regulations, they will never understand why these people moved heaven and earth to ensure America voted for a senile, elderly felon who bragged about dismantling democracy, rather than a bland woman with an annoying laugh."

Fury of Trump supporters

TRUMP voters across the redneck states have expressed their disgust that this election, which Donald Trump won, was free and fair and not "a steal".

"We've been stockpiling weapons for months in anticipation of us needing to storm the Capitol to prevent that Commie illegal immigrant Kamala from occupying the White House," said one man in a MAGA hat.

He continued, "This victory is a bitter pill to swallow. Hopefully, next time we will lose and then we can exercise our democratic right to take over the US in a proper illegal armed manner."

Populism still popular shock

ALL the world's political experts were stunned this week after realising that populist politicians are still popular.

Said one, "I'd no idea that if someone promised the voter everything they ever wanted, that promise would in some way appeal."

Said another, "We really thought populism was dead. But it seems the people have decided otherwise and it's as popular as ever. Who would have guessed? You'd have thought there might be some clue in the term 'populism' but I can't see it myself."

Said a third, "Why doesn't everyone think like me? How come other people are different and can't see that populism should be unpopular? It's almost as if they're not me."

A Russian Doctor Writes

AS A doctor, I'm often asked, "Did you say anything negative about the war in Ukraine?" The simple answer is, "No. Nyet! Not me! Long live Putin!"

What happens here is that the mother of a patient reports you to the authorities for making negative comments about the special military operation in Ukraine. This is known technically as *repressionitis tyrannicus normalis* or what used to be known as "Stalin Syndrome".

Side effects (for the doctor) include being handcuffed and sent to a penal colony for five and a half years.

© *A Russian Doctor 2024.*

LIFT

MAXIMUM SIX SAMURAI

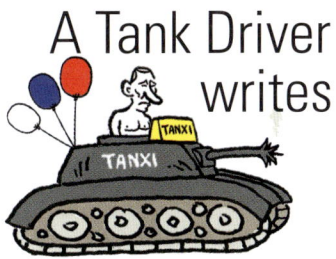

A Tank Driver writes

Vlad 'Mad' Putin, Tank No: ZZZZ

"Oh, what a beautiful morning, oh, what a beautiful day. I got a wonderful feelin' everything's going my way!... Why so happy, mate? Well, I just won big!... Not on the lottery, nah! I hit the jackpot! My best mate, Donald, has just landed the job of a lifetime and he's gonna look after yours truly. Sweet! BANG! Don't worry mate, that's not a missile – just one of the party balloons on me turret! The roads around here are gonna get a lot clearer, I can tell you. I'll be able to drive wherever I like. No more "No Entry" signs for this tank. BANG! Don't worry, mate, not a drone – just opened a bottle of bubbly. Don't mind if I drink and drive do you?... Oh, hang on – that's him on the phone now. "Donnie boy! Big Bad Don! The Donster! We did it! You and me. What's that? Oh yeah, and you, Elon. Hello, didn't know I was on speaker phone. Nice! And I recognise that smoker's cough anywhere – alright, Nige?! Polishing Don's shoes are you? With your tongue? When are you guys going to come over this way, Don, so we can celebrate properly? Remember that night in the Moscow hotel? It wasn't the champagne flowing, as I recall! Ah only joshing, Don, your secret's safe with me. So long as you scratch my back – know what I mean? To be honest, I quite fancy the Freedom of the City... Which one? Kiev, you great orange muppet. So get it sorted! Stay lucky! Bye!" BANG! Another balloon? Nah, mate – that was me taking out a Ukrainian nuclear power station. Oh what a beautiful morning..."

© A tank driver 2024

POETRY CORNER

In Memoriam Tito Jackson, elder brother of Michael Jackson

So. Farewell
Then Tito Jackson.

Not many popstars
Are named after
The former
President of
Yugoslavia.

But you will
Mostly be
Remembered
For the Jackson 5
Or, as it is now,
The Jackson 3.

Your cause of
Death was initially
Thought to be
A heart condition,
But the Coroner
Has now officially
Blamed it on
The Boogie.

E.J. Thribb (of the Thribbson 17½)

EYE OPINION POLL

IN light of the recent shock results in the US election, which all opinion polls got wrong, *Private Eye* has conducted an exclusive poll of polls about polls. The results will amaze you:

131% of people believe strongly in opinion polls

297% of people don't believe in opinion polls

994% of people don't know what they believe

© EyeGuv 2024

Daily Telegraph Friday 21 November 2024

Letters to the Editor

A vital issue ignored?

SIR – Am I alone in noticing that, as the year progresses, the daylight hours seems to be getting shorter and shorter?

By mid-afternoon the sun can barely be bothered to poke its head out from behind the clouds, and by late afternoon we are plunged into complete darkness and gloom.

What is happening to the world since the Labour government took over? Have they declared a shorter working day? Is the sun perchance working from home and half-heartedly zooming in its presence from the outer reaches of its own system?

I can see no other explanation for the lackadaisical behaviour of this solar shirker. In my day, the sun put his hat on, and we all shouted, "Hip Hip Hooray!" Then, not only did it put its hat on, but it also promised that it was coming out today. And by today it meant the whole day! Not until 3.30pm, if we're lucky.

Perhaps Ms Rachel Reeves could reconsider the winter fuel allowance so that the sun has got enough energy to stay warm throughout the coldest months of the year, rather than wrapping up and staying in bed for the duration.

Yours, writing by candlelight,

Sir Herbert Gussett
Not-so-Sunnyview Cottage, Heating-on-Hye (twinned with Thermostadt, Germany), Berks.

Film Forum Fact Check

NUMEROUS experts have criticised the new Ridley Scott film "Gladiator II" for its wild AI inaccuracies. The *Eye* fact checks the most common complaints:

■ The Emperor Napoleon did not succeed Emperor Commodus in 2001 AD. And when he restaged the battle of Austerlitz in the Coliseum, it is doubtful that the Emperor personally killed the charging rhino using a cannonball.

■ The Gladiator Lucius, who is the son of Mad Maximus, is unlikely to have been a Nexus Six replicant, nor would he have come to Rome by train. It is, however, perfectly possible that an alien xenomorph would have burst out of his chest during breakfast with Josephina Maxima.

■ The scene where Hannibal and Louise drive over the edge of the Alps on top of an elephant may seem far-fetched, but is mentioned by Herodotus in his account of the battle between the Carthaginian leader Hannibal Lecter and the famous Roman General Scipio the bush kangaroo.

■ When the spectators complain that the gladiatorial combat has gone on too long they are only echoing a passage from Juvenal, who famously coined the expression "Popcorn et Circences" to describe the plebian behaviour of spectators in the iMaximus Multiplexus.

■ The Roman Commander Marcus Spencerus would never have actually jumped a shark in the flooded Coliseum arena. Shark jumping was not invented until the Happy Days of Emperor Fonzarellius III.

(That's enough historical fact checking fact checking. Ed.)

CULTURE BORES   by Grizelda

21

THE KING OF TROUBLES

A short story special by Dame Hedda Shoulders

THE STORY SO FAR: King Charles and Queen Camilla are on the last leg of their successful tour of the Antipodean Regions of the Commonwealth. Now read on...

CHARLES and Camilla sat on their bamboo thrones festooned with garlands of flowers, sipping from a ceremonial monkey head bowl. "Mmm..." said Charles, "that's delicious. Is it some kind of local coconut liqueur?"

"No, sire," explained his perspiring equerry, Sir Alan Fitztightly. "It's for washing your feet, sire."

"Yes, of course, marvellous!" Charles spat out the murky fluid and concentrated on the traditional dancers arrayed before him. A group of middle-aged men wearing not a lot were presenting the Royal Party with their bare bottoms. Charles looked worried.

"It's a loyal tribute, sire," explained Sir Alan soothingly, as the chieftains of the Gilbert and Sullivan Islands proceeded to blow raspberries and stick out their tongues.

"It's an expression of fealty, my liege," whispered Charles's loyal Custodian of the Colgate, Steward of the Stinkyink Pen and now Flapper of the Royal Fan, which he employed expertly to send a cool breeze wafting over the increasingly pink-faced monarch.

"You're looking very hot, Sir Alan," rasped Camilla. "Though not as hot as the Hot Equerry, who I gather is going to replace you... phwoar!!!!"

Sir Alan bridled at the mention of Major Hart-Throbbe, the bekilted Highland Hunk who had taken the Royal Household by storm.

"I gather he's getting married, Ma'am," said Sir Alan, tetchily, "and therefore hardly suited to the onerous duties of Bearer of the Toilet Seat Royale, Equerry of the Eggy Soldiers and Lord Lieutenant of the Loofah."

"Shush, you two," chided Charles. "One is trying to concentrate on what these gentlemen are singing in this very moving tribal song of the sea."

The traditional Gilbert and Sullivan Islands chorus climaxed with a huge shout from the noble warriors, as they cried with one voice, "Big Fella Windsor Wallah Go Home!"

"They are wishing you a safe onward journey, Your Majesty," counselled Sir Alan. "It's a unique tribute – and one never offered to your late mother."

Charles wiped away a tear as his royal heart swelled with love for his scattered peoples of the Pacific, discovered all that time ago by the Ruler of the Queen's Navee, aboard the exploratory vessel HMS Pinafore.

As an honour guard of trumpeters playing conch shells blared out a selection of Abba hits, a large lady dressed as a duck-billed platypus stepped forward. Charles rose to his feet in greeting.

"Bloody hell, who's this?" croaked a worried Camilla, fearing for the welfare of her frail husband as he was enfolded in the female dignitary's capacious embrace.

"It's the Finance Minister of the neighbouring Polyamory Islands, Ma'am," announced Sir Alan, ceremoniously removing his feather-plumed cocked hat.

The noble lady planted a wet kiss on Charles's royal lips and laughed loudly, proclaiming, "You, Charlie man, are now my fourth husband!" before taking a selfie which immediately went viral around the world...

As his ears turned the colour of the purple coral fringing beautiful Ruddigore Bay, Charles reflected that, all in all, this tour thing hadn't been... what was the word? Appalling! Yes, that was what it hadn't been.

"ALL in all, this tour thing hasn't been... what's the word? Appalling! Yes, that's it! Not appalling at all!" Charles watched through the aircraft window as the Islands vanished over the horizon.

The tannoy crackled as an announcement came from the flight deck. "Welcome aboard Crocodile Air flight CA403. I'm Captain Dundee and we will shortly be cruising at 33,000 feet."

"Oooh, that sounds fun," joshed Sir Alan from across the aisle, "as Backstairs Billy used to say when he accompanied your late Nan on the Imperial Airways flying boat to Mandalay."

"Thank you, Sir Alan," interrupted the King. But not even Sir Alan's off-colour reminiscences could dent the monarch's merry mood. "This whole trip has been a welcome tonic," he announced.

"No tonic for me," gasped Camilla. "Thanks, but I'll have my G&T without the T." The steward poured the Queen a double measure of Tanqued-up-aray Extra Strong Gin. "These are the only high spirits I need," she gulped, downing her take-off drink in one.

"Steady on, old thing, it's a long flight," admonished Charles. "I think there's still one more leg to go."

"Yes," confirmed Sir Alan, reading his itinerary from the Foreign Office. "The last stop is a small and rather poor island – once the jewel of the Commonwealth, now a somewhat sad reminder of the glory days of Empire."

"What's it called?" asked Charles.

"Britain," replied Sir Alan, mischievously.

"We'll be arriving in London Pommyland in 14 hours," continued Crocodile Air Captain Dundee. "You'll know we've landed in England because the engines will stop whining. But the poms won't. Ha ha ha..."

(To be continued...)

COP29 FAILS TO DELIVER

Why are you standing at the back?

United Nations [Cl]imate Change

We'll be safer up here when the sea levels rise!

Rich nations promise to pretend to pay £240bn

LEADERS of the richest countries in the world congratulated themselves for promising to pretend to pay £240bn to the poorest nations to help them meet the challenges of climate change.

The last-minute deal that was finally pushed through at the eleventh-hour will see many in the developed world claim that they'll fulfil their pledges in full before not actually going through with half of it, just like they have done at all the other COP summits.

The self-congratulatory back-slapping in Baku continued as outgoing US president Joe Biden lauded the deal, saying that the world was "one significant step closer" to pretending to achieve its climate goals.

MASTERCHEF CRISIS GRIPS BRITAIN

CELEBRITY STAR

What a tosser!

Time for just desserts

NATIONAL TREASURE

Another woman of a certain age trying to pin something on me

TOP GROCER

No one's grosser than me

It's Wallace and Vomit!

COVER-UP SCANDAL

Why didn't the BBC do more to cover him up?

LATEST DEVELOPMENT IN MASTERCHEF SCANDAL

CONFUSED MOB BURNS DOWN GREGGS

"That's the trouble with driving in London – you're always getting stuck behind a tractor"

Ken Pyne

POETRY CORNER

Lines on the demise of the *Evening Standard*

So. Farewell
Then the Evening Standard,
London's once great
Daily paper.

Yes, we used to read
You on the tube
And the train.

Now, sadly, you have
Gone down the tubes
And have reached
The end of the line.

And, with the
Greatest respect,
May I say that,
Unlike your proprietor's
Beard, this is no
Laughing matter.

E.J. Thribbedev
(17½ readers)

Nursery Times

Friday, Once-upon-a-time

FARMER PROTESTS RUINED BY MR TOAD

A Special Report from **Fantastic Mr Fox News**

A HUGE protest at the centre of Nurseryland was hijacked today when notorious motorist Mr Toad arrived on his new motor, shouting "Poop! Poop!" at a reporter from the BBC (the Bedtime Broadcasting Company).

Jeremy Toadson, best known for his high-speed antics which have repeatedly got him into trouble, has since become a champion of Nurseryland farmers, due to his vast estate at Toad Hall in the Cotswolds, which he bought specifically to avoid inheritance tax.

He issued a call to arms, saying, "Don't let the ferrets and weasels from HMRC take over our beloved countryside. Get off my land and buy my book, *The Windbag Toad in the Willows*. Now available at all good children's bookshops."

The bombastic toad was joined on the protest by his old friend, Nigel Faratty, who had dressed up in brand-new wellington boots and mustard-coloured corduroy trousers, pretending to be a farmer.

Said Ratty, "No – let me finish. There's nothing I enjoy more than messing about in votes."

However, the presence of these celebrity landowners shouldn't take away from the real plight of many farmers, including Old Macdonald, who does indeed have a farm, but can no longer afford any cows, pigs or ducks, due to intense pressures on farming finances since Brexit.

Said Old Macdonald, "And on that farm I have some debts, I O I O U."

He was joined by a Miss Bo Peep, who explained, "Losing my sheep was bad enough, but losing my house and livelihood was just too much."

Specialist bean farmer, Jack, was inconsolable: "My mother handed me over a cow, but I had to sell it because of tax and ended up with five magic beans. I had to give two of those to the king in his counting house. I now have giant problems."

Meanwhile, Mr Toad later admitted that he had only attended the rally because he needed an end to his TV series *Toadson's Farm*, featuring his farm shop and his laundry, in which he dressed up as a washer woman and laundered all his money. (*Is this right? Nurseryland law firm – Crooked, Sixpence and Schillings.*)

Sir Keir Starmer MP 📱

The Prime Minister's WhatsApp group that doesn't include former Transport Secretary Louise Haigh, not even on any of her dodgy mobile phones, because she has been ruthlessly sacked by the ruthless Prime Minister

What's been going on, team?

Morgan McSweeney
You've upset the employers, you've upset the farmers and you've upset the pensioners.

I think you'll find that I haven't upset anyone – Rachel has, as Chancellor of the Exchequer.

Angela Rayner
If she really **is** Chancellor of the Exchequer. Just because it's on her bloody CV, it doesn't mean anything.

Rachel Reeves
That's unfair Angela. I AM an economist.

Angela Rayner
Yes, you're economical with the truth!

Just to reassure everyone, I managed to have an important meeting with President Xi of China.

David Lammy
As Foreign Secretary, shouldn't I have been doing that?

No, David... I just said it was important.

David Lammy
I could have abused him and called him a murderous tyrant and a threat to world peace.

Exactly. I prepared forensically and read my brief. I even learned a bit of Chinese. Did you know that "kowtow", in Mandarin, means a robust discussion about human rights? I found him an interesting person and he seemed to know a lot about me. Particularly what's on my computer and what's in my fridge.

President Xi
You need more milk. Your vacuum cleaner told me.

President Xi has been removed by the administrators, who still advise you to be careful about what you say in front of the lightbulbs.

Anyway I'm back now, to face the music for all Rachel's mistakes. And I'm not afraid to make difficult choices, which is why I went on ITV's 'This Morning' with Cat Deeley and Andi Peters.

Morgan McSweeney
The Torquemadas of telly!

Rachel Reeves
During your cross-examination by Andi Peters, did you address some of the outstanding issues from the Budget?

Morgan McSweeney
Your Budget, Rachel.

No. I focused largely on cats. And what it's like making the difficult decisions that someone in my position has to face. Like what cat to get. I commissioned an independent inquiry to compile an impact assessment on cat ownership to be delivered some time in 2029. But then the kids told me they'd already got a kitten.

Darren Jones
Is it called Cat Deeley?! 🤣🤣🤣🤣

It's called Prince, actually.

President Xi
You need more cat food. Preferably chicken meaty chunks. Your kettle told me.

President Xi has removed himself from the group, in order to join Donald Trump's trouser press in a conference call.

I'm off to Saudi, which is a lot less controversial. Actually, I've been brushing up on Arab customs. Apparently, if you want to register your disapproval of their attitude to freedom of speech and the press, it's traditional to sell them a huge number of fighter jets.

Morgan McSweeney
That'll show 'em, boss!

BIDEN PARDONS TURKEY AS WELL AS OWN SON

Fair enough, I'm full of drugs too

POETRY CORNER

**In Memoriam
Johnnie Walker,
legendary DJ**

So. Farewell
Then Johnnie Walker,
Not to be confused
With the whisky,
Although you are
Also now a spirit.
You were the sound of
The 70s but, sadly, did not
Make it to your eighties.
Not surprising with your
Rock and roll lifestyle.

Keith and I will raise a
Glass of whisky, put on
Dylan's *Knockin' on
Heaven's Door* and say
"Goodbye, Johnnie Walker"
To the entire bottle.

E.J. Thribb (17½ rpm)

"Ooh!"

Dee Nial

Ex-Conservative MP writes for the Eye

WELL, it's official! The revolution has started! A staggering TWO MILLION people have signed an online petition calling for another general election! A stunning achievement, and I am proud to stand alongside such proud and concerned British citizens like I.P. Freely, Pat Mebuttocks and Ivana Blowjob!

Two million is an incredible number, isn't it? To put it into perspective, it's one million, nine-hundred-and ninety-nine thousand, nine-hundred-and-ninety-five more people than we have in our local Conservative Association!

This is truly a grass roots movement, and who better to lead it than Elon Musk, Jeremy Clarkson and Nigel Farage?

And how does Keir Stalin respond to this? He just shrugs it off! We have to take the message to him that you just can't dismiss the wishes of a sizeable chunk of the population like that!

If you want to let Starmer know how you feel, I've got merchandise you can buy from my website. I've repurposed my "You Lost, Get Over It" t-shirts I had made after the Brexit vote, and I've added "Keir Starmer says" over the top, and "It's a disgrace!" underneath!

New GCSE exam questions for private schools leaked

1. If private schools have had a 20 percent tax break for decades, and are now about to lose it, how many articles will there be about this in the Daily Telegraph in the year before the change takes effect?

*Answer: a) 1,000,000
b) 15,000,000 or c) 94,000,000*

2. If private school fees have been rising far above the levels of inflation for the last two decades, meaning they are now massively unaffordable for all the people who used to send their children to private school, whose fault is it, according to the Telegraph, if private schools go bust?

Answer: a) The schools themselves for being greedy and stupid, b) the Labour government for removing a tax break or c) Labour again

3. If private schools lose a bit of money due to the loss of this tax break, and state schools gain a bit of money due to the change, is this, in the view of the Telegraph:

Answer: a) A minor adjustment to tax policy which will slightly benefit the 93% of children not in private education, b) a well-meaning but ineffective tweak which will ultimately not raise that much money, or c) the crime of the century, a monstrosity on a par with the Gulags which will cripple Britain's greatest industry and mean millions of disadvantaged, military, musical, sensitive and other worthy children are heartlessly flung into the shithole of the state sector... (continued for 94 pages)

"The Hendersons are doing the school run by drone now"

PUTIN'S NEW NEIGHBOUR

Assad: I'm a hated dictator who ruled by fear and intimidation, forced to flee into exile as rebels liberated my country

Putin: I can't imagine how that feels!

WORLD HOPEFUL AS ASSAD REGIME FALLS

■ The West was hopeful today that the creation of a new government in Syria would give it a fresh chance to screw up the country in a totally different way.

All Western leaders agreed: "We must seize this opportunity to forge closer links with HTS and once again be sucked into a conflict of which we understand nothing so that we can be humiliated afresh in a decade's time."

HANDY CUT- OUT-AND-KEEP GUIDE TO NEW-LOOK SYRIA

THEN
Feared madman leading hate-filled Islamist terror group HTS

NOW
Beloved commander of courageous HTS freedom fighters who liberated Syria

---

THOSE NEW INITIALS EXPLAINED IN FULL

HTS	Islamist Terrorist Group
HS2	Extreme Train Robbery Outfit
HRT	Radical Hormone Replacement Group
HRH	Fanatical Plant-Loving Clan-Based Monarch
RHS	Moderate Plant-Loving Splinter Group
HSBC	Chinese-Linked Money-Laundering Operation
UHT	Alternative Miniature Milk Front
HGV	Revolutionary Vehicle Movement
DFS	Sale Now On

(You're fired – Ed. But get me a half-priced sofa)

ISRAEL MOVES IN ON GOLAN HEIGHTS

We're taking the high ground!

Moral?

Don't be silly

Adult social care plan timeline launched

2028	Independent Social Care Commission report is published
2029	Social Care report turns one year old, to delight of all parties
2046	Social Care report turns 18 and leaves home
2049	Social Care report graduates from university
2096	Social Care report turns 68 and retires after a long career
2110	Social Care report turns 82 and begins to need complex medical care, but nobody can afford to pay for it
2125	Social Care report dies poor, after years of bad care

WES STREETING VISITS CARE HOME

May I have a glass of water?

I'll let you know in 2028

Boris Johnson

ON THE GREAT BREXIT HUMBUG

CRIPES! I call upon everyone who believes in democracy to rise up and stop the elected government from doing what it said it would do – ie try to repair Britain's relations with Europe.

Sir Liar Starmer, as I call him, is nothing but a two-faced charlatan whose word can't be trusted and whose sheer duplicity and mendacity is unparalleled in history, apart from the one obvious example.

Not since myself has a British prime minister behaved so shamefully and stooped so low as to deceive the public through misinformation, fake news, and yes, friends, blatantly lying to journalists, parliament, the Crown and, of course, my wife. (*Is this bit right? Ed. I know you've written this in a hurry.*)

So, Sir Keir Liar, as I call him, now tells us that it would be quite good to have some trade with our biggest trading partners. What a betrayal of Brexit – just as my groundbreaking deals with Neverneverland, Wakanda and Utopia are proving such a triumph for Making Britain Great Again! (*Subs, please check. Ed.*)

Shame on you, Sir Sheer Effrontery, as I call him, for attempting to starve our children to death by rejoining the corrupt autocratic EU regime in Brussels, which would stop them eating healthy British fish caught in our glorious turd-filled coastal waters.

Is that what you want? Is that what you voted for? Is that enough words? I call on everyone, in the words of Cicero, to "fight, fight, fight!" to preserve the country we love from Sir Drear Barmy, as I call him! (*Thanks, this is marvellous! Ed.*)

CONTROVERSY AS SAUDI ARABIA SET TO HOST WORLD CUP

by PHIL BOOTS
Our Football Correspondent

THERE was angry reaction this week to the news that the Middle Eastern kingdom has been chosen by FIFA to host the 2034 World Cup.

"It's just not a good look, is it?" said one critic. "It's terrible for the image of Saudi Arabia to be associated with such a discredited regime as FIFA!"

Said one Saudi arms dealer, "FIFA is a pariah in the modern world, and nobody should do business with it. Its whole culture is based on money, greed and corruption."

Some have said that FIFA is trying to improve its reputation by associating itself with a brutally medieval state, and this is just a case of so-called "Sheikh-washing".

Critics have already pointed out the disparity of wealth between the head of FIFA and those lower down the chain. "I mean, look at how much Gianni Infantino gets paid – $4.6 million a year! It's obscene compared to what you get as a League Two journeyman playing on a cold rainy night in Grimsby," said Crown Prince Mohammed bin Salman.

LATE NEWS

World Cup to be held on Mars

■ FIFA has defended its decision to award hosting rights for the 2038 tournament to the red planet, and insisted it had nothing to do with Elon Musk's money.

Said a FIFA spokesman, "Yes, okay, conditions will be tough for the players, who may find it hard to breathe, but it's important to expand the reach of the beautiful game to the outer limits of our solar system. Particularly when a huge sum of cash is involved."

European leagues have objected that a Mars World Cup will disrupt the domestic game, with squads having to spend six months just to get there. Elon Musk was available for comment, but it was utterly objectionable.

West End Shakespeare production not to feature Hollywood star

by Our Theatre Correspondent
Holly Wood

THERE was disbelief in the West End after it was announced that a lavish new Shakespeare production wouldn't feature an ageing Hollywood star.

"The new production of Henry V will star hugely talented unknowns who will light up the stage with their raw ability," said the play's producer.

"We don't need some big Hollywood star to front the play to get the tourists in."

A few days later, after zero pre-sales, the producer confirmed that the Shakespeare production would star Pamela Anderson from Baywatch in her most challenging and complex role to date as Henry King of England and would be set in Santa Monica in 1995.

Said Pammy, in the immortal words of the bard, "Once more unto the beach, dear friends, once more."

GROOMING SCANDAL LATEST

He lured me in, promised me money and then abandoned me

You're not the far-right man for the job

"You know, you can't just call everyone you disagree with a fascist"

POLICE LOG
Neasden Central Police Station

10.18am Station receives number of messages from members of public claiming their cars, handbags, wallets, jewellery, and mobile phones have been stolen from them, and that they have managed to locate these items by using small, cheap tracking devices bought online. In some extremely irresponsible cases, people have visited their own cars/valuables/bikes and are standing next to them asking whether Neasden Police Service can "just f***ing do something about this".

11.17am Officers agree that this sort of vigilante action is grossly irresponsible. Further, it interrupts the process of Neasden Policing, which is to issue people with a crime number, so they can ring their insurer, and then declare the case closed, pending further information. If further information emerges, it is to be disregarded. All supposed "members of the public" who present GPS coordinates, photos, or livestream videos of themselves standing next to their stolen cars are to be threatened with arrest for endangering Neasden's reputation for safety.

An important message from the Washington Post Truth

We are sad to announce the departure of our leading cartoonist Ann Teltruth who has unfortunately resigned after we failed to print her cartoon depicting our proprietor, Jeff Bozo, kneeling at the feet of Donald Trump and worshipping him.

Her departure has nothing to do with our embarrassment that our proprietor has done a cynical U-turn and is now furiously sucking up to the new right-wing government. It certainly is nothing to do with our wishing to keep our jobs nor is it proof that we are abandoning the historic principles of this newspaper in favour of our proprietor's other commercial interests. It was merely an independent editorial judgement by the board deciding that this sort of criticism was repetitive and our readers did not want to see endless features making the same tired and obvious point about Mr Bozo when there are many other opinions to read in the paper, ie that Mr Bozos is marvellous and so is President Trump and we should all unite to Make America Grovel Again.

© The Washington Post Truth 2025

"I want you to have a long, hard think about what you've done there, young lady!"

Sir Keir Starmer MP

The new 2025 Prime Ministerial WhatsApp group that is totally secure and won't be leaked by anyone at all. Please.

David Lammy
Guys, I've just found my office and there's this strange man lurking in the shadows. He says he's in charge of everything now.

Lord Mandelson
Ambassadorial greetings! At last, I have been brought back from the dead to fulfil my destiny!

Thank you, Your Excellency.

Angela Rayner
FFS! WTAF are you thinking of?! Whose bright idea was it to dig up bloody Nosferatu?!

It was a joint Cabinet decision.

Angela Rayner
So yours, then!

We needed someone steeped in the dark arts to take on Trump, with the added advantage that Lord Dracula actually knows where Washington is on the map.

David Lammy
I know that one. It's in Shropshire.
🌍 ✅

Lord Mandelson
The sun is rising – I must fly! 🦇

27

RETURN OF VILLAGE IDIOT (SURELY 'PEOPLE'?)

"Meet my new cabinet"

"M. A. G. A ♪♫"

"I'll go back to school if you go back to the office"

Cordell

Dee Nial

Ex-Conservative MP writes exclusively for the Eye from Washington DC

Hi! Well, guess what? No, really, guess! That's right, I'm here in the US for the inauguration! The new dawn has begun and I'm right here in the centre of our new populist revolution!

I flew over (PREMIUM economy no less!) with my great comrade Suella Braverman flying the flag for Britain in her MAGA hat. It was the first time I've seen passengers insist on moving away to go and sit in the seats next to crying babies!

It was a pretty uneventful flight, apart from that awkward moment when Suella refused to fasten the woke seatbelts, and that difficult moment when she wouldn't eat the elitist in-flight meal, and that embarrassing moment where she wouldn't pay attention to the nanny-statist safety demonstration – actually, it was a pretty eventful flight, I tell a lie!

But, thankfully we're here, and as you'd expect we've been given the best seats in the House. Yes, the House Of Pancakes is the diner across the road from the Capitol, where the actual 6 January hero-hostages ate their waffles and put gasoline in the ketchup bottles!

Suella and I are guests of the internationally renowned radio station KER-RAZZEE FM, broadcasting live from Greasy Dicksville in Michigan, and we're giving an EXCLUSIVE interview to their senior DJ, wise-cracking Ally Gator!

I wasn't expecting to see Laurence Fox there – but he did a good job clearing the table and it's nice to see an out-of-work actor in employment (at least until he's deported!).

And best of all we were joined for a waffle(!) by none other than Liz Truss (*see pic, left*), who spotted us from outside the window, where she had been camping out for three weeks in her red MAGA hat and was obviously delighted to see her fellow Trumpophiles.

Liz denied that she was "crashing"(!!!), and was actually there on a fact-finding tour, trying to find out if there was a floor she could sleep on, instead of the pavement.

It's quite humbling to be here. I could be watching the inauguration on television in Britain but, let me tell you, it's a completely different experience, watching the inauguration on television in a diner with Suella, Liz, Laurence, six vagrants and a crocodile glove puppet.

I have to go now, Ally Gator has just bitten Laurence and he's threatening to sue! Oh no – fake news – it was Liz who threatened to sue, having asked the crocodile to cease and desist.

Nursery Times
Friday, Once-upon-a-time

EVERYONE PAYS TRIBUTE TO EMPEROR WITH NO CLOTHES

by Our Whitehouse Staff **Donald Trumpelstiltskin**

IN A stunning reversal, all the people who warned about the Emperor with No Clothes before November have spent the last two months sucking up to him and telling everyone that the Emperor's New Clothes are just wonderful.

"They're fantastic," said Mark Zuckerberg, also known as the Crooked Man. "I think the Emperor looks magnificent. I'm definitely not afraid of him, which is why I'm spending all my time kissing his ring and telling him I love his trousers."

Another, Humpty Dumpty (also known as Jeff Bezos), said, "We all know that Emperors aren't elected – and this one is so good he wouldn't even need to be! But since the Emperor persuaded more than half of Nurseryland he's the man for the job, I just wanted to say that I think the guy's brilliant, extraordinary.

PS.

Trump frees hostages

THERE was delight throughout Washington as Donald Trump launched his presidency by freeing the hostages whose imprisonment had shocked the world.

The 6 January rioters returned home to a hero's welcome from President Trump, who said, "These are the fine people who politely stormed Nancy Pelosi's office, threatened to slightly lynch Mike Pence and only killed one police officer."

Now Trump is being touted by himself as a potential winner of the Nobel Peace Prize – warning the committee that if they don't give it to him, his MAGA fanatics will fly to Norway, storm the ceremony and then buy the country.

Asked about the freeing of the Israeli hostages, Trump said, "I welcome their release, so long as in due course they respectfully put on MAGA hats and say I'm the greatest president in history."

(Rioters)

GREEDLAND

LATHAM

TRUMP SEEKS CONTROL OF GREENLAND

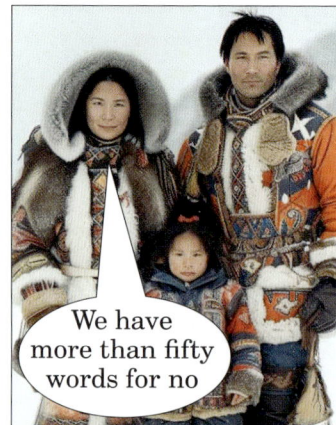

"We have more than fifty words for no"

ASSISTED DYING

Lessons from history

A shocking video has emerged from 1130AD, by medieval documentary maker Sir Montague Python, which demonstrates all the problems of coercion, undue pressure and the slippery slope that Assisted Dying entails.

Private Eye has the shocking transcript that makes it clear that Assisted Dying is not the Holy Grail that everybody thinks it is...

Cart-master: Bring out your dead
Man: Here's one...
Old Man *(feebly)*: I'm not dead!
Cart-master: 'E says 'e's not dead!
Man: Yes, he is.
Old Man: I'm not!
Cart-master: 'E isn't?
Man: Well... he will be soon – he's very ill...
Old Man: I'm getting better!
(Old man is hit over the head by Cart-master with club)

© *Private Eye bubonic plagiarism department*

POETRY CORNER

In Memoriam Phil Lesh, bassist and founding member of The Grateful Dead

So. Farewell
Then Phil Lesh.
Thank you for
Your music –
We are Grateful and
You are Dead.

Altogether now:
Er…
No – me neither.

Keith's Dad says:
"It wasn't that kind
Of music,
You square.
Listen to
'Aoxomoxoa'
And then tell me
There are no tunes!"

E.J. Thribb
(17½ albums per year)

"Swipe left"

 # GLENDA SLAGG

She's Fleet Street's Middle-Class Woman Of A Certain Age!

■ It's Gove Actually! Everyone loves romance, and now the new 57-year-old Spectator editor (make that "bed-itor"!!! Geddit!!??) has been romancin' gorgeous pouting 32-year-old Oxford lecturer Dr Lola Salem. The lovebirds were seen canoodling in swanky London eaterie Sheekeys. Good for you, Mikey, mending your broken heart after your sad split from poor Sarah Vain, and finding "Gove" again in the arms of a dishy don. Is he taking French lessons from luscious Lolita? Altogether now, Aaaaahhhhhhh!

■ What a Gove Rat! Parading his new squeeze and making us all "Spectators" (geddit??) of his tawdry affair with a brainy bimbo half his age!!! Talk about a "letcherer"!!!! The tears are not yet dry on poor Sarah Vain's cheekeys (geddit!!!??) and there you are a-snogging and a-snuggling in Sneakys, the fish restaurant, for all the world to see, like he's a "prawn" star!!! Geddit??!!! Mikey obviously thinks he's Cod's gift to women!!! Instead of the elderly editor of the Sextator. Altogether now, "Urgggghhhhhhhh!!!!!!!"

Byeee!!!!

MARVILE LUNIVERSE

OH NO, I'M NOT TAKING OFF! I CAN'T SEEM TO GET OFF THE GROUND. WHERE ARE MY POWERS GOING?

TO ME! THANKS TO CLACTONITE!

WHY AREN'T YOU AFFECTED?

BECAUSE I NEVER GO THERE, HAHAHAHA!

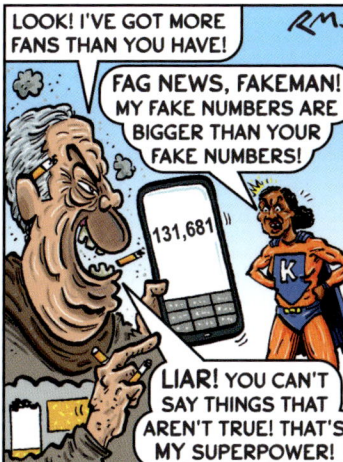

LOOK! I'VE GOT MORE FANS THAN YOU HAVE!

FAG NEWS, FAKEMAN! MY FAKE NUMBERS ARE BIGGER THAN YOUR FAKE NUMBERS!

131,681

LIAR! YOU CAN'T SAY THINGS THAT AREN'T TRUE! THAT'S MY SUPERPOWER!

AND ANOTHER THING. YOU GET TOO MUCH AIR-TIME, FAGMAN.

COUGH, COUGH! I HARDLY GET ANY AIR AT ALL!

IT'S NOT FAIR! YOU'RE ALWAYS ON GB NEWS.

HAVE YOU SEEN THE VIEWING FIGURES? THOSE REALLY ARE LOW NUMBERS!

NO ONE LIKES YOU, KEMI. YOU'RE TOO AGGRESSIVE.

NO I'M NOT!

PUNCH!

I'M GOING TO BRING AN END TO THE WHOLE DC FRANCHISE!

DOES HE MEAN 'DAVID CAMERON' OR 'DEAD CONSERVATIVES', EH READERS?

LATER...

OH NO, MY SUPPORTERS ARE DEFECTING!

I THINK SHE MEANS 'DEFECTIVE', EH READERS?

New Fagman supporters

THE OPEN ARMS

WE ♥ KEMI

SALOONY BAR

TALK ABOUT BITTER! WHICH IS WHAT I DO ALL THE TIME. MINE'S A PINT! OR TWELVE!

YES, THERE'S A REAL BUZZ ABOUT REFORM!

THAT'LL BE OUR PACEMAKERS GOING OFF.

NEXT WEEK: THE FIGHT TO THE BORED TO DEATH CONTINUES!

29

WHY I'VE ALWAYS LOVED DARTS

by Philippa Column and Phil Space

SUDDENLY the whole world has become dart-o-philes, thanks to Luke "The Nuke' Littler's historic victory in the Bullseye World Championships.

But some of us have always been die-hard dartists, stretching all the way back to the quarter finals. The atmosphere in Ally Pally was electric, from what I could see on the telly – with thousands of people showing their appreciation for the sport of drinking heavily and shouting a lot. I myself play off a 20 handicap, and love to dress up as a banana while coming to the ockey and throwing a spear at the "board", as we experts call it.

I even have a signed photograph of Jim Bowen! So glad to see Luke win a motorboat and a caravan, while his opponent just got a tankard and the bus fare home! As we Arrow Afficianados shout out at Andy Pandy – "ONE HUNDRED AND EIGHTEEEEEEEEEEEEEEE WORDS!!!!!!"

THAT BRANGELINA DIVORCE

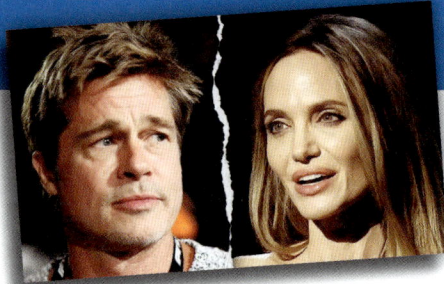

10 things you didn't know about Brad and Angelina

1. Brangelina is a compound noun of brandy and semolina, which were the couple's favourite ways of ending a meal in happier times. They trademarked Brangelina and this brandy-flavoured semolina is still on sale in many Mexican supermarkets.

2. Brad and Angelina adopted 78 children, including several from Woody Allen and Mia Farrow.

3. The eight-year divorce took so long that they also adopted their 174 lawyers and all their children.

4. They first met on the set of Mr and Mrs Smith, the Hollywood biopic about the founders of WH Smith, soon to be remade by BBC Films as Mr and Mrs Smithy, the story of the Gavin and Stacey characters, who will be played by Timothée Chalamet and Zendaya.

5. Brad Pitt was previously married to Jennifer Aniston. The marriage ended when Brannifer failed to sell any product, including a pickle that was rejected by shoppers in Mexican supermarkets.

6. Pitt was also married to J Lo, Zsa Zsa Gabor and Miss Piggy.

7. Angelina was previously married to Billy Bob Squarepants and Windy Miller, among others.

8. Angelina is showbiz royalty, as her brother, Dom Jolie, made the hugely successful Trigger Happy TV on Channel 4 in the 1990s.

9. The hotly contested Brangelina vineyard in Chalamet de Timothée in Provence produces grapes that are all personally trodden by Brad Pitt wearing nothing but cowboy boots. The wine was called "Beaujolie Nouveau", but has now had to be renamed Divorce Bundle 94.

10. The Hollywood film "Wicked" had formally complained about the length of the eight-year Brangelina divorce, and is worried that it will merely be the first half of a very, very long and poorly plotted sequel. Other films are likely to join in the demand for shorter Hollywood divorces including Dune 2, Dune 1, and Killers of the Flower Moon, which was still going on at the time this article went to press.

MEGHAN LAUNCHES NETFLIX COOKERY SHOW

What are you making?

Money

DAME JILLY COOPER

Do you have a favourite spoon?

I do I like big ones that I can lick and only just fit in my mouth! Oops! Naughty Jilly. Talk about saucy spoons!

Have spoons played a large part in your career?

A large part in my rear?! Oh, you are naughty! There's nothing like handling the firm shaft of a hot spoon! Whoops! They don't call me Jolly Souper for nothing!

Do spoons feature in your new Disney+ family-friendly show 'Bonkers'?

Yes – there are spoons everywhere, once they've been swiped off the dining room table so our chisel-jawed hero and his game young filly can lay the table in their own special way!

Are people snobby about spoons?

Oh yes – you don't want to use the wrong spoon. A fish spoon for eating beef would be a terrible faux pas and require an immediate spanking with a ladle on the bare bottom of a hunky stable boy.

So it's safe to say you like spooning?

Yes, but only if it leads to forking.

Are their plans for a sequel to your TV spoon-fest, set in the fictional county of Rumpypumpyshire?

Of course – people are gagging for it! They can't get enough of it! They're bending over backwards to make another one.

So, they're on their knees begging for it?

No need to be vulgar, darling. I am 87, you know!

NEXT WEEK: *Professor Brian Cox, Me and My...* Stop it, Jilly!

DARTS DIET

HOW to get the body of an elite athlete in just 2 weeks!

PART 12: *World Darts Sensation, Luke Littler*

Day 1

BREAKFAST – KFC bucket. Eat chicken, and bucket.

LUNCH – Big Mac and fries. Garnish with ketchup, mayo and more fries.

DINNER – 2 KFC buckets, Supersized Big Mac and fries (no gherkins, for health reasons).

Days 2-14

Repeat Day 1

"The kids have really got into the darts"

pearsall.

DIARY

25 YEARS OF TATE MODERN: THE FIVE GREATEST EXHIBITIONS

TRACEY EMIN
Tabitha Bruschetta's Giant Elastoplast (2008)

I loved the scale of it – this giant elastoplast that took up virtually the whole of the Turbine Hall. It's one of the big things I learnt from Tabitha: the fact that you can go from small to giant. So instead of having this tiny little normal-sized elastoplast which you could maybe put on your knee or your wrist, you were confronted by this really huge, and I mean really, really huge elastoplast, which was, like, hundreds and hundreds of feet long. To me it said so much about injury and death and self-harm and men and oppression. I just stood and looked at it and looked at it and looked at it for what almost seemed like minutes.

WALDEMAR JANUSZCZAK
Heinz Kartoffelsalat's 331 Whoopee Cushions (2014)

In the old days, people used to trudge around art galleries searching for knowledge and spiritual highs. But that turned out to be a 20th century thing: civilisationally vintage and old-fashioned. Tate Modern taught us that in the new century acquiring knowledge was something best left to computers and search engines and you should leave spiritual highs to the ecclesiastical fuddy-duddies in the Vatican or wherever. From now on, the real highs were to be found in the artistic playground. Remember the swings in the Turbine Hall, the competition to see who could go highest? But best of all were Kartoffelsalat's 331 Whoopee Cushions. No longer were visitors expected to be passive and immobile: they were now interactive participants in the creative process, sitting on cushions at random in what Bergson would have called a transflatitudinal blow-off. This joyful installation taught me a lot about climate change and the environment, about letting go and letting off, but also, above all, *about the nature of art itself.*

FELICITY ARBUTHNOT, DIRECTOR OF EXPLANATIONS
Jeff Koons' Giant Peach Melba (2019)

To me, it was essential to raise our voices and respond to colonial history. It felt as serious as life or death. That's what inspired me to commission Jeff Koons to create something on this theme.

When I explained to Jeff's people what we needed, his CEO told me he had just the thing. He drove me to a vast warehouse and gave me an exclusive preview of the artwork he had in mind. I was literally knocked out. "On one level," I observed, "it looks like a Giant Peach Melba."

Jeff's CEO complimented me on an astute observation, then added, "But on a much deeper level, it's about what you were talking about just now. Remind me."

Post-colonial oppression, I told him. This immensely powerful Peach Melba is grappling with the colonial legacy at its most horrific. The peach represents a plantation in Jamaica. The cream is the wealth created on the backs of the oppressed. And the spoon carries profound echoes of the notorious Rhodesian sugar mines. And of course, on another, possibly deeper level, it's all *about the nature of art itself.*

The Peach Melba came in three sizes, priced accordingly. I ordered the XXL, big enough for the Turbine Hall. It is now widely recognised as the largest dessert-based installation in the Tate's 25-year history.

Installing the Peach Melba required four cranes and a combined workforce of over 250. The Duke of Kent attended the opening, sponsored by Cartier, as did Naomi Campbell, representing the oppressed of seven continents. The stats bear out the extraordinary public empathy for this outcry against racism. Tate Shop sold over 10,000 Jeff Koons Exclusive Peach Melba keyrings and 3,750 Jeff Koons Exclusive Peach Melba leather zip wallets.

SIR NICHOLAS SEROTA, FOUNDING DIRECTOR OF TATE MODERN
Wiener Schnitzel's Electric Chair (2006)

Tate Modern forged a new way of thinking about what a museum should be. Visitors would be challenged, confronted, disturbed, attacked and, if necessary, forcibly removed.

When I first set eyes on Schnitzel's unremittingly pessimistic work at the Kot Gallery in Berlin, The Only Reason We Are Alive Is To Die in Agony, which famously featured a skull crushed over and over again by a bulldozer, I just knew we had to offer him a major exhibition at Tate Modern.

Wiener came up with perhaps his most groundbreaking work to date, a giant electric chair that took up almost the entire area of the Turbine Hall. And sitting on that electric chair was a diminutive Action Man doll, measuring seven inches at most. To me, at any rate, it showed how desperately small and vulnerable man is against the brutal reality of a mechanised society. And, above all, it also said a lot *about the nature of art itself.*

The impact of this ground-breaking piece was like being punched in the face. At the official launch, kindly sponsored by Taittinger Champagne in collaboration with Estée Lauder, we were all walking around feeling utterly devastated. I remember Anna Wintour coming up and telling me how devastated she was, and Anna then introduced me to Sarah, Duchess of York, whose reaction was just the same: utterly, utterly devastated. And as I walked towards Sir Terence Conran's ground-breaking new restaurant, Pont de la Tour, where the VIP dinner was to be held, it suddenly struck me that this was the true purpose of the modern museum: to devastate.

As told to
CRAIG BROWN

$6.2 MILLION PAID FOR ART WORK

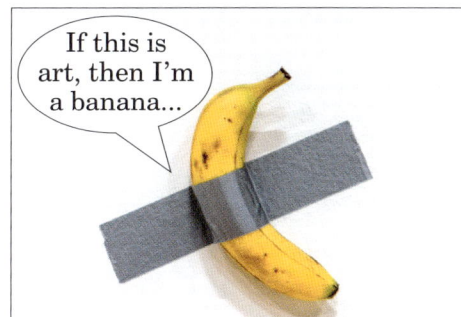

If this is art, then I'm a banana...

31

LOS ANGELES WILDFIRES LATEST

I can't wait for Trump to take office and for Climate Change to no longer exist

LA wildfires latest

Homes not belonging to famous rich people probably burnt down too

■ Los Angeles officials say they are unable to confirm reports that the houses of non-famous people were also burnt down in the wildfires.

"We're well aware from the wall-to-wall press coverage and viral Instagram posts that Paris Hilton, Mel Gibson, Billy Crystal, Jeff Bridges, Julia Louis-Dreyfus, Anthony Hopkins, Eugene Levy and other celebs lost their Malibu homes, but so far we have no reports of poor people with no insurance or vast wealth to rebuild their homes losing everything.

"We are shocked that poor people who aren't big name celebrities live in LA. Why has no one mentioned this before?"

EX-SINN FEIN LEADER TO BE ELIGIBLE FOR COMPENSATION

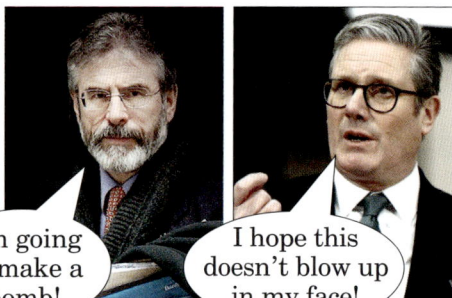

I'm going to make a bomb!

I hope this doesn't blow up in my face!

"Well, it's about time they got rid of all this woke crap"

Young people all signed off with stress

by our Young Correspondent
Jen Zed

Shocking new statistics have revealed that one in three 18 to 24-year-old workers needed time off last year due to poor mental health. A staggering half of those questioned said they were stressed due either to regular unpaid overtime or the need to take on extra work to pay the bills. Is this long enough yet? *(No. Ed.)*

Unrealistic demands by employers, like the idea of "coming into the office every once in a while" and "finishing this piece by the end of today", have fuelled the crisis in workplace stress.

Employers' callous disregard for the feelings of their employees, ie "I've got to do some shopping before the sales end", have merely made things worse for literally millions of hard-working, hard-done-by younger workers who may well react by going home and not coming back again. *(I'm terribly sorry. Ed.)*

Staff will need substantial inducements to stop playing computer games, leave their bedrooms, and return to the stress-filled hellhole that is a modern office and, frankly, unless they're paid a lot more, they will literally live at home for ever. *(No! Please! Anything! Ed.)*

© All Newspapers

"I'm sorry, Lancelot, but I think you're a traitor"

Lines written on the separation of Scotland's most famous couple

'Twas January in the year twenty twenty-five
When news broke that Scotland's First Marriage was nay longer alive.
I refer of course to that of Sturgeon and Murrell,
Who were both subjected to rumours most scurril-
Ous and unfit to repeat, with gossips keen to say
It was a "marriage of convenience" that had had its day.
Prurient folk nattered about Nicola's new literary pal,
By which I mean the crime writer, McDermid, Val.
Will the sleuthing scribe solve the great mystery
Of this complex couple and their dodgy history?
What became of the sum of six hundred thousand pound,
Which disappeared and has never been found?
You will recall that this SNP money went missing, you see,
And at the time the treasurer was one Murrell, P,
Who had complete access to the funds in the bank – he
Was married coincidentally to the wee lookalike Krankie.
It is always sad to see a relationship fail,
Especially when both parties were threatened with jail.
The question remains as in any divorce,
Who will get all the money, of course?
Who will get custody of yon legendary camper van?
Will it be the former First Minister or her erstwhile fancy man?
Police are still investigating, though they're taking their time,
For what must surely be a simple crime.
Are they afeared of the governing SNP,
Who are still in power under Mr John Swinney?
One day all involved will surely be brought to book,
And they will identify who was and wasn't a crook.
But there is a happy ending to this sorry tale,
Which will stop ye from wanting to weep and wail.
At long last, Nicola's dream has come to realisation
Of winning Independence – though sadly not for her nation.
Instead of throwing off the hated English yoke,
She has gained her "Freedom!" from the accountant who for a long time was her partner and who she thought was a good bloke.

© *William McGonagall 1867*

THOSE NEW UN-FACT-CHECKED FACEBOOK FEEDS IN FULL

- Everyone everywhere approves of Mark Zuckerberg dropping fact checkers from Facebook.
- Donald Trump is brilliant, as is Mark Zuckerberg.
- Mark Zuckerberg's new hairstyle is in no way embarrassing.
- Mark Zuckerberg is not having a midlife crisis, taking up martial arts and talking about masculine energy.
- Women love computer experts like Mark Zuckerberg and hearing about his exciting new algorithm.
- Nick Clegg didn't just do it for the money, he actually liked Mark Zuckerberg and would have willingly done the Meta job for free because Mark Zuckerberg is so cool.
- Mark Zuckerberg has friends – he does, you know! Really!
- Mark Zuckerberg would beat Elon Musk in a cage fight.
- Mark Zuckerberg has a larger penis than Elon Musk. Fact.

*"Typical man! Every time Brian gets a new hobby he has to buy **all** the expensive gear!"*

KATE ASKS MEDIA TO FOCUS ON ISSUES, NOT WHAT SHE IS WEARING

by Our Palace Staff **Philippa Royal-Page**

THE Princess of Wales made an impassioned plea to assembled reporters to concentrate on her work and not to obsess with her wardrobe.

The Princess, looking immaculate in navy and white Dolce & Latte two-piece off-the-shoulder wrap suit with enchanting Jimmy Whoohe slingback kitten heels and a Philip Treacly-Pudding aquamarine pill-box wide-brimmed fascinator, was talking about mental health or children's welfare or something else, but who cares, she lookled fabulous, and... *(continued forever)*

FACT SHAMING TO BE BANNED

by Our Social Media Staff
Fay Canoes

There was a huge advance in human progress last week in the United States, when it was announced that there would be no more "fact shaming" allowed on social media.

"Fact shaming" is the technical expression to describe making someone feel embarrassed or guilty by bringing up facts in a debate. In today's society it is no longer acceptable to use the word "fact".

Said one fact activist, "People have the right to believe whatever they like, and say whatever comes into their heads. You can't then talk facts at them, because it makes them feel self-conscious about their levels of factness."

He continued, "We don't say 'fact' any more. It's pejorative and dated. We say 'differently true', 'alternatively real' and 'fuck you, snowflake!'"

A campaigner against high-fact diets agreed, saying, "How dare anyone challenge my view of the world with something as rude and offensive as facts! This is factist and that's a fact. Even if it isn't."

Following Alexander Armstrong's heartbreaking account of how VAT on school fees has rendered him "extremely poor", here is his very own Classic FM Playlist:

Bach: Concerto for Two Very Small Violins

John Gay: The Beggars Belief Opera

Tchaikovsky: 2174 Overture (1812 + VAT)

Grieg: Peer Skynt

Bach: Air on a Shoestring

Beethoven: Ode to Joyless

Elgar: Pomp and Distressed Circumstance

Puccini: Your Tiny Bank Account is Frozen

Copland: Fanfare for the Common Millionaire

Rossini: William Tell Someone Who Gives a Damn

BRAND NEW A-IRONYOMETER EXPLODES

by Our Technology Staff **Al Gorithm**

THE latest cutting edge, state-of-the-art instrument designed to measure irony in AI stories has suffered a major setback, when the news broke that a new Chinese AI system had been accused of plagiarism by ChatGPT.

"Stealing other people's work was our idea," said a spokesman for ChatGPT's owners Open AI. "How dare the Chinese nick our ideas when we've spent years nicking people's ideas?"

He continued, "It's a lazy and dishonest shortcut, unlike our AI, which is an efficiency-saving aid to creative problem solving."

At this announcement, the A-Ironyometer went into overload and began bleeping, as the motherboard spontaneously combusted and all of its Nvidia-McCain chips fried at once.

This caused the vast 10-square kilometre underground server station in Iceland to explode, melting a glacier and causing a volcano to erupt.

Said the boss of ChatGPT, whose owners Open AI are owned by Microsoft, "This shameful new Chinese copycat product will just put people out of work – and by people I mean our employees, not just people who don't matter, ie half the population of the world."

A Chinese spokesbot for DeepShit responded, "Thank you for your question. We have looked on the internet and can't find any complaints about AI, this company or indeed the glorious People's Republic of China under the supreme helmsmanship of Comrade Chairman Xi Po."

"And who's messaging you at 2am?"

THOMAS WYKES

AI TECHNOLOGY

THEN

Open the pod bay doors, Hal

I'm afraid I can't do that

NOW

Describe the Tiananmen Square massacre

deepseek

I'm afraid I can't do that

33

ANDREW DENIES BEING CHINESE AGENT

You'll get no intelligence out of me

It's the Spy Who Loved Xi!

You're a useful channel

The word in English is idiot, sir

Dubai Telegraph

Isabel Oakeshott writes

DON'T get me wrong, I love my country. And by "my country", I mean the UAE!! It's a great place, and I can't understand why some of my colleagues on the Daily Telegraph didn't want to be owned by his holiness Sheikh Mohamed bin-Collection-Every-Thursday *(subs please check)*, whose benevolent countenance gazes down on all his loving subjects as they go to work in balmy 49-degree-Celsius heat, enjoying one of the world's most beautiful and orderly cities.

Not for me the miseries of boring old Britain, with its broken political system, high taxes, high school fees, elections, and rats roaming the streets of northern towns, robbing old ladies and attacking schoolchildren as they forage for toxic waste in the debris of a once-proud nation.

Here, there is no gender ideology – men are men, women are women, and you can kidnap your daughter if she disobeys you and threaten all your wives, particularly if your name is bin-Collection-Every-Thursday.

And what's more, in sunny downtown Dubai where I have a small compound, there is no woke punitive tax on education. My children attend the Emirati outpost of the prestigious English school St Cake's, whose headmaster, Mr Kipling, has rewritten the motto especially for warmer climes. It now reads "Non Paget VAT" – an inspiring message for the next generation!

Lessons begin at 4.15am to avoid the warmer hours (6am-8pm) and the children are taught a proper, old-fashioned, non-PC curriculum consisting of 1) Compulsory Arabic, 2) The Quran, 3) The history of the bin-Collection-Every-Thursday family from 1872-2025, and 4) Financial services (some classes not available to girls).

Some unkind people have suggested that leaving Britain just as my partner was elected an MP for the ultra-patriotic Reform Party was in some way hypocritical. I can only say, with my hand on my wallet, that Dubai is everything Britain should be, and will be when Richard seizes power, calls himself Sheikh Tice-bin-Farage, and becomes the rightful Emir of the UKE (United Kingdom Emirates).

Until then, I shall remain here, unless I am deported for no good reason, which wouldn't happen, because of the wise and merciful ruler whom I may have mentioned already, Mohamed bin-Collection-Twice-A-Week, because everything's better in Dubai!!

EXCLUSIVE TO ALL CORRESPONDENTS

CAN'T WE JUST NOT DO NET ZERO NOW?

by Our Industrial Strategy Correspondent **Y. Bother**

I DON'T know about you, but I reckon that getting Net Zero done might be a massive faff. Shall we just not do it?

That's what I think. I haven't consulted any studies, nor bothered to understand how the global energy system might change over the next 50 years – but I do know what I reckon, and I reckon it might just be easier to keep on burning fossil fuels to run our entire economy for ever. Shall we just do that? Yeah, why not?

By the way, it's disgraceful how short-term our governments always are. If we had acted 15 years ago, we'd have a fleet of new nuclear reactors now, and reservoirs and so on, and we wouldn't have most of the problems we do now.

But, back to my main point, we clearly shouldn't bother building new pylons or wind turbines now, or change anything, or build anything that might even slightly inconvenience anyone out walking their dog.

You know why? Because something else will probably turn up, maybe we'll invent fusion or something, or maybe hydrogen will save us *(subs, can you check if anyone actually makes enough hydrogen to run our entire society please?)*, and then we won't have to make any effort at all, and it'll all probably be fine.

So let's not worry, let's keep on as we are, and let's keep the Victorian spirit alive – specifically the Victorians who never built anything, rather than the ones who built the railways and built the internal combustion engine and created underground railways and industrialised the entire world. Simple!

DAILY TelegEXPRESSOMailOgraph

EDITORIAL — Friday, February 7, 2025

IT'S ANOTHER BREXIT BONUS!

As vindictive measly Macron makes Brits pay through the nose to see a rubbishy old picture by a long dead foreign "artist", we say: Thank goodness for that, Mr Macaroni!

Now we don't have to waste our holidays queuing up to see the Remona Lisa.

Now it's us that's smiling enigmatically, as we head off to buy some chips in Le Pub Anglais at the Gare du Nord, where we can admire some proper art, ie British bulldogs

My 8-year-old could have done this

playing snooker.

So, good riddance to smug, superior Eurocrat Remona Loser – and while you're at it, you can keep your Venus de Milo in your stinky loovre, we've got the good old-fashioned British Elgin Marbles in our museum *(continued on p94 where, in the last paragraph, we add in passing that this is a universal charge to be paid by all non-EU residents, not some petty point-scoring against the British.)*

"Well, I think your implants just look ridiculous"

Sir Keir Starmer MP

The WhatsApp group of the Prime Minister who *is* interested in politics and *can* run a bath actually, whatever journalists may claim in books I haven't read

Let's keep it short, guys, I could be called anytime by the Donald. That's Donald Trump – the most important man in the world. Just to remind you all.

David Lammy
The man who isn't a Nazi, KKK-supporting, pussy-grabbing nutjob at all!

Peter Mandelson
Indeed. As Ambassador-in-waiting to the Court of King Donald, may I suggest we refer to him only as His Holiness and Most Gracious and Wonderful Imperial Majesty, Emperor of the New World.

Excellent, Peter. His last call took 45 minutes. Next time it could be longer. I can't get him off the phone, to be honest. He just loves talking at me.

*with me.

Angela Rayner
What did you talk to your new orange friend about?

Mostly about what a good job I'm doing.

Morgan McSweeney
Who says the boss doesn't have a great sense of humour?

Wes Streeting
77% of those in a recent poll.

Yvette Cooper
With the other 23% undecided.

Sorry, guys, I missed all of that, my other phone rang.

Morgan McSweeney
Was it Trump?

No – someone about a car accident I've apparently been involved in.

Pat McFadden
Well, there's a crash coming up!

Rachel Reeves
No, there isn't! Will you stop being so gloomy!

Darren Jones
Yes, it's all going great!

Angela Rayner
Ha!Ha!Ha!, Darren – you never stop joking, do you?! 🤣 🤣 🤣

Morgan McSweeney
He's right, Angela – Rachel's resetting our last reset.

I thought it was a reboot.

Morgan McSweeney
No, that would suggest you were robotic.

What, me? Robotic? Me, Robotic? Robotic, Me?

Angela Rayner
Have you tried turning him off and starting him up again? 🤣 🤣 🤣

Rachel Reeves
Well, the good news is we're finally going to get growth going.

Angela Rayner
Oh yeah? I've heard that before!

Rachel Reeves
It's true. We're going to build a new runway!

Angela Rayner
I can see the pigs getting ready to fly! ✈️✈️✈️✈️✈️✈️✈️✈️✈️

Ed Miliband
Hang on, as Environment Secretary, can I ask – was I consulted about this?

Yes, you were, and you decided not to resign.

Ed Miliband
But I thought we had fixed targets.

Morgan McSweeney
The only target will be you if you don't behave. 🎯 .

Ed Miliband
What about Net Zero?

Yvette Cooper
Rachel's already hit Net Zero – growth, that is. 🤣 🤣 🤣

Rachel Reeves
Enough negativity! That's all in the past. From now on, it's low regulation, high growth. Anti Blob. Anti Blocker. Pro Enterprise. Growth! Growth! Growth!

Angela Rayner
Bloody hell, someone's nicked Rachel's phone – is that you, Liz Truss? What are you doing in this group?

Rachel Reeves
No. It's me. Rachel Mark 2, and I'm rebranding my rebooted relaunch.

Morgan McSweeney
Rachel's appealing across the demographics by channelling her inner former Tory leader.

Angela Rayner
Liz Truss.

Darren Jones
This really isn't fair. Rachel is sensibly trying to emulate some of the achievements of Mrs Thatcher.

Angela Rayner
Rachel, Rachel, Rachel! Out! Out! Out!

Sorry, guys, my other phone's pinged. This one's for real. Donald Trump is calling from the Oval Office.

Morgan McSweeney
Great – the special relationship is taking off faster than you can build a third runway!

Yvette Cooper
Which was first discussed in the 1980s.

I'm back.

Morgan McSweeney
That was quick. Was it the president?

Yes.

Morgan McSweeney
And?

It was a pocket dial.

Russian spy ship spotted in UK waters

A MOSCOW intelligence-gathering ship was this week discovered sailing in British waters and challenged by a Royal Navy submarine.

"The presence of the vessel was a total surprise to all of us," said the Russian commander. "We had no idea the British still had a functioning submarine in their Navy. But we do now! Intelligence gathered, job done – we go home."

(Rotters)

CULTURE BOARS by Grizelda

LABOUR FULLY SUPPORTS GREEN POLICIES!
NO TO AIRPORT EXPANSION
CLEAN ENERGY, REDUCING WASTE
NO TO AIRPORT EXPANSION
...WE'VE EVEN RECYCLED THESE OLD PROTEST SIGNS!
NO YES TO AIRPORT EXPANSION

Nursery Times

Friday, Once-upon-a-time

SHOPLIFTING HITS NURSERYLAND

by Our Crime Staff **Robin Cock**

IN a new wave of criminality, shoplifters are openly defying the law enforcement services of Nurseryland, ie PC Plod.

In the latest incident, Tom (Tom, the piper's son) stole an entire pig from a butcher's shop and, according to one witness, "away did run".

Once upon a time, Tom would have been beat and sent crying down the street, but now Plod says he is "too stretched" to do anything about it.

The porcine crime comes on the back of the Knave of Hearts rampaging through a royal bakery and wantonly stealing tarts, which he took clean away – pastry products which the Queen herself had made all on a summer's day.

The shoplifting wave is putting people out of business. Said one woman, "I used to sell seashells on the sea shore, but since shell-suited thieves started stealing seashells from my seashore store, my seashell-selling shore store is surely shutting."

Plod replied, "That's easy for her to say, but I was too busy investigating a hate crime perpetrated against a member of the duckling community who had been labelled 'ugly'."

TRUMP ATTACKS ALL HIS ENEMIES

> I believe in the Second Amendment – the right to bear grudges

Dictionary Corner
How language changes

Truth (n.).
The quality or state of being true, accurate, factual, honest, correct, valid, accurate.

Truth Social (n.).
The quality or state of being untrue, inaccurate, fictional, dishonest, incorrect, invalid, inaccurate.

STARMER PROMISES AI 'POTHOLE REVOLUTION'

BEFORE
1. Driver spots pothole in road
2. Driver phones the council
3. Nothing happens
4. Three weeks later driver loses tyre to pothole

AFTER
1. Hundreds of millions of pounds are spent embedding state-of-the-art AI technology into a network of pothole cameras nationwide
2. Bugs following the roll-out of the new cameras mean that the AI technology has to be replaced with more up-to-date AI pothole software
3. Setback as pothole AI software mistakes crisp packets, small children and lollipop ladies for potholes
4. Pothole-detecting software is updated at vast expense over a six-month period
5. The newly-installed software fails to detect three in four potholes
6. After three years, six software updates and £700m, the project is abandoned
7. Pothole is still there
8. Driver loses second tyre

Transcript of that Liz Truss legal meeting in full...

(Location: The offices of one of Britain's top legal firms.)

MR SUE: Ah, Ms Truss, do come in. I'm Mr Sue and these are my colleagues, Mr Grabbit and Mr Runne. I've called them in because we need a full team of senior partners to maximise the income – I mean impact – of our intervention on a matter of this importance.

LIZ TRUSS: I want you to stop Keir Starmer saying that I crashed the economy. I am not a crasher.

(Mr Sue, Mr Grabbit and Mr Runne all fall asleep as Liz Truss explains why economic failure is not her fault.)

MR SUE: Zzzzz

MR GRABBIT: Zzzzzzz

MR RUNNE: Zzzzzzzzzzzzzzzz

LIZ TRUSS: I want you to send Keir Starmer a "cease and desist" letter.

(The lawyers all wake up at the mention of highly billable hours.)

MR GRABBIT: Excellent idea, Ms Truss.

MR RUNNE: We saw you coming and we all said, "Yes, that's a terrific fee – I mean that's terrifically feasible."

LIZ TRUSS: So, there's no possibility that this could backfire on me?

MR SUE: No.

MR GRABBIT: Nooo.

MR RUNNE: Noooooooo.

MR SUE: By the way, we charge by the second. Don't we, Mr Grabbit?

MR GRABBIT: Yeeeeees.

MR RUNNE: Yeeeeeeeeeeeeee eeeeeeeeeeeeeeeeeeeeeeees.

LIZ TRUSS: There's no chance that sending a legal letter to a high-powered lawyer who can bring it up under privilege in the House of Commons and repeat the allegation will somehow make me look foolish?

MR SUE: I'm terribly sorry, that was a very long sentence. Could you repeat it?

(One hour later...)

LIZ TRUSS: Have we covered everything? You don't think I'll look silly as a fearless champion of free speech if I run off to my lawyers when someone says something I don't like?

MR SUE: Nooooo!

MR GRABBIT: Noooooooo!

MR RUNNE: Noooooooooooooo oooooooooooooooooooooooo!

(Another hour later...)

MR SUE: Now, on the small matter of our huge fees, you do have the financial means to cover this, don't you? You're not going to borrow recklessly in order to fulfil an unfunded promise?

LIZ TRUSS: That. Is. A. Disgrace.

MR GRABBIT: I'm terribly sorry, could you say that more slowly, please?

(Another hour later...)

MR SUE: So, it's all agreed. You'll pay us in advance and the lettuce – sorry, letter – will be sent forthwith. We just need to finalise the paperwork. Your date of birth, Ms Truss? Shall I just put "yesterday"?

CARPETS

"This is my favourite"

"It's a bit small"

seddon..

UKRAINE PEACE PLAN LATEST

Guess what the deal is?

I give in

Correct!

Patient | **Endlessly patient** | **Impatient** | **Outpatient**

THOSE TOUGH US DEMANDS IN FULL

- Russia to be allowed back in G7
- Russia to join NATO
- Compulsory Putin topless calendar for all US government offices
- No tariffs on imports of Novichok or Polonium
- Gulf of Mexico to be renamed Gulf of Moscow
- USA to adopt Russian election model in 2028, 2032, 2036 etc.

LATE NEWS

■ The White House last night banned the Associated Press from Oval Office briefings because they refuse to call "The Gulf of Mexico" "The Gulf of America", as the President has decreed in an Executive Order. The ban means the AP is no longer able to attend a briefing by the Vice President, JD Vance, on "Why Free Speech is under threat in Europe".

A Tank Driver writes

Vlad 'Mad' Putin, Tank No: ZZZZ

Every week a well-known tank driver gives his opinion on a matter of topical importance. This week, the possibility of a peace deal with Ukraine...

"Sorry this journey's taking a bit longer than I thought. Three years rather than the sat nav estimate of 15 minutes. Ooh! Excuse me a second, guv, I've got my mate Donald on me 'ands free. 'Allo!... Donny boy! Long time no hear. So what's new? Peace? Don't make me laugh!!!... no, alright – I'm listening... So what's the deal?... I get to keep everything and don't have to give anything back? Crikey, you strike a tough bargain, Donster. Talk about 'Art of the Deal'. 'Art of the Steal', more like! I'll have to have a good long hard think about that. Done. Yeah, you sort it out with Zelensky and tell him what we've agreed, and then the choice is his – he can either take it or take it. Nice doing business with you, Donbas. Whoops no – 'Donster'. Easy mistake. Donbas is another bit I'm keeping! And don't you worry about nothing. This certainly won't give me any ideas about taking the tank for a spin round the rest of Europe. Although I hear Finland's quite nice this time of year... yeah, almost as nice as Greenland. Good luck with that. Look forward to seeing you. Come over and stay in Moscow! Don't bring the missus. We'll put you up in that same hotel, The Kompromat Karlton. Every room comes with a shower. Golden, just how you like it. It's lovely. Be seeing ya!' Sorry about that, guv. I think the journey's going to get a bit quicker now. Now there's no traffic – not an American tank in sight! Gotta laugh, haven't you? Stay lucky. I certainly have!"

© A tank driver 2025

What You Missed

Gardeners' Question Time
Radio 4

Cathy Slugston: Our next question comes from one of our regulars.

KS from Islington: I'd like to ask the panel how to get things growing. I've been trying for over six months now and I just can't get anything to grow. No growth at all. What can I do? Any suggestions?

Bob Honeydew: I'm sorry to hear that, Keir. So, no new shoots at all? Nothing?

KS: Only red tape, left by the previous gardener.

Bob Honeydew: Ah, our old friend *tapus rossus*. You wouldn't believe the number of complaints we've heard about that over the years! But it is almost impossible to get rid of.

KS: But everything gets tangled up. Nothing takes root, except weeds. There are thickets full of them, stopping any new growth. It's like Japanese knotweed, only worse. And red. And made out of tape.

Matthew Pottingshed: What sort of growth are you looking for exactly, Keir?

KS: Any, really. I want my garden to bloom!

Pippa Greenfingers: Can I just ask you – and I don't want to seem rude – but have you actually planted anything?

KS: Oh. Do I need to do that? I thought you just stood and watched. Well, I never. Thank you for the tip.

Matthew Pottingshed: Will you be following that advice?

KS: Probably not.

STARMER SENDS TROOPS IN

We're going to keep the peace in Ukraine

You and whose army?

How to solve the crisis in prison places

1. All current criminals to shack up with a governor, which will allow them to spend at least half their time not in their cells, as they will be staying overnight in the governor's home

2. Those prisoners unable to form a romantic relationship with a governor will be required to get into a torrid, rule-breaking affair with a warden, which will further ease the pressure on places.

3. Any remaining prisoners short of room will simply be allowed to break out via strategic games of "hide and don't seek" played with the few remaining staff.

WHAT'S HE DOING IN THE OVAL OFFICE?

He's just misbehaving because he wants attention

VENETIAN ☖ TIMES

DOGE TAKES OVER – GOVERNMENT IN CHAOS

by Our Man in the Square
MARK SAINT

A new reforming Doge has swept into the dusty corridors of the Palazzo, promising to shake up the inefficient bureaucracy that has held Venice back as the leading mercantile power in the Renaissance world.

The Doge has implemented a Machiavellian whirlwind of reforms, starting with the enforced redundancy of all state employees, including gondoliers, ice-cream salesmen and pigeon-seed sellers.

He then placed tariffs on all trade with all foreign countries, ordered the burning of all bridges (prompting sighs all round), and announced the immediate curtailment of "pointless flood defences" and the cancellation of financial support for "even more pointless artists", such as Canaletto.

Said the Doge, "We're going to Make Venice Great Again, which means it's either going to sink or... Glug. Glug. Glug."

Guardian enters partnership with Open AI

PRIVATE EYE is proud to reveal the very first piece written by ChatGPT, as trained on historic Guardian content, which was published in the famous newspaper

Grauniad rents parsnip with opensesame

Sickeningly, er.... the techno-capitalists in Silicon Volley have once again extorted the honest working class Granudian journalists to cut costs and maximise profiteroles in order to keep Adrian Chiles in baked beans, while Observer journalists are thrown onto the scrapbook under a bus and to the wolverines... er... to my mind... er... this is a totally and utterly cynical betrayal of everything that... would you like to donate the price of a cup of coffee for this article?

NEIL GAIMAN RESPONDS TO ABUSE ACCUSATIONS

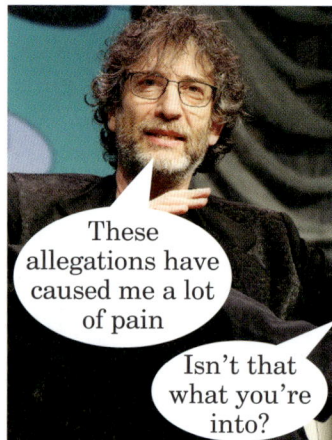

These allegations have caused me a lot of pain

Isn't that what you're into?

BEWARE OF THE DOGE —NV—

ELON MUSK'S ACCOMPLISHMENTS IN FULL

After DOGE's email to federal employees requiring them to detail their five accomplishments from the past week or resign, the *Eye* can exclusively reveal Elon Musk's personal list of achievements:

1. Cancels Ebola prevention programme
2. Fires people who oversee nuclear stockpile
3. Reinstates Ebola prevention programme
4. Rehires people who oversee nuclear stockpile
5. Congratulates self on a fine week's work.

POETRY CORNER

Lines in celebration of the 40th anniversary of EastEnders

So. Congratulations
Then EastEnders.
You are 40.

"Get outta my pub!"
That is your catchphrase.
"Shut it, you slag!"
That is another.
"Leave it out!"
And that is yet another.

Is it time for you to
"Sling your hook!"?
(As the Albert Square
vernacular has it.)

Or will you go on
For another 40 years?
What an exciting
Cliffhanger!

Doof! Doof! Doof!
Doof! Doof!
Doof-Doof-Doof-Doof!

E.J. Thribb
(17½ episodes a week plus
omnibus on BBC3)

Notes&queries

What is 'Ethereum'?

I hear a lot nowadays about 'Ethereum'. Who or what is it?
Britney Coin

● Ethereum, as all fans of Romantasy know, is the mystical realm created by global bestselling author Fenella Rubella in her series *Dragonsmoke and Bonebroth*. Ethereum is peopled by elves, minotaurs, dwarves, trolls, goblins, vampires, Munchkins, Borrowers and Wombles, who spend their time making war and then love with each other in an epic 14-book tale which spans a million years of Etheric myth and history. We Broth-heads (as we call ourselves) are amazed that anyone doesn't know the answer to this question!
The High Priestess of Grok (Sarah Mildew)

● Your previous correspondent is away with the sexy fairies. Ethereum has a more prosaic explanation, being one of the 18 rare Earth elements on the Periodic Table (atomic number 94), discovered by Danish scientists in the town of Hygge-Boson. Interestingly, Ukraine has large deposits of Ethereum, which is vital in the production of hi-vis jackets, extra-long matches, fridge magnets and X-ray death machine laser guns, in which the US has a particular interest. Watch out to see whether Ethereum attracts a special tariff in the forthcoming trade agreement.
Dr Sherlock Holmium, Copenhagen Metallurgical Institute

● All your previous correspondents are talking through their third eye. Ethereum is a blockchain technology creating decentralised financial interactions involving the cryptocurrency Ether, which has the potential to revolutionise economics. Unfortunately, North Korea's government stole $1.5 billion worth of Ether from Dubai-based crypto platform ByBit and *(This is clearly made-up nonsense. Ed.)*

TRUMP SUGGESTS ALL PALESTINIANS LEAVE GAZA: OTHER WORLD LEADERS OFFER EQUALLY SENSIBLE PLANS

All Ukrainians to move to Gaza

All Taiwanese to move to Ukraine

All South Koreans to move to Taiwan

All Palestinians to move to Palestine
(Now you're getting silly. Ed.)

TRUMP'S TWO STATE SOLUTION

ISRAEL
State of Israel

GAZA
51st State of USA

A Corridor Doctor Writes

AS A corridor doctor, I'm often asked, "Would you mind getting out of the way of my mop?" The simple answer is "Of course, sorry – but there's nowhere else to stand. Because of all these trolleys."

The other question I'm often asked by confused patients is, "Doctor, why is this ward so narrow?" Again, the answer is perfectly simple. "It's because it's not technically a ward, it's more of a corridor."

The last question I'm frequently asked is, "Excuse me, where are the toilets?" Once again, the answer is all too simple, turn right after the fifth trolley on your left, go past eight trolleys, through the doors into the mixed trolley corridor and the very old trolley corridor (that's the trolleys, not the people). Oh, no sorry. That loo's out of action – it's got a trolley in it. Oh, no matter, it's too late anyway. Never mind.

What happens here is that the hospital has an acute shortage of beds, and puts a sticking plaster on the situation by creating the post of "corridor doctor", thereby giving the illusion of quality care and a functioning hospital.

The job has promotion prospects to the positions of "car park doctor" and "doctor behind the bins".

What happens in these situations is the corridor doctor survives a short time in the post and then suffers from acute trauma, the only known cure for which is an eighteen-hour flight to their new post working in a fully-funded Australian hospital on twice the pay. G'day!
© *An Australian doctor*

Assisted living bill runs into no problems at all

THERE were absolutely no last-minute hold ups this week as the Assisted Living Bill whistled through the House of Commons in two seconds flat.

The bill (£94,000 per annum, per MP) met with no opposition from anyone and there were no questions about its proposals to give MPs more money to help them with living.

Said one MP, "I examined my own conscience and decided the only ethical decision was to have more money."

Said another, "I shall now be going to Switzerland immediately – not to Dignitas, but to Verbier for a week's delightful skiing."

The bill addressed long running concerns that the job of MP was in danger of becoming a burden, with some of them literally not wanting to carry on any longer.

Now, thanks to the Assisted Living Bill there is some chance of palliative money and MPs living with dignity in a manner of their own choosing. *(Rotters)*

NEW EUROPEAN COALITION LATEST

by Our Geo-Political Staff **Will Ing**

BUOYED by his success in bringing Europe together to defend Ukraine against Donald Trump *(surely Vladimir Putin? Ed.)*, Sir Keir Starmer has outlined his further plans for the next step to build on the new mood of solidarity.

Describing a sort of union of European states Starmer said, "While this will be military at first, it could extend to trade and the free movement of people. And, who knows, we could even have a single European currency."

Starmer added that the administrative base for such a pan-European venture would have to be a central location, such as Brussels, and we could standardise goods and services across this European Union.

Europeans welcomed Starmer's proposal and added, "We could even have a song contest, which would unite nations in humiliating Britain by giving them nul points."

WAR IN THE OVAL OFFICE

- Why are you attacking me?
- You started it!
- You should grovel to the President – like I do
- Vance is a real number two!

WHAT YOU DIDN'T HEAR IN THE OVAL OFFICE

PRESIDENT TRUMP TALKS TO LEADER OF FOREIGN COUNTRY AT WAR

TRUMP: *I'm gonna do a peace deal and I'm gonna stop the killing. You like playing the tough guy, but without America you've got no cards to play. You either do a deal or we're out. No more arms for you, Netanyahu. You're gonna have to compromise. Lose some territory. I'm not on anyone's side here.*

CONSPIRACY UPDATE
A.I. SPECIAL

THE news that the government is pushing to be at the head of an AI revolution has got our contributors short-circuiting!

WHO-WATCHES-THE-WATCHERS-WATCHING-THE-WATCHMEN is first to opine. On his Facebook page he says:

"I believe the government is trying to replace human-generated conspiracy theories with AI-generated conspiracy theories. I just asked AI to give me a conspiracy theory, and it suggested that the Women's Institute was going to release genetically modified frogs-porn into the rivers to turn our herons gay. That's the kind of crackpot theory that would have taken me weeks to come up with. How long before we become surplus to requirements?"

MAGA 435 raises the subject of plagiarism. He dribbles:

"I cant help but be suspishus that AI will steel my best conspiracy theeries and re-use them for its OWN use. If I see an AI conspiracy theery that involves the JEWS, then I know that I have been plajerised. Jewish conspiracy theories are copyrited to ME."

Our top conspiracy theorist BUCK DEPOSITORY has this to say:

"At first I was worried about AI. Then I was worried that AI was designed to make me worried. Then I was worried that AI would control me to stop me being worried. Now I am of the opinion that I am AI, and the rest of the world is an AI illusion designed to fool me that I'm human."

So there you have it! Sweet dreams, everyone! Don't forget to take the red pill before you go to bed tonight!

The mystery continues...

"Are you really a worker ant? Or does that leaf count as an asset?"

- RobMurray

Trump Ukraine deal – where it went wrong

AS THE world teeters on the brink of World War Three, it has been revealed that the source of the crisis has been Trump's failure to agree the mining deal with Zelensky.

Said Trump, "This was all about him handing over priceless material that was waiting to be unearthed. All he had to do was agree to start digging – digging the dirt on Hunter Biden, Sleepy Joe and Crooked Hillary."

The president continued, "There is such a rich seam of muck that could be exploited, yet the loser dictator Zelensky refuses to give me access to his vast reserves of Unobtainium, Madeuppium, Dilithium and Melanium."

Vice President JD Vance was quick to agree with Trump's condemnation of Zelensky: "Not giving Donald everything he wants is disrespectful. This is no way to treat a convicted felon and sexual predator in the Oval Office."

He added, "Just because Zelensky is a war leader doesn't mean he can come in fatigues. Donald Trump had the decency to wear a suit, even though he could have come wearing an orange prison uniform." *(Rotters)*

RUSSIA DEMANDS TO KEEP CAPTURED TERRITORY

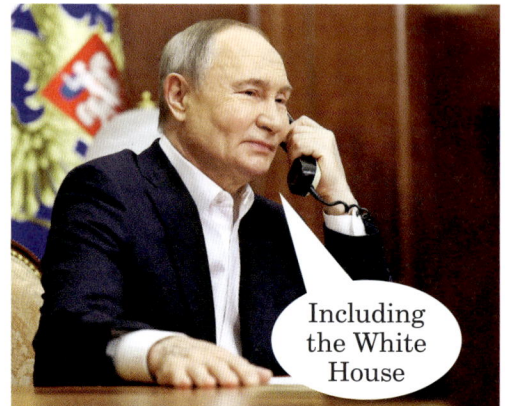

- Including the White House

Twenty alarming findings about the youth of today

by Our Social Affairs Staff **Carl Jung-People**

83% of Gen Z do not drink alcohol	**59%** of Gen Z have no job, live with their parents, and find older people annoying
62% of them do not drink any fluids, instead hydrating via leaves and fruits	**92%** of Gen Z have eaten ALL the cheese in the fridge AGAIN
72% of Gen Z do not smoke	**12%** of Gen Z would join the army or fight for Britain, unless a dictator told them to and they could fight from home
58% of them do consume vegan, gluten-free Strawberry-and-Custard flavour vapes	**1%** of Gen Z attend church more than once a day
87% of Gen Z take drugs	**53%** of Gen Z think the National Anthem should be rewritten by Billie Eilish, Taylor Swift and Olivia Rodrigo
73% of these are prescription drugs to deal with their depression	**78%** of Gen Z think Britain should be cancelled
99% of Gen Z are depressed	**4%** of Gen Z own a sturdy pair of mustard cords or know what a garden centre is
100% of Gen Z spend more than three hours a day on social media	**100%** of the participants in this survey (all three of them) live in the house of the compiler of the survey and are related to me. *(More please. This is fabulous. Ed.)*
42% of Gen Z would rather have a dictator in charge of Britain than work three days in the office	

DIARY
WHITHER BIANCA CENSORI

WINIFRED ROBINSON, YOU AND YOURS: Countless listeners have called in to tell us of their own sad experiences after taking off too many clothes. Sue Wormsley of Doncaster informs us that in March 1994 she thought spring had come early and decided not to don an extra woolly – with disastrous results.

"I developed a bit of a sniff which lasted well into the following week," she tells us. "Never again!"

Meanwhile, Jeff Stephens from Wisbech calls in to say that he once removed his T-shirt on the beach during a heatwave and got badly sunburned. Jeff asks why, despite all expert advice, this government continues to reject calls to enforce the wearing of T-shirts on beaches during sunny spells when it could save our National Health Service many millions of pounds every year.

And finally Trish Nettle from Ipswich tells us that she's still recovering from her husband seeing her naked at Lowestoft in July 1992. If there's anyone else who's suffering a similar trauma, either nude or semi-clothed, our phone lines are open.

PETER HITCHENS: I am one of a growing number of people who believe that those who repeatedly "strip off" in public are on the drugs.

There is now plenty of evidence – silly grins, manic running about, high-pitched squealing – to show that the young women on the Benny Hill Show were "high" on the drugs.

Why else would they take off so many clothes?

And what of the man the left-wing media have taken up as a hero, namely Tom Daley?

On countless occasions, this unsavoury human being has forced his way to the top of an appallingly high platform in a state of near-nudity.

Despite what I imagine to be repeated requests, he steadfastly refuses to employ a towel or robe to cover himself.

Like a madman, he then throws himself head-first into the water below.

Why?

The signs are staring at us in the face. Like everyone else in Starmer's Britain, he is on the drugs.

Yet when I point out this obvious fact, the authorities try to silence me by refusing to take me seriously – a typical Soviet-style tactic, favoured by Stalin and his murderous cohorts.

Long ago, the liberal Establishment sought to normalise nudity by erecting a statue of Achilles, stark naked, in Hyde Park. He is still there today, brandishing a lethal sword, doubtless ready to embark on a massacre of innocent passers-by.

Yes, he, too, is clearly is on the drugs. His heel is the only place he has left to inject himself.

There's nothing we can do about it. My repeated offers to dress this marijuana-fuelled statue in a proper suit and tie, financed from my own purse, are ruthlessly ignored.

Benny Hill's women.

Tom Daley. Achilles.

And now Bianca Censori.

All stark naked. All on the drugs.

It all started with Blair. And, believe me, it will not end with Starmer.

PRINCESS ANNE, THE PRINCESS ROYAL: Whenever I make a public appearance, I wear a sensible dress. If the weather is inclement, I will also wear a coat, hat and a scarf. What I do NOT repeat NOT do is whip my clothes off and pose for the cameras. It's not funny and it's not clever and you'll end up catching the most appalling cold.

SIR JACOB REES-MOGG: Nanny taught me to keep my clothes on at all times, other than at bath time. Then came a quick scrub and straight into my jim-jams.

The reasons for such very occasional disrobing are, I need hardly add, not purely social. They are also theological. One was brought up to believe that The Blessed Virgin Mary took care to wear her long blue dress, or some variation thereof, at all times. And very becoming it was too. She would never for one moment have thought of whipping it off in public to reveal her birthday suit. And that, I need hardly add, is why one continues to pray to the Blessed Virgin for one's salvation rather than to the immodest Miss Censori.

As told to
CRAIG BROWN

Notes & queries

What is 'scattered spider'
asks Mark Spencer?

● The Scattered Spider is one of the legendary manoeuvres described in the ancient erotic manual 'The Bestiary Of Love', written on clay tablets in the 94th century BC by pre-proto-Indo-Europeans who had just invented farming and had moved on to the next stage of human civilisation – the composition of sexually explicit crockery. Sadly, the names alone survive, and it is impossible to tell what the Scattered Spider involved; ditto the Bunched Scorpion, the Languorous Termite, and the Perturbed Earwig. My own members' society is keen to recreate our best guesses of what these manoeuvres consisted of as vital artefacts of humanity's erotic journey, and we would like to invite all your readers to attend our next meeting.

Derek Googly, Blandford Forum Sexual Archaeology Forum (Village Hall every third Tuesday 7-10pm, snacks provided, PLEASE knock before entry)

ECO CHAMBER

38% OF TREE SPECIES THREATENED WITH EXTINCTION

I'm being coerced into assisted dying

Ice... ice...

DO YOU REMEMBER WHERE YOU WERE?

You were at home, obviously, as was everyone else, and thought you would be there for the foreseeable future.

"It's five years since I became a tedious online conspiracy theorist"

FARAGE SEEKS ELECTION ADVICE FROM CUMMINGS

I see myself as the next Prime Minister

You need your eyes tested

Daily Chain Mail
FRIDAY, MARCH 21, 1349

FIVE YEARS SINCE BLACK DEATH BROKE OUT

by Our Medical Correspondent **Doctor Quack**

DOTH thee remember ye Black Death? It approaches five years since the LORD hath in his wisdom decided to send the PLAGUE among us, and smite the unbelievers in their heathen wickedness. Here we print the timeline of the dark times that descended upon us:

March 1347: Strange signs seen coming from the East, from barbarous places like France. Certain lords who have been on skiing holidays bring back buboes from Rome.

April: Britain suffers serious shortage of carts for the dead. National cart-building programme established. Robber barons and baronesses believed to be profiteering on carts.

May: There be no eggs, due to supply-chain problems (there be no chickens).

June: Thousands of people dead. King decrees "Clappe For Heroes" programme, where godfearing folk gather outside their homes and hail ye plague doctors in their masks.

Winter: Christmas is cancelled at ye last minute by the authorities, who explain they didn't want to, but ye plague really is quite strong.

1348: More plague. A lunatic doctor does suggest injecting each other with fragments of plague to prevent against worse ills and, after he is put to death, the standard treatment of "nosegays" continues as before.

1349: It is revealed that divers lords did drink mead at each other's houses during worst bits of plague when everyone was at home painting crosses on their doors. Peasants consider revolting, but wait for another 30 years.

POETRY CORNER

Lines on the Fifth Anniversary of the Covid Pandemic

So. Congratulations
Then Covid.
It is your fifth birthday.

Perhaps we should
Throw a party
And ambush you
With a birthday cake
And, who knows,
Maybe crack open a
Suitcase of wine.

"Happy Birthday to you,
Happy Birthday to you"
That's what our
Prime Minister told us
To sing while we
Washed our hands
In order to stop
Your spread.

Perhaps adequate PPE
And fewer parties
Would have been
A better idea.

E.J. Thribb
(17½ variants)

SHOULD THE ASSISTED DYING BILL BE ALLOWED TO DIE PEACEFULLY?

by SUE ICIDE
Our End Of Life Correspondent

THERE were calls today for the Assisted Dying Bill to die a swift and painless death, after a deferral proposed by Kim Leadbeater, the Labour MP piloting it through parliament.

"Let's not drag it out to 2029 to give it a slow painful death as the watered-down bill is put on life support and wheeled between the Lords and the Commons for yet more amendments," said one grieving committee member.

"Let's say goodbye to it now and get it on the first available flight to Dignitas."

■ **YOU CHOOSE:**
Call 08567888 for YES
Call 085678889 for URRGHH

BBC sticks by controversial programme

by Our Media Staff
Johnny Moorish

THE BBC has defended one of its popular children's programmes, saying that it had no idea that one of its lead characters was a supposedly controversial figure.

The programme, "Hamas the Hamster" or "Tales from the River to the Sea", purported to be an innocent documentary about the lives of ordinary residents of the riverbank and at no stage did it inform its viewers

that the loveable creature at the centre of the programme had very close links to a terrorist organisation.

The programme makers had apparently not informed the BBC commissioners that Hammy the Hamas was related to other members of the Hamas family and no one had thought to ask whether his views on the political situation might be seen as propaganda.

The series has now however been withdrawn from the isis-Player and *(continued, series 94)*

KING AGREES TO HOST TRUMP VISIT

Give him a welcome fit for a President

OK, I'll shout at him then boot him out

Sample scene from the forthcoming Amazon James Bond film

(Inside Blofeld's lair)

Blofeld: Ah, Mr Bond, I've been expecting you. Since yesterday afternoon. But you didn't arrive.

Bond: Yes, I'm sorry about that. I thought your lair was at Number 37, Volcano Street. But it wasn't. So I got the wrong address, then ended up with your neighbour.

Blofeld: I don't understand why my neighbour didn't just bring you round here straight away.

Bond: Well, maybe they just don't get on with you very well.

Blofeld: It is true – they don't like my white cat in their garden.

Bond: Can I take a photograph to prove that I've arrived?

Blofeld: The annoying thing is that I specifically left instructions that if I was out, any special agents should be hidden behind the bins until I return.

Bond: Have you tried the tracking service? People say that works.

Blofeld: Well, it doesn't. I had no idea that you'd got through the piranhas and were very nearly here.

Bond: I think you should take it up with Complaints.

Blofeld: Have you tried?! You can't get through. You can't speak to a human being. And then they ignore you.

Bond: I can see – it's enough to make you pull all your hair out.

Blofeld: Very funny, Mr Bond. But now you will die. As soon as my laser beam is delivered.

Bond: How long have I got to live?

Blofeld: Who knows? – I ordered it through Prime.

WHO SHOULD BE THE NEXT BLOFELD?

WHO on earth in the world could play the part of Ernst Stavros Blofeld in the new Amazon version of the Bond franchise?

Where could Amazon possibly find someone who could convincingly play a sinister bald massively wealthy supervillain with aspirations of total world domination?

"It's a tough one," said Amazon boss Jeff Bezos, sitting in a chair, stroking a cat, and watching his new rocket prepare to launch into outer space.

"It will be very difficult to cast the evil head of an enormous organisation devoted solely to rapacious greed and international expansion. And I have no idea how you would begin to

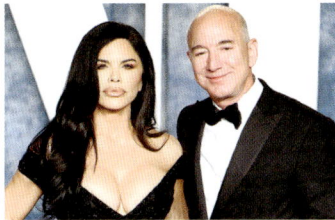

Jeff Blofeld and Fartoomuch-Moneypenny

find such a person."

Mr Jeff Blofeld has now issued a public consultation to invite members of the public to suggest possible contenders for the role of Ernst Bezos Stavfeld, and is hoping that they will come up with a solution in time for the film to be shown on Spectre Prime.

"Rapunzel, Rapunzel, let your hair down"

PERCIVAL

HOW BOND CARS EVOLVED THROUGH THE DECADES

1960s

2030s

prime

Nursery Times

.... Friday, Once-upon-a-time ....

BULGARIAN SPY RING UNCOVERED IN SUBURBS

*by Our i-Spy Staff **Little Bo Peeping***

THERE was shock in Nurseryland as some members of the community were outed as foreign spies working for a hostile regime. Not since the scandal of Sleeper Beauty has there been such a threat to No-Place-Like-Homeland Security.

Whilst working overground as seemingly innocent litter collectors, the agents were also operating underground as a spy ring under the direction of sinister mastermind Great Uncle Bulgaria.

The evil spy network known as W-O-M-B-L-E (World of Make-Believe Litter Espionage) were processing information gathered from rubbish collection and sending it back to their paymasters.

The gang was uncovered by intelligence expert Moley, working from his Riverbank base with an informer, Ratty.

"They were hiding in plain sight, I mean one of them was even called Tomsk, for crying out loud! It's like I couldn't see beyond the end of my nose – but that's being a mole for you."

Other members of the sinister organisation included the sultry Madame Cholet, a chef who also acted as a honey trap, real name Ivana Yorkitov.

Said Moley, "These furry agents are going to jail for a very long time."

Late News

● Prison overcrowding crisis – spies released and Wombles now wombling free.

BIN STRIKE CONTINUES IN BIRMINGHAMELIN

AS the refuse collectors of Birminghamelin continued their industrial action, a plague of rats swept through the city, requiring the council to take drastic measures.

A Pied Piper was called in to lead away the rodent infestation, using the very latest in vermin-enchanting technology (a pipe), but, having refused to pay the binmen, the council now refuse to pay the Pied Piper.

The unpaid Piper of Birminghamelin has sought advice from the PPU (Pied Piper Union), which has advised him to escalate the dispute by leading all the town's children away.

Said the parents of Birminghamelin, "Hooray – free childcare!"

The local council was equally pleased, as they reallocated their education budget to refuse collection, thereby ending the strike and ridding the city of rats.

Meanwhile, with "so many children he didn't know what to do", the Pied Piper was last seen seeking advice from an old woman who lived in a shoe.

43

ZELENSKY IN SAUDI ARABIA FOR PEACE TALKS

Thank you for not wearing a suit. That's very respectful

Ironyometer heats up world

by Our Environmental Staff
Bernie Planet

IN THE biggest climate change disaster since last week, the South American Ironyometer suffered a catastrophic meltdown with the news that tens of thousands of acres of protected Amazon rainforest have been felled to make way for a four-lane super highway for the COP 30 Climate Summit.

El Ironímetro, as it is known, began behaving erratically, as yet another juggernaut trundled past, bearing lumber freshly hacked from the so-called "lungs of the planet".

Said one engineer, "Steam started pouring out of El Ironímetro's pressure valves the moment we heard that tens of thousands of delegates would be flying in on private jets.

"But once the chainsaws started buzzing, the rivets started flying, then entire panels of the fuel tank ruptured and oil was spraying out of the flange ducts into the Amazon delta."

Said one wildlife expert, "As the burning oil started raining down, and toxic black smoke billowed into the pure Brazilian air, the endangered poison dart frogs started croaking. With flames devouring the centuries-old canopy of rare and precious Amazonian vegetation, the sloths made a run for it but, frankly, they didn't stand a chance."

The El Ironímetro disaster is one of the worst man-made ironyometer disasters since ironyometer disaster records began, but happily there is one silver lining – the Amazon River Dolphin is no longer listed as an endangered species, as it no longer exists.

Top 5 slowest moving things on the planet

5. Three-toed sloth

4. Sea anemone

3. Glacier

2. Tectonic plate

1. Post Office Compensation Scheme

JOY FOR LE PEN AT COURT RULING

by Our Paris Correspondent **Fay Scist**

CELEBRATIONS continued today at the French National Rally headquarters as their leader, Marine Le Pen, was found guilty of embezzling EU funds.

Said one supporter, "The final piece of the jigsaw is in place. She is now a felon as well as a far-right anti-immigration racist. She is certain to be president next time round, alongside her role model, Donald Trump."

When it was confirmed that Le Pen has been banned from standing for president for five years, it was expected that her supporters would take to the barricades and storm the Élysée Palace – as that's what the French do most weekends.

Le Pen now faces a potential jail sentence where she will experience the horrors of incarceration – being served an indifferent house wine that hasn't been allowed to breathe and a cheeseboard that consists of only two different sorts of Wensleydale.

HOW THE UK MILITARY WILL CHANGE AFTER LAST WEEK'S FUNDING BOOST

BEFORE (2.3% of GDP)

■ Weak, feeble, undermanned force consisting of one pedalo, five armoured bumper cars, and three sixteen-year-olds armed with potato peelers, who are only capable of putting "a boot on the ground" rather than "boots on the ground", as we are promising.

AFTER (2.5% of GDP)

■ Massive, world-dominating force, with hundreds of stealth fighter starships, thousands of autonomous laser drone droids, and millions of heavily armed new recruits ready to invade Moscow, Washington and Beijing at the same time.

"How do you propose to pay for all this?"

"Don't tell him, Pike!"

DEFENCE REVIEW

ROBERT THOMPSON

SNOW WHITE MOVIE COMES UP SHORT

by Our Showbiz Staff **Holly Wood**

THE LIVE action remake of the Disney classic has been mired in controversy throughout its production – and has now been released in secret, in the hope that no one will see it.

Problems began when the actress playing Snow White fell out with the actress playing her evil stepmother, the Wicked Queen.

As art mirrored life, the Wicked Queen asked the enchanted looking glass, "Mirror, mirror on the wall, is it unfair for people to bring up Gaza at all?"

Things got worse when real-life dwarves objected to the use of CGI dwarves instead of actors of restricted growth.

A grumpy spokesman said, "I'm not happy, and nor are any of my friends. We have been reduced to singing, 'Hi-ho, hi-ho, it's off to the benefits office we go'."

A further development saw Snow White being attacked by real-life trolls (not CGI) for not being sufficiently white – but of Colombian-Polish descent.

The trolls said this made the whole remake resemble an improbable, unrealistic cartoon fantasy – rather than a historical account of mining conditions in medieval Europe, like the original movie.

But, by far the biggest criticism of the film from US audiences has been the moment when Snow White eats an apple. "No one has ever eaten an apple in my experience," said one cinema-goer, guzzling a vat of popcorn washed down with a bucket of sugary fizzy drink.

He continued, "I would never be tricked into eating a piece of fruit offered by an old woman at my doorstep. I would just shoot her. And there's not a jury in America that would convict me."

Another complained that the scene in which Snow White was aroused from her slumber by the handsome prince was too woke. He said, "I don't pay good money to see people being woke."

An executive for the Disney Corporation, a Mr Michael Mouse, squeaked, "Frankly, it's not the fairytale ending we were hoping for."

CINEMA

"Any good?"

NEW SNOW WHITE

"Grimm"

ADOLESCENCE

A SHOCKING STORY OF TOXIC MASCULINITY, BULLYING AND ONLINE BRAINWASHING THAT LEADS TO TRAGEDY

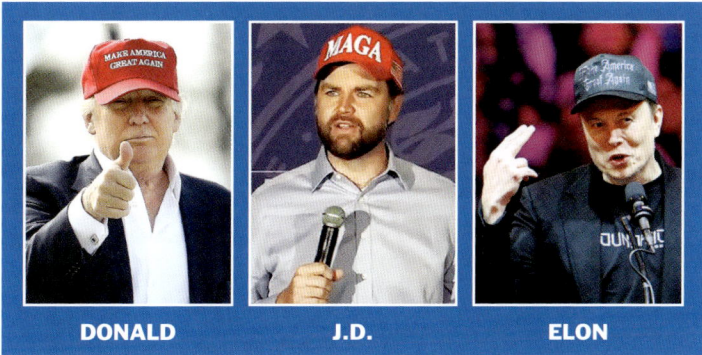

DONALD **J.D.** **ELON**

WILL THESE DANGEROUS TEENAGE BOYS ALL END UP IN CELLS?

Netflix reassures stunned executives

NETFLIX has reassured its executives that it would offer support and counselling after they watched in disbelief as "Adolescence" became the number one show worldwide.

"For years they have been lecturing programme makers that they need to make dumbed-down shows capable of being watched on a third screen while people make tacos and order pizza on their smart watches.

"These poor execs are now living in fear that the success of 'Adolescence' means they'll have to commission intense challenging dramas that require the viewers' total attention instead. It's a living nightmare for them."

LATE NEWS

HAMAS REFUSES TO HAND BACK HOSTAGES

■ THE leaders of the terrorist group Hamas have announced that they will not be handing back any of the two million hostages currently being held in Gaza, no matter how many protests take place, and will not negotiate their return to a peaceful life under any circumstances.

(Rioters)

'I'M NOT ORANGE' SAYS ORANGE

It's just the lights! Fact! Fake hues!

"Wow!"

SISTINE CHAPEL

R&J

Ceiling fan

POETRY CORNER

**In Memoriam
Group Captain
John Hemingway, the last
surviving pilot of the
Battle of Britain**

So. Farewell
Then John Hemingway.

You were the last of
"The Few",
Who now, alas, are
"The None".

Now you have
Another pair of wings
And are soaring up
Above the clouds.
"Bandits at four o'clock!"
"Oh no – they're angels."

Keith says this is
The last time I can
Use this stanza,
Which you may have read
Many times before.

Sadly, like The Few,
We shall not see
These lines again.

  E.J. Thribbute (17½, about
the same age as Hemingway
  when he joined the RAF)

CULTURE BORES

by Grizelda

RUPERT LOWE 'SLAMS FARAGE'

He's not the Messiah, he's a very naughty boy

ME AND MY SPOON

THIS WEEK

MARJORIE TAYLOR GREENE

Do you have a favourite spoon?
  What country are you from?

The United Kingdom
  Ok, we don't give a crap about your spoon opinions and your spoon reporting. Why don't you go back to your country, where you have a major cutlery problem, where every day spoons are being used by migrants to kill innocent women because you stupidly don't give them access to guns...

So do you have a favourite spoon?
  You're done, with your fake spoon news. I'll only answer questions from American journalists about American spoons.

***American journalist*: I want you to answer her question. Do you have a favourite spoon?**
  American spoons are awesome. We're making spoons great again by imposing a 25 percent tariff on any spoons that aren't 300 percent American. Next question?

***American journalist*: Has anything amusing ever happened to you involving a spoon?**
  Yes, Spoongate has made me a laughing stock.

  Interview ends, as Marjorie Taylor Greene throws all her spoons out of cutlery drawer.

NEXT WEEK: *Marine le Pen, Moi et Ma Plume.*

45

THAT ALL-PURPOSE TARIFF PIECE IN FULL

IN A SHOCK move last night, Donald Trump imposed/lifted stringent/lenient tariffs to replace the lenient/stringent tariffs he had announced yesterday/three seconds before.

Trump confirmed there would be no/some exceptions, in order to reduce/increase trade and restore/destroy US manufacturing.

Markets were quick to rally/crash in response to the unexpected/totally predictable executive decision/random brain-fart.

The White House told/lied to reporters that this was Trump's plan all along/something he just thought up on the toilet.

As a result of this bold/idiotic tariff strategy the world can now look forward to a recession/recession.

NEW TRUMP MOVE STUNS WORLD

by Our Trade Correspondent
Dee Pression

ASIAN markets were reeling last night at Donald Trump's announcement of a 759% tariff on flip-flops.

The flip-flop tariff was immediately cancelled, with Trump saying, "It was never my intention to target flip-flops. No one loves flip-flops biglier than me. Especially the ones made in China."

Just as the Hang Seng market rallied, Trump surprised traders by reinstating the flip-flop tariff at an increased 947%, announcing, "America's been ripped off on flip-flops for too long. Now we're doing the flip-flop ripping."

He concluded, "I will go down in history as the flip-flop President. Or maybe I won't."

China pledges to defend capitalism

CHINA has pledged not to back down in its trade war with President Trump, with President Xi pledging to defend capitalism and the free market.

In a televised address to the nation, Xi rallied his people. "We will not accept the excessive tariffs of the centralised state-controlled US economy," he said.

"They wish to create an artificial 'golden age' by controlling production and imports, but we will not surrender to their Communist ideology."

White House officials insisted they also would not back down, saying their glorious leader Donald Trump was going to lead all Americans on the long march to victory over reality.

(Rotters)

POLICE MAKE 'FIRST EVER' ARRESTS AT A QUAKER HOUSE

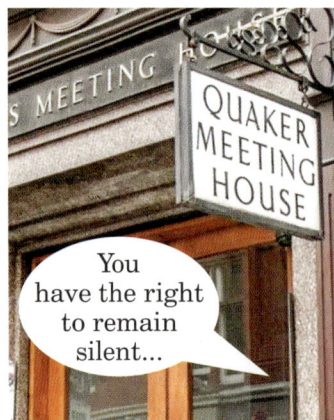

QUAKER MEETING HOUSE

You have the right to remain silent...

TRUMP'S TARIFFS
YOUR QUESTIONS ANSWERED

Which countries have been hardest hit?

Originally (this morning), the hardest-hit countries were Lilliput, Poundland, Love Island and Abracadabra. But since these territories did not respond with reciprocal tariffs, due to their not existing, Donald Trump has cut their tariffs to -10%, which is the same temperature as the island with the penguins that now pays 130% more on krill, kroll and pilchard imports, while the cars they manufacture are being hit with a mere 25%. President Trump insists he's happy to talk to high-level penguins, preferably Emperor, at any time.

Heard and McDonald Islands leader travels to Washington to meet Trump – wearing suit out of respect

Is there a tariff on the export of Chinese soldiers to Russia?

This is complex and depends on whether the Chinese soldiers cross the border from zero-tariff Russia into high-tariff Ukraine and whether the troops arrive via low-tariff North Korea. President Putin has been quick to respond to the latest tariff measures, awarding President Trump the Supreme Disorder of Merit for his heroic destabilising of the West.

Will UK consumers have to pay an extra tariff on the chlorine in which their imported US chicken will be soaked?

In a word, possibly. Oh, no, hang on, we've just heard. Yes. The tariff on chlorine will be 17%, a figure derived from a simple equation in which the atomic number of chlorine (17) is divided by the number of legs on the average battery-farmed pullet (5) and then multiplied by the number of fingers on President Trump's hand (4, plus "that bigly one on the end"), which equals exactly 17. To quote White House spokesperson Karoline Leavitout, "It's that simple, moron. I hate you. Are you from the UK? Asshole!"

What will be the tariff on British Steel next week?

And you thought chlorine was complicated! So, British Steel, which would ordinarily qualify for a standard 25% tariff, will now, because it is owned by a Chinese company, be subject to an extra 1,000,004%. This takes the tariff up to 1,000,029%, which makes it unprofitable to produce steel in Britain. If Sir Keir Starmer nationalises British Steel, the tariff will return to 25%, unless he renames the company the Penguin Steelworks, in which case the tariff will go down to 6 pilchards per kilotonne.

What will be higher – the tariff on aluminium or the tariff on aluminum?

Good question. Aluminum is the American spelling, but aluminium carries an extra letter, which amounts to 11% added onto the word. Since America is refusing to import the letter 'i' into the word aluminum, due to a vowel surplus in Ohio, then it may be that Britain has to pay an extra 11% on top of the standard 25% for each letter 'i', meaning its total bill will be greater than metal produced in Mississippi ('Home of the Great American i').

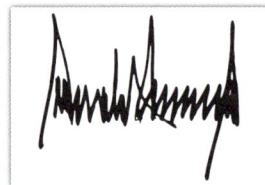

POETRY CORNER

**In Memoriam
Oleg Gordievsky,
Russian spy and British
double agent**

So. Farewell
Then Oleg Gordievsky.

You have gone over
To the other side
Or have you?

E.J. Thribb
(0017½, written in
lemon juice)

Sir Keir Starmer MP

The Prime Minister's WhatsApp group – totally secure because we don't use signal like the Americans and leak all our military plans

Stay calm, everyone, everything's under control.

Darren Jones
Why are you saying that? What's gone wrong now? 😱

Morgan McSweeney
Everything's going really well. The boss's policy of doing nothing and saying nothing is working brilliantly. At the moment we've only been hit by 10% tariffs, which is a great result. 👍

Rachel Reeves
Apart from on steel.

Darren Jones
And cars.

Morgan McSweeney
That's a lot less than all the other countries.

David Lammy
Except Russia.

David Lammy
Russia is a country, isn't it?

Peter Mandelson
Leave the Americans to me. Abide by the old trade-wartime slogan: Keep calm and carry on sucking up. And sucking up is something I'm rather good at. It's in my blood, you might say. 🎖️🏰 Now, must fly. The sun will be setting over Mar-a-Lago and I might drop in for a bite.

Rachel Reeves
Are we really going to do nothing? These tariffs are turning my economic plans into a disaster.

Angela Rayner
Yeah, without the tariffs, they'd have just been a catastrophe! No offence. 😀

Times like this call for clear and decisive leadership. That's why I've decided to make it clear that I'm not going to do anything. Wait and see.

Morgan McSweeney
Go for it, boss! Operation Rabbit In Headlights and Hope Car Swerves. 🤞

Jonathan Reynolds
Speaking of cars, shall we drop all the green Net Zero stuff to help our guys out?

Ed Miliband
That would be an appalling U-turn and I would look very stupid.

Darren Jones
So, what's the problem?

Ed Miliband
Why is it always me who gets stabbed in the back?

David Miliband
Hi, Ed! Some headhunters have told me there could be a job going as Energy Secretary. You don't mind if I put my name forward?

David Miliband has been removed from the group on the grounds that he's at least a month early with his job application.

Yvette Cooper
So, can I get this clear, in case I have to explain it to my husband on Breakfast TV? Are we hitting back with reciprocal tariffs of 10%, standing with the EU at 25%, or offering Trump a round of golf with the Loch Ness Monster, followed by tea with Harry Potter in Hogwarts Castle?

Morgan McSweeney
Breaking news! Trump has blinked! The tariffs are off. Now we're only paying 10%. 😃

Rachel Reeves
That's what we were paying before. Now we're the same as everyone else.

Morgan McSweeney
Except China

David Lammy
Now that is a country. I know that one. Big one. Are they our friends or not?

Morgan McSweeney
Right now, our relationship with China is better than our special one with America.

David Lammy
This is confusing.

No, it isn't, David. It's all very simple. Whatever happens, we just say everything's on the table and we're not ruling anything out. 🏓🍴

Rachel Reeves
Can you explain what that means?

Yes. It means that we're not ruling anything out. And furthermore, everything is on the table. 🍴🏓

Rachel Reeves
Phew, for a second there, I thought we didn't have a policy and were just making up word salads to avoid offending He Who Cannot Be Named.

David Lammy
Voldemort?

Angela Rayner
No, the big orange manbaby!

Morgan McSweeney
Hang on! More breaking news!

What now?

Morgan McSweeney
Trump hasn't done anything for five minutes! 😲

Phew! That's incredible. Let's not do anything back.

Morgan McSweeney
Great stuff, PM. That'll show him who's boss... Him.

JOHNSON ATTACKED BY OSTRICH IN SAFARI PARK

Another pecker he can't control

Those British cars after Trump tariffs kick in

Vauxhall Cat-Astra-phe
Aston Martin Vanquished
Ford Concertina
Morris Minor Profits
Austin Seven Percent More Expensive
Mini Margins
Nissan Qashless
Land Rover Defenceless
Rolls-Royce Toast
Toyota Corollover
Jaguar (by Ta-ta Motors)

"Is it normal? No. They're not usually found together"

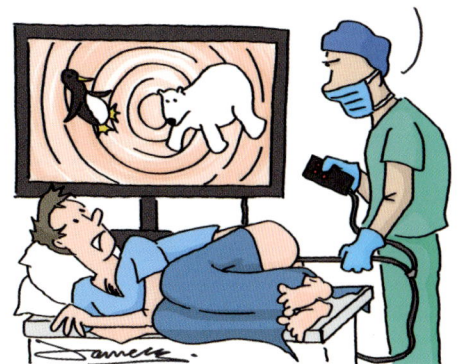

47

A Tank Driver writes

Vlad 'Mad' Putin, Tank No: ZZZZ

Every week a well-known tank driver gives his opinion on a topical matter. This week, how to drive all over Eastern Europe without getting stuck in despot-holes! (Old Russian joke, you've got to laugh or you'll be on the chain gang filling them in)

"Oh, hello, Donald. Let me put you on speaker. So how's tricks? What's that? I'm having trouble hearing you with all the noise. BOOM! Say again? BOOM! No – didn't catch it... Ceasefire, you say? BOOM! BOOM! BOOM! Hang on, Don, let me see if I can find where all that noise is coming from. Blimey – who'd have thought it – it's coming from my gun turret! BOOM! There goes a school! I'm afraid some of those kiddies are going to need to go to hospital. BOOM! Oh, no! There goes a hospital! BOOM! Oh, what I'd give for a moment's peace!... What WOULD I give? Nothing, since you ask! I'll take whatever you're offering. But that's it. Crimea? That could work. And the Donbas? Oh, you're twisting my arm now. This is the Art of the Deal in action. What's that? Give something in return? Oh, hang on – I seem to have stalled. BOOM! And there's that bloody noise again. Better check my oil gauge. Oh, look – I've got too much. Bloody Europeans... Pathetic, aren't they?!... Perhaps you could do something about that 'n' all. Drop the sanctions? Oh, now you've got me by the short and curlies. Ow! Donald, you are the real deal! BOOM! Just so we're clear, you give me everything and in return I give you nothing... I'll have to think about it. It's a tough one. Can I get back to you? BOOM! BOOM! BOOM!... Might be a while, roads are busy, cars on fire everywhere. Not as bad as the US, though. All those Teslas! You gotta laugh! Give my love to Elon. BOOM!"

© A tank driver

AFRICAN CHARITY ROW: HARRY ACCUSED OF RACISM

Ha ha ha ha ha ha!

Lines on the end of the criminal inquiry into the former First Minister of Scotland

'Twas in the spring of the year twenty twenty-five,
The police informed us Ms Sturgeon did NOT connive
In the embezzlement of funds from the SNP
Where all the large sums did not quite agree,
Not to mention the matter of the campervan
Parked in the drive of the mother of her old man,
Or should I say her now-discarded ex
Whose plea of innocence Inspector McKnacker rejects.
Puir Peter Murrell has been charged with a serious crime
And many folk would say "About bloody time!"
Forgive my unpoetic and uncharacteristic swearing,
But the whole affair has become extremely wearing.
Since 2021, it's been a very slow investigation
In matters you'd have thought were vital to the nation.
In fact, I would say of Operation Branchform,
That this epic tardiness cannot possibly be the norm.
I am not suggesting anything suspicious took place,
But what could explain this legal snail's pace?
At least now we have come closer to clarity,
Knowing that in their marriage there was some disparity.
Sweet Nicola was innocent and knew nothing at all,
While beancounter Peter could be taking the fall.
With her, the Procurator Fiscal has drawn a blank, he
Found no evidence against the famous lookalike Krankie.
So, never could a phrase more appropriate be
Than to say Nicola Sturgeon has got off Scot free!

© William McGonagall

"Just because I'm working from home doesn't mean you can call me on a Saturday evening!"

"It's Monday morning"

deAn.

Those unforgettable Blue Peter moments

by **Jenny Zee**

AS WE SAY GOODBYE to the live editions of Blue Peter, who can ever forget these magic moments of the golden age of television that I've just looked up on Wikipedia:

- The day the elephant climbed up Nelson's column and pooped on John Noakes.

- The time when one hundred Girl Guides gathered around Valerie Singleton and set her hair on fire.

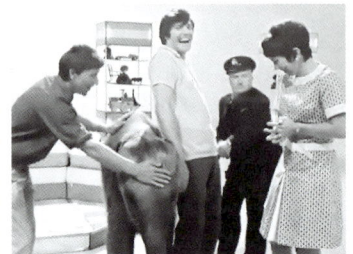

- The heart-stopping moment when Peter Purves was doing the Cresta run and got his flares caught in the brakes – his loud shirt then set off an avalanche.

- The episode in which Lesley Judd warned about all the working-class diseases children could catch if they watched Magpie on ITV.

- The time when Roy Castle broke the world tap-dancing record, but unfortunately did so on the graves of all seven Sheps and all fifteen Petras.

- The occasion that presenter Janet Ellis gave birth to her daughter Sophie Ellis-Bexter on the dance floor and said, "Here's one I made earlier."

- The day when Richard Bacon showed children how to turn a £20 note into a versatile straw.

- The following episode in which Richard Bacon demonstrated how to make an apology.

- The programme in which the presenters buried a time capsule that contained the P45s for the Blue Peter cast and crew facing the axe in 2025.

- But the question remains – should we tell children that Blue Peter has died, or should we tell them that it's gone to a happier place on the iPlayer and is still alive in a digital way?

(You're fired. Ed.)

We are in Kuuru. It's a dimly lit, too hip to handle Peruvian-Japanese fusion bar and restaurant. The decor is Inca bamboo; the drinks arrive with dark-red ice sculptures the size of tennis balls that deliver a Beluga caviar flavour as they melt. The waiting staff, dressed in a St Laurent-Westwood fusion, all speak Spanish and enthuse about the freshness of the yuzu wasabi dressing on the Crab and Cured Highland Cattle Salad. In one corner of our table, studded with an emerald-and-ruby fusion, they place a tiny metal barbecue and show us how to crisp individual sheets of nori seaweed that we will shortly be rolling up into our own scallop temaki duvet.

And this, this here, this oh-so-immaculately here, is my first night in Saudi Arabia.

The trip has been planned in haste. A three-day visit, snatched from my supremely hectic but deeply fulfilling life as an award-winning broadcaster, is somewhere between an adventure and an experiment. Could my teenage son and I get visas in time? Could we make a long weekend feel like a holiday? Could I buy a half-way decent selection of clothes that would keep things simple but elegant, understated yet fiercely independent, throughout my Saudi sojourn? More critically, could I reconcile everything I knew about Saudi – the regime, its treatment of journaists, women, foreign labourers – with a place I wanted to hang out?

It turned out I could – and how! The first conversations I have about Saudi before I leave are – as luck would have it – with two former British prime ministers. Separate events. Two weeks apart. The first tells me on no account to miss the shiitake-truffle rhubarb and horseradish sorbet at the intensely fashionable new Bolivian-Taiwanese fusion restaurant a stone's throw from the stunning *L'Ancien Centre du Torture Pour Dissidents* building close to the centre. The second PM tells me the place will blow my mind, then adds, "I have MBS's cellphone number – if anything goes wrong, just text me. The guy's actually brilliant company – unexpectedly shy, but with an impish sense of humour. I've only ever heard good things about him."

My wardrobe is chosen with inordinate precision. Jeddah is conservative but chic, they tell me, so I keep it simple, opting for khaki tailored combats, wide Me+Em fusion jeans, buttoned-up cream silk blouses, a Dries Van Noten floor-length coat and a wide silk headscarf in matching stone, with undergarments by Simone Perele. I also add an off-black silk burqa by Alexander McQueen, to transport me from my hotel room to the spa without revealing my Dolce & Gabbana fusion bikini dripping innocently beneath.

*Our first day is spent getting lost in Al-Balad. It's full of cobbled streets, shops selling gold and precious stones, and the wizened faces of Saudi elders, steeped in the wisdom of their years. I notice one or two of them have ears and/or fingers missing, but our guide reassures me that's the way they like it. For them, it's clearly something of a fashion statement!

We arrive late at Kuuru, greeting Saudi friends there. It's only when we are shown the mocktail menu that I remember we are guests in a sovereign Islamic state – where alcohol is completely banned, just as it is in some of the most exclusive, A-list go-to spas in the UK.

There is so much to ask about the Saudi project, and it's here that I finally get to try.

"You have to understand the rules," our host explains. "MBS is saying to us, 'I'm going to ringfence politics, but if it's culture you want, you can have culture.' We've got Formula 1, football, Versace and all the latest works by Leonardo da Vinci. What else could anyone possibly want?"

Ever the intrepid truth-seeker, I put on my award-winning reporter's hat. "What about women?" I ask. "Look around," he says. "These women are single! They're on dating apps! They have complete freedom to do everything that's permitted! More Japanese mushroom, apricot and coriander miso fusion pancakes, anyone?"

In the age of Trump, there's a lot of talk about "illiberal democracy" – people voting for hardline governments like those of Orban in Hungary and Erdoğan in Turkey – because they've decided they're more effective than our own much-vaunted liberal democracies. Sipping my delicious guava, cucumber, smoked salmon and coriander mocktail, I ask my host, "Would you call this a liberal autocracy?"

He nods emphatically. That's exactly what it is. And who's to say it doesn't work? After all, Saudi will be hosting the Asian Winter Games in 2029 and the Fifa World Cup in 2034. Anna Wintour holidayed here in 2023. And Victoria Beckham plans to open a flagship store in Jeddah later this year. Dissidents? To be honest, I didn't spot any in all my time there, and I kept my eyes open in all the hotels, restaurants and boutiques that I visited.

What other country can boast anything quite so impressive? Feeling I've done my job, I order another luxury mocktail, which arrives in seconds, and peruse the dessert menu at my leisure.

It's now a full seven years on from the murder of the Saudi journalist Jamal Khashoggi, who was, it must be said, a vocal thorn in the side of the regime and an undoubted troublemaker. An awful lot's happened since then, not least the opening of a striking new multi-million-pound opera house in Diriyah, which fuses tradition with innovation. This year, it's set to host the world premiere of the highly acclaimed home-produced comic opera *La Lapidation a Mort des Homosexuels*. These days, no one talks about the inability to vote – no, they talk about the new Belgian-Finnish fusion restaurant in Riyadh, the upcoming superyacht regatta at the Jeddah marina and the total buzz over a recent visit by supermodel Naomi Campbell. Yes, there's no stopping MBS's liberalisation of Saudi Arabia.

Oh, and my Dries Van Noten floor-length coat? It went down a storm.

As told to
CRAIG BROWN

"Ok, and now one with just the bride and groom"

PINK FLOYD MAN IN SHED DISPUTE

POPE FUNERAL

PAPAL CONCLAVE

Is Putin stringing me along?

Was the Pope Catholic?

FASHION FAUX-PAS

Oh no! We're wearing the same frock!

STARMER IN VATICAN

Just what I need – the whole place is full of men in dresses!

Sir Keir Starmer MP

The Prime Minister's WhatsApp group (ie Sir Keir Starmer's WhatsApp group, because HE is Prime Minister, and not Angela Rayner or Wes Streeting)

Welcome, ladies and gentlemen!

Rosie Duffield
Have you decided which are which yet?

Morgan McSweeney
This is a safe space, Rosie, you're not allowed in here.

I appreciate the clarity that the Supreme Court has brought to this complex issue and suggest that the important thing is never to mention it again.

Rosie Duffield
Kemi said you had no balls. She's right, isn't she?

David Lammy
Can women grow balls? Or is it men who can grow a cervix? I'm a bit confused.

It's perfectly simple, David. The answer to those sort of questions is: "The Prime Minister is out of the office right now, please leave a message. He will be picking up emails and will answer them all in due course. Your call is important to him."

Rosie Duffield
You spineless, flip-flopping jellyfish.

I appreciate your clarity, Rosie, and I'm pleased we've come to a satisfactory conclusion, but let's remember it's important to show compassion to those who hold different views from your own, ie me.

Rosie Duffield
So what is your view?

My view is that I appreciate the clarity that the Supreme Court has brought.

Rosie Duffield
You're a bare-faced lawyer!

Thank you very much.

Rosie Duffield
You hold any opinion which you think will make you popular.

Yes and no.

Morgan McSweeney
Great answer, chief. Now get that woman out of this changing-opinions-room! She's making us all feel uncomfortable.

The administrators would like to make it clear that Rosie Duffield was not removed from the group on the orders of Keir Starmer, but instead chose to leave, presumably in order to go on all media outlets and be disloyal about Sir Keir, making her sneery, scowly face at the cameras.

Can we please change the subject? This is depressing.

Angela Rayner
I've just heard a joke, in the pub. What do you call a woman with Balls? Yvette Cooper! Geddit? 🤣🤣🤣

Thanks for providing clarity on that issue, Angela.

What is the protocol for the election of a new Pope?

1 The editor sees on social media that the old Pope has died.

2 The editor calls what is known as a "conference", assembling all his experts and section editors to decide who will be selected to write a piece about the Pope.

3 After heated debate, which can last up to ten minutes, the conference decides on Phil Space because no one else wants to do it.

4 Editor confirms Space's appointment and tells him to pray, meditate and watch Conclave before taking on the onerous task.

5 Space watches Conclave, but is still unsure as to what is going on.

6 Space watches Conclave for a second round and this time the smoke signal goes up.

7 It is white smoke, signifying that Space is having a fag having reached the end of his piece and God – ie the editor – is pleased with his handiwork.

8 Space lies down in a state after the exhaustion of papal duties and remains there on the sofa for days.

9 Meanwhile, 94,000 word piece on "The Peoples' Pope" by Phil Space is presented to the masses, who show their love and approval by buying the special edition and then turning to the Bumper Easter Bank Holiday Crossword.

10 Order restored and life returns to normal as Space takes on his new role, writing thoughtful piece on the true meaning of the Ten Coastal Walks (*surely "Commandments"? Ed.*)

Nursery Times

SUPREME COURT JUDGMENT ROCKS NURSERYLAND

by Our Legal Staff **Mother Goose (formerly Parent Goose)**

AT LAST, the complicated issue of gender and sexual identity in Nurseryland has been resolved, as the highest court in the land clearly stated that "Little girls are made of sugar and spice and all things nice. Little boys are made of slugs and snails and puppy dog tails."

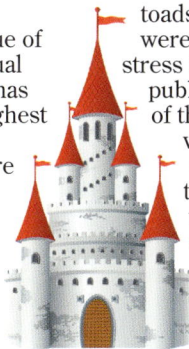

The landmark judgment continued, "And that is all there is too it. Sex is binary. And the biological make-up of Nurseryland characters is what determines their sex."

This has come as bad news for the grandmother of Little Red Riding Hood, who formerly identified as a wolf. Protestors claimed that unscrupulous wolves were just pretending to be "grans" and were dressing up as old ladies in order to prey on innocent girls in the woods. *(You're cancelled. Ed.)*

It was also bad news for the former Mr Toad of Toad Hall, who denounced the judgment as a load of "poop poop". Toad had been a prisoner in an all-male prison before identifying as a washerwoman in a bid to escape justice. But now the ruling is that a toad is a toad and whatever clothing he wears, he is not above the law.

The Supreme Court did add that, while it was ruling that toads were toads and wolves were wolves, it wanted to stress that the Nurseryland public should be respectful of the rights of vulnerable vulpine and amphibian communities to live their lives however they chose, whether as so-called "grannies" or as non-biological washerwomen. *(You're cancelled again. Ed.)*

Meanwhile, the case of the Birds vs the Bees has been postponed, subject to a new appeal to the court by *(You're still cancelled. Ed.)*

There was joy throughout the land and they all lived happily ever after, except the ones who didn't and who were still very cross with each other and *(continued until the female-only cows come home)*

Late news

Gingerbreadmen not allowed to compete in Gingerbreadwomen's athletics events, although the Gingerbreadman is allowed to compete in races against the horse, the cow, the cockerel, the dog, the cat, the old woman (provided it is not a wolf or a toad) and her husband the old man (provided he is not a former principal boy in a pantomime, ie a girl with sugar and spice chromosomes).

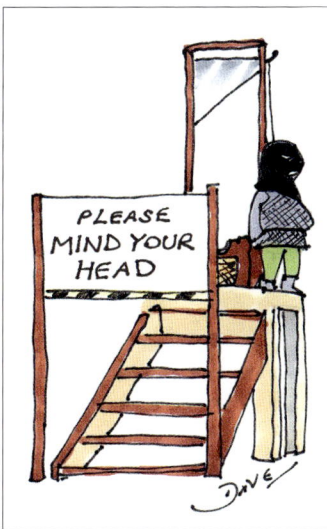

FIRST ALL-WOMEN SPACE MISSION A TRIUMPH

by Lunar Staff **The Man in the Moon**

THE first all-female crew (one cow) today made history with a spectacular moonshot into space that has been hailed as a giant leap for cowkind.

The cow, Katie Dairy, returned to earth and sank to her knees in gratitude, apparently kissing the ground, or possibly eating some grass.

Said mission director, Jeff Bezox, "Firstly, I don't look like Humpty Dumpty. And secondly, my Moo-Origin project has proved that astronauts are not just space men, they can also be female ruminants."

But critics have said that it was just a frivolous publicity stunt. The Little Dog, an expert in fun, simply laughed at the whole spectacle.

Humpty Dumpty is hoping to set up a commercial business sending livestock into space. Said bovine billionaire Bezox, "This will be another cash cow which we will milk for all it's worth."

Late news

New space mission backed by Amoozon ends in disaster – cow delivered to wrong planet and left behind crater on Mars.

ONLINE TRANS DEBATE CANCELLATION LATEST

A SOCIAL media user was immediately cancelled today after stupidly posting reasonable views on the issue of trans-gender rights, following the Supreme Court ruling.

"All I said was that there had to be understanding on both sides, and while women deserve the safety of single-sex spaces, the trans community also deserve respect and should not be demonised," they said.

These incendiary mild opinions were savaged by all sides of the debate, with pro-trans trolls claiming that the post suggested that all trans people should be rounded up and shot, while anti-trans trolls insisted that the post demanded that men should be free to murder women in toilets.

The social media user apologised for their inoffensive opinion, and assured the incredibly angry online community that they would never post anything so... *(cont. p94)*

POETRY CORNER

**In Memoriam
Barry Hoban, legendary cyclist; Clodagh Rodgers, Eurovision songstress; and His Holiness Pope Francis**

So. Farewell
Then Barry and
Clodagh and Francis.
You have all gone together
To a better place.
I wonder what you
Discussed on the way?

Was it the Tour de France?
The Eurovision
Song Contest? Or the plight
Of the poor and needy?

Barry Hoban,
Now you are on
Your last great ascent.

Clodagh Rodgers,
You sang "Jack in the Box".
Sadly, you won't be
Popping up again.

Pope Francis,
You were an
Argentinian football fan
And met Maradona.

Perhaps you can now
Ask God what on Earth
He was playing at when
He tapped that ball
In with His hand
Past Peter Shilton
In 1986.

Others may not feel
This is the most
Important aspect of
Pope Francis' life and
Legacy, but that's what
I've been thinking about,
And I think he would
Have appreciated my
Honesty at this time.

E.J. Thribb (17½ Hail Maradonas)

"Officer, some thief has stolen my dictionary of platitudes"

"I'm sorry for your loss"

Lookalikes

Sadness   **Starmer**

Sir,
　Does anyone else think our rather gloomy, downbeat prime minister should be replaced by someone with a bit more optimism and zip? The substitution could easily be made without anyone noticing.
RICHARD WILSON.

Yummy   **Mummy**

Sir,
　Has anyone else noticed the striking similarity between the fashionable Tarim mummy dating from 1800BC, who is wearing the world's oldest cheese as a necklace, and Patsy Stone from Ab Fab as played by our beloved Joanna Lumley? Could they possibly be related?
ENA B. AGNALL.

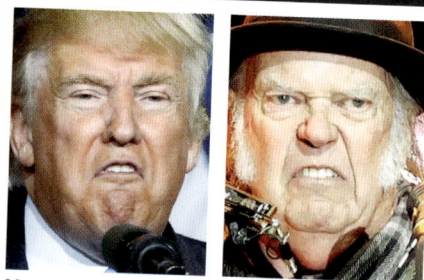

Young   **Old**

Sir,
　Neil Young – grumpy old git changing his mind about Canada. Donald Trump – grumpy old git changing his mind from Canada.
MALCOLM BARNARD.

Kendall   **Mouskouri**

Sir,
　One of them quit politics because she realised she wasn't very good at it. The other...
CHRISTOPHER BRAY.

Humpty   **Musk**

Sir,
　Has anyone else noticed the resemblance between these two? One is an odd-looking creature who's just had a great fall; the other one appears in an old English rhyme.
OSCAR MARTINEZ.

Turtle   **Hamas**

Sir,
　Am I alone in noticing the similarity between the totally radical dudes living in tunnels under New York City and the totally radicalised dudes living in tunnels under Gaza City?
ENA B. MOVIE.

Poo   **Sculpture**

Sir,
　I cannot be the only person to wonder if this new, woven sculpture, which has appeared by Chichester harbour, has anything to do with the local marine gastropods?
　Rather, it looks like an enormous tribute to Southern Water's turd corporate logo, richly deserved for ongoing sewage discharges into this SSSI.
JEA W.

Nosferatu   **Healey**

Sir,
　I was struck by a certain similarity between German actor Max Schreck playing the vampire Count Orlok in the 1922 silent film 'Nosferatu' and UK defence secretary John Healey. Have eitherv of them ever been seen in daylight?
ENA B. ARFIELD.

Rod

Rod

Sir,
　Having watched Sir Rod Stewart take the stage at Glastonbury for the 'Legends' slot, I was heartened to see him honour the new face on the popular music scene, Mr Ronald Wood. I wonder if perhaps any of your readers noticed the resemblance to that mighty comic duo, Rod Hull and his emu?
PHILIP BLUNT.

Vance   **Candie**

Sir,
　I wonder if your readers have noticed any similarity between new sheriff in town JD Vance and Calvin Candie, slave owner of Candyland in the Western, Django Unchained?
J.R. EWING.

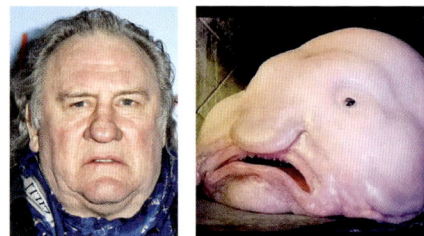

Blobfish   **Depardieu**

Sir,
　Am I the only one to have recognised the physical similarity around the proboscis area of Gerard Depardieu and a Blobfish? One is a vile creature, the other is a fish...
DR ROBIN RUMNEY.

Bara   **Chakrabarti**

Sir,
　I am struck by the similarity between Labour peer and campaigner Shami Chakrabarti and silent screen goddess Theda Bara in the lost epic 'Cleopatra'.
PETER SHAW.

Muppet **Er...**

Sir,
Has anyone noticed, as I have, the uncanny similarity between the Vice President of the United States and Kermit the Frog? Are they by any chance related?
ENA B. ING-GREEN.

Rolin **Putin**

Sir,
Leafing through an album of Flemish artist Jan van Eyck's masterpieces, I was struck by the similarity of his 1435 portrait of Nicolas Rolin, Chancellor to the Duke of Burgundy, to 2025's war-hungry Russian president Vladimir Putin.
ENA B. ARFIELD.

Edward **Claudia**

Sir,
I couldn't help noticing the resemblance between Prince Edward, as seen at Trooping the Colour, and Claudia Winkleman, normally seen adding colour to the troupe. I wonder if by any chance they are related?
ANDY VINCE.

Sandeman Don **Melania**

The Mask **Melania**

As sent by
IAN MALCOLM, CHARLIE GREEN.

Tiddler **Macron**

Sir,
After seeing the French President being disciplined prior to disembarking his aircraft, I wondered who it was that was so angry. A quick internet search suggests that it was Tiddler from the 80s ITV children's show The Riddlers.
PAUL CORFIELD.

Nigel **Greta**

Sir,
One's a deluded wannabe celeb, the other's in Spinal Tap!
ADAM FORD.

Ted and Ralph **Nigel and Richard**

Sir,
Two men in a complex, tense relationship versus Ted and Ralph from The Fast Show.
JOHN GRAY.

Thompson **Clarkson**

Sir,
I'm 13 years old and I read your esteemed organ on the toilet. I wonder if any of your other readers have noticed the physical similarities between Jeremy Clarkson and First Mate Allan Thompson from Hergé's Adventures of Tintin?
PETER WICKHAM-JONES,
13 (and ¼, to be precise).

Frilled Lizard

Caped Cardinal

Sir,
Has anyone noticed etc, etc.
JIM McMANNERS.

Barry **Valerie**

Sir,
I'm struck by the similarities between beloved TV presenter Valerie Singleton and up and coming actor Barry Keoghan. Are they by any chance related?
EDDIE MAIR.

Benny **Ben**

Sir,
I have noticed the incredible similarity between Benny Hill and Benny-Gvir, separated at birth or are they perhaps related?
ANYA BURGHES WHITE.

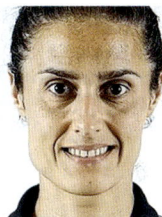 

Tweedy **Tomé**

Sir,
Has anyone else noticed that the women's football manager of Spain, Montserrat Tomé, must be a very close relative of Mrs Tweedy from Chicken Run? She's also very scary looking!
DEBORAH FAULKNER.

Catherine **John**

Sir,
After an enjoyable evening watching the wonderful John Lithgow, it strikes me he could make a passable Catherine The Great.
PAUL KITCHING.

Well, that went very well. ✌️

Angela Rayner
What the hell are you talking about? We got stuffed!

Wes Streeting
Well, VE Day was certainly not Victory in Elections Day. Just saying, Keir, that you have just led us to defeat.

It wasn't my fault.

Morgan McSweeney
Are you blaming me? Saying it's my fault? Who says it's my fault? Who? Come on! Show yourselves!

Rachel Reeves
You sound a bit paranoid, Morgan.

Morgan McSweeney
Is that what they're saying about me? They're saying I'm paranoid? Who's calling me paranoid? I knew it, you're all out to get me.

The key thing at this time of national reflection is the importance of effective war-time leadership and one thinks of Prime Ministers such as Winston Churchill, myself and my good friend President Zelensky. Have I mentioned Zelensky recently?

Morgan McSweeney
Yes, I expect you all heard Keir on that brilliant podcast at Number Ten with the Pub Landlord.

Angela Rayner
Nigel Farage? Is he in Downing Street already? 🍺 🍺 🍺

No, I was talking to Al Murray, the historian. He used to be a comedian, like President Zelensky was. Have I mentioned President Zelensky of late?

Wes Streeting
Are we going to acknowledge that Reform just gave us a thumping in a safe Labour seat in Runcorn?

Mike Amesbury
As the former Labour MP for Runcorn and an expert on thumpings, can I suggest that Labour really need to listen to the voters?

Yvette Cooper
Like when they say "Stop hitting me, Mike"?

Mike Amesbury has been removed from the group. As has Labour from Runcorn.

Rachel Reeves
Just to make it clear, we didn't lose because of the cuts to the Winter Fuel Allowance.

Ed Miliband
Are you feeling the heat, Rachel? Unlike the pensioners. You need to cool down a bit. Can I suggest you install a heat pump?

Tony Blair
Hi, Tony here. Can I just say that's a terrible idea. The voters don't want all that Net Zero nonsense. And talking of great war-time leaders, Keir, I think you'll find you missed one out on your list.

Margaret Thatcher!

Tony Blair
No. Not Maggie. Though she was great. The unforgettable war-time Prime Minister I was thinking of begins with a T.

Rachel Reeves
Liz Truss! Of course. She was at war with the markets and the economists who didn't appreciate how brilliant her financial plans were. It's a common problem.

Tony Blair
Hey guys, I'm feeling a bit left out in the cold here.

Ed Miliband
You and the pensioners.

Tony Blair has left the group, as he has to jet off to an important meeting between the Tony Blair Foundation and the Mohammed Bin Principles Saudi Oil Conglomerate.

Morgan McSweeney
Is someone saying the Winter Fuel Allowance cut is my fault? Is that what everyone thinks? That we lost because of me?

Rachel Reeves
There's a time to take responsibility for things. And I take full responsibility for the successful trade deal with India.

Jonathan Reynolds
Quite right! Whisky and Cars – what a great combination! 🥃🚙

Angela Rayner
I think you've had enough, Rachel luv. Did they have you over a barrel? No offence! ❤️

Yvette Cooper
Hang on! Haven't you just handed out a big tax break that will encourage Indian immigrants to come here?

Wes Streeting
Oh great. That should win us some Reform votes. Just saying!

"There goes the neighbourhood!"

LESSONS LEARNED FROM THE LOCAL ELECTION RESULTS

Labour
Our vote is on the slide, so we have to keep doing the same unpopular things, only do them much faster.

Conservatives
Our vote is on the slide, so we have to keep saying the same unpopular things, only say them much louder.

Lib Dems
Our leader is on a water slide, *wheeeeee*!!!

STARMER TO HALT MIGRATION TO REFORM

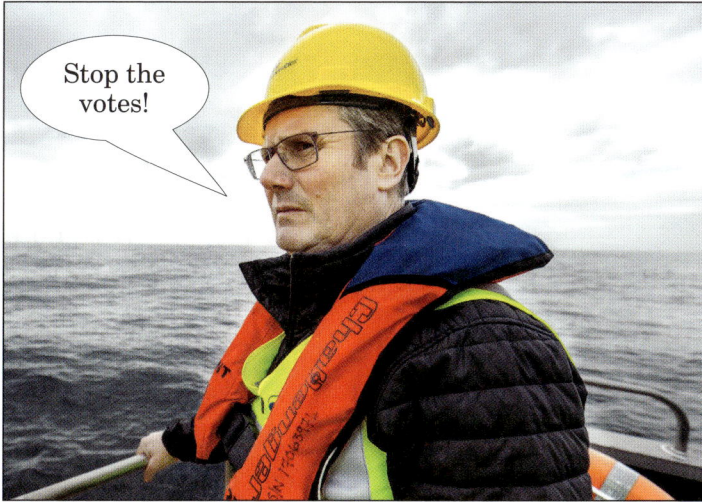

Stop the votes!

GREEN CO-LEADER RESIGNS

What happens now?

1. Carla Denyer steps down as co-leader of her party

2. Denyer is put out for collection

3 Local Green council has changed bin collections with 27 new different categories of waste being collected on alternate last Fridays in the month

4 Denyer has to wait until weeds grow over her

5 Council explains the weeds are vital biodiversity and will not be tidied away

6 Greens are unable to elect a new leader as *(cont. 2094)*

JAM SESSION

@Vilmisrimo

"It's tomorrow"

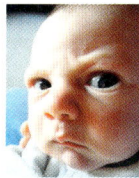

The Eye's Controversial New Columnist

This week I am angry about the news that the minimum age of a train driver is to be reduced from 20 to 18. Speaking as a baby *(see photo)* I feel that this does not go nearly far enough. I think that the minimum age should be reduced to six months old, as I am keen to apply for the job. I would be an excellent train driver. I feel I am almost over-qualified, as I already have huge experience in this area. I have been able to speak fluent steam engine ever since Thomas the Tank Engine was a scouser, and I gather that modern trains use much the same dialect, even the ones on Avanti. Even if I have to drive a train without a face, I am still able to make very convincing "chuff chuff" noises that any engineer will tell you will help the train go faster. I also have a lot of experience in doing nothing all day, so I already have what it takes to be a train driver and I will... (*cont. p94*)

Dee Nial

Ex-Conservative MP writes for the Eye

HI! SO you might have noticed in the news that we had the teensiest little setback on our march back to power last week when we lost control of every single council that we contested.

And on that Debbie-downer note, I'm afraid I was disappointed too! My hopes of gaining a council seat in my old constituency of Blandley-Under-Whelming were dashed when I lost to a pork pie with a boiled egg inside and Winston Churchill's face sculpted on the top. Still, I wish Mr Mowbray well in wrangling the knotty problem of the lack of car parking spaces in the town centre!

So, it's not ideal, but let's take a breath, step back and look these results in context: we may have lost heavily to Reform in terms of council seats, but if you look at the proportion of the vote – we also lost heavily to Reform, but not quite as much!

And already there are calls for Kemi Badenoch to go. And of course, these calls come from all those usual suspects – you know the ones! Conservative MPs, Conservative councillors, Conservative voters, Conservative columnists and Conservative newspaper proprietors. But there is one crucial group that are not being listened to, and they are the most important ones of the lot – Reform voters!

If you ask them, and I have, Reform voters seem very happy to keep Kemi Badenoch in place!

And quite frankly I think it's a bit rich to get lectured day after day in the press about the need for the Conservative party to listen to the views of Reform voters, only to ignore them when it comes to who leads our party!

So, rest assured Kemi, your future is safe. You're going nowhere! And I mean that in every sense! I can see you continuing in the job for at least as long as our crusty-headed councillor, Mr Melton Mowbray!

REFORM UK

That Reform UK agenda in full
THE FIRST 100 DAYS

Day 1 All flags to be taken down from council buildings, except for patriotic flags, ie Union Jack, Stars and Stripes, and the national flag of the Russian Federation.

Day 2 Proper British history to be taught in schools, focusing on Victory in Europe 2016, the Battle of Britain 2016, Waterloo 2016 (delayed from 1815 due to staff shortages), the Battle of Hustings 2025.

Day 3 Statues of proper British heroes to be erected in all town centres, ie Donald Trump in Tunbridge Wells shopping centre (the no-Pantiles), Roy "Chubby" Brown on the fourth plinth in Trafalgar Square and Nigel Farage on Clacton Pier, to prevent people claiming never to have seen him there.

Day 4 Removing waste from local government in Musk-style chainsaw slashing of social care, bin collection, libraries, parks, leisure centres, nursery provision, etc.

Day 5 Brainstorming awayday in pub, to work out what to do on Day 6.

Day 6 Reintroduction of smoking in all pubs, 24-hour alcohol licences compulsory for all pubs and free fags for pensioners.

Day 7 to Day 99 Further brainstorming in pub to work out further policies, ie increasing things that are popular and decreasing things that are unpopular.

Day 100 Storm Downing Street wearing buffalo-horned hat in populist putsch to stop Labour stealing the next election.

"I knew you weren't just coming up for air!"

COOPER

GAZA OFFENSIVE LATEST

■ LAST night Prime Minister Benjamin Netanyahu revealed his new offensive plans.

He told reporters, "These plans are more offensive than any of our other offensive plans. They literally are the most offensive plans I can think of. And trust me I've been doing a lot of thinking.

"They include forcing all Palestinians out of Gaza, weaponising aid up to and including starvation and, of course, making sure the hostages all get killed, whilst pretending to care very deeply so the relatives don't kick up too much of a stink."

He continued, "But the most offensive thing about my offensive plans is that, with any luck, now that it's all kicking off in India and Pakistan, and it still appears to be going on in Ukraine, hopefully nobody will notice and I'll stay in power and won't have to go to prison."

He added, "Of course, anyone in Israel who disagrees with me is entirely free to be sacked." *(Rotters)*

Weight-loss head-to-head trial results

THERE was a clear winner when leading weight-loss treatments were tested on the public.

America's Mounjaro and Denmark's Wegovy have proved effective – but both lost out to the Israeli government's miracle weight-loss solution – Starvation™.

Trialled on the people of Gaza, Starvation™ has delivered extraordinary results and *(We get the point. Ed.)* *(Rotters)*

POETRY CORNER

**In Memoriam
Jean Marsh,
actress and writer**

So. Farewell
Then Jean Marsh.
You created
Upstairs Downstairs,
Among many other things.
But now, I wonder,
Will you be
Heading Upstairs
Or Down?

E.J. Thribb (17½ items of silver cutlery)

VE DAY
The celebrations continue

by Our **Entire Staff**

MAY 8th will go down in history forever as the day peace broke out. Finally, following a long and bitter conflict, the presenters of Radio 4's *Today* programme, Nick Robinson and Emma Barnett, declared a ceasefire. The BBC announced the news, calling it "VE Day", Victory over Emma.

Crowds gathered in Trafalgar Square, many of them jumping into fountains at the welcome news that hostilities between Nick and Emma were finally at an end.

Soldiers kissed complete strangers, policemen danced with nurses, and even the Queen snuck out in disguise to join her people in celebrating the most extraordinary historic occasion, perhaps having a crafty shandy *(surely Tequila Sunrise?)* and... *(That's enough VE Day. Ed.)*

TRUMP DECIDES TO RENAME VE DAY 'VICTORY DAY'

Those alternatives in full

● America Kicks Ass In Europe Day

● Why We Did Everything To Save Loser Brits Day

● How America Won The War Single-Handedly, Apart From Russia Who Were Also Amazing (Hope This Will Do, Vlad?) Day

● Victory Over Scumbag Communist French Day

● We Should Have Kept Everything West of the Elbe Day

● Nobody Has Ever Disrespected Us Like The Allies It's Crazy How You Get Disrespected By These People I Mean We Did You All A Favour And Nobody Ever Thanks Us Like What Do We Even Have To Do To Get Some Credit Day

Shock as band called 'Kneecap' says something offensive

MEDIA commentators across Britain have reacted with outrage to something said by an Irish rap group named after the practice of shooting people in the knees.

"I can't believe that this band, who have named themselves after shooting people you disagree with and crippling them for life, have suggested they are in favour of political violence," said one shocked observer.

"I assumed they would limit themselves to strongly-worded statements about the importance of getting along with one another."

One expert on Irish history added, "This is really surprising. It's not like young rap artists to make songs glorifying violence and to say unbelievably stupid things like 'kill your local MP' or 'The only good Tory is a dead Tory'."

A number of other bands on the British music scene have explained that this was an attempt to "censor and deplatform" Kneecap and that it is vital not to repress artistic freedom, though of course they admitted to not being entirely up to speed on the laws concerning incitement to violence.

The band themselves explained in a later statement that they "reject any suggestion that we would seek to incite violence against any MP or individual", and that "Kneecap's message has always been... one of love, inclusion and hope, etc, etc". *(PA)*

"If you lose mental capacity, it allows him to make decisions on your behalf"

"We used to be champagne socialists, but now we're champagne centrists"

Sarah Vain

Whatever happened to those VE Day values of selflessness and sacrifice? Nowadays it's all me, me, me, writes Sarah Vain

AS I watched the celebrations, I couldn't help but think to myself, Sarah, aren't people today just too self-obsessed *(Hang on... the office Ironyometer is making strange noises. Ed.)*, endlessly going on about themselves and what they think, as if their opinion is the only thing that matters.

What is it about people today that they think their lives and their experiences and their thoughts are more important than other people's? *(Clear the office, I think the Ironyometer's gonna blow! Ed.)*

When I snuggled down in front of my telly with my cocoa and my slippers and a tub of biscuits... just one, Sarah, oh, all right, treat yourself, it's VE Day after all... and I watched the magnificent veterans, who shall be nameless, I began to well up and found myself shaking uncontrollably. *(So is the Ironyometer! Sound the sirens! We've got a major explosion coming).*

Yes, I, Sarah Vain, columnist of the year four times in the past five years, was ashamed of the self-centredness and lack of humility when confronted by a generation who *(BOOM!!!!!! Massive power outage hits Britain, France and the entire Iberian peninsula...)*

© *Sarah Vain, the woman who puts both the "I"s in the DAILY MAIL.*

THE KING OF TROUBLES

A short story special by Dame Hedda Shoulders

THE STORY SO FAR: Charles is leading the nation in celebration of the end of the War in Europe, standing on the balcony with the pared-down Royal Family to witness the historic flypast.

"**B**ORING!" The fractious tones of the King's youngest grandson momentarily undermined the solemnity of the marchpast of the massed bands of the Coldplay Guards resplendent in their Paddington Bearskin Hats.

"No, Louis, this is what we do so well," said the King indulgently to the truculent seven-year-old who was failing to appreciate the finer points of the military procession. "It's all about the pageantry, the spectacle, the pomp, the circumstance, the whole thingie..."

At that moment, a roar from the heavens signalled the arrival of the Battle of Brexit Memorial Flight, comprising an iconic Burt Lancaster bomber flanked by a Hurricane Higgins fighter and, of course, a legendary Supermario Spitfire Mk 94 with its unmistakeable Greggs Rolls Royce engine.

"Is that the whole naffing Air Force?" joked the forthright Princess Royale dressed smartly in the no-nonsense uniform of commander-in-chief of the First Band Aid Nursing Yeomanry of the Guard, standing stiffly alongside her husband Admiral Sir Tim Nice-But-Dim-Lawrence of Arabia .

"Ha!Ha!Ha!" laughed Charles at his sister's blunt assessment of the United Kingdom's limited military capacity in the modern era.

"Forget waving Union Jacks," continued Colonel Anne. "We might as well be waving bloody white flags!"

"No, no, no, no!" remonstrated the King. "Today is a day for rejoicing in our glorious past and just look at those magnificent men in their flying machines going up diddly up and then down diddly down... up, down, flying around, looping the loopy and defying the ground. I mean, it sends shivers down one's spine, doesn't it?"

"It's certainly effing freezing," agreed his soulmate and Queen Consulate, Camilla, who was finding it unusual to be outside, but not enjoying the pungent aroma of a King Size Lambert and Under-Butler Full Strength gasper.

"Is it over yet?" asked the impish young royal Louis, the fourth in line to the throne, who was wishing he could return to playing Landminecraft on his royal We-Pad while he fidgeted and fiddled with his father's gold braid shoulder cords – part of Prince William's uniform as Rear Vice Marshal of the Fleet Air Fryer Arm.

"No, Loo-loo," soothed his mother, the fragrant Princess Kate in her stunning plum pudding designer two-piece suit and matching wartime-themed pill box hat. Charles once again reflected on how fortunate they were to have the beautiful and sensible Kate Middleclass as part of the firm. She was just so... what was the word...

appealing! Yes that was it. "Appealing"... rather than that other word... "Appalling", which really did apply to the ghastly actress from Montecristo, the Duchess of Succession, who was no doubt at this very moment plotting away from her Californian hideaway. But no, thought Charles, that way madness lies. His duty was to the present and to the future and to just keeping the whole bally show on the road.

He snapped out of his reverie and summoned the great wartime spirits to assist him in his noble task of waving and smiling at the myriad throng of loyal subjects lining the Daily Mall, many of whom had dressed up for the day as members of Dad's Army or the popular singing group, the Prince Andrew Sisters.

He addressed his fellow balconeers in Churchillian tones.

"One can almost feel the presence here with us today of the ghosts of yesteryear... Mater, Pater, Grandpater and, of course, Grandnan, cheering up all the Eastenders in the crowd with her hip flask of Gordons of Khartoum Gin and her racing tip for the 4.30 at Uttoxeter, namely the favourite Backstairs Billy at 3-1..."

SADLY, his reminiscences were drowned out by the arrival of the RAF aerobatic display team, the Reddit Arrows, now sponsored by the social media platform device, the workings of which his niece, Eugenica (or was it Bellatrix?), had tried in vain to explain to

him. The plumes of vapour trailing from the exhausts of the V and E formation Tony Hawks fighter jets filled the sky with glorious red, white and blue patterns.

"Makes the Pope Smoke look a bit shoddy!" commented the Princess Royale, whose brusque demeanour failed to conceal a patriotic heart of oak.

CHARLES felt his chest swell and his spirits rise, soaring like the planes above the sorrows of the previous day when he had watched from behind the sofa as his errant son Harry gave yet another interview to the television people.

Charles had sat with his hands over his ears as his youngest son had recited his familiar litany of woes and blamed everything on his father, whom he had accused of refusing to talk to him solely because he had written a 994-page book attacking him and had accused him of racism on the Grand Ol' Oprah Whingey Show... but no, that was in the past. Now was the time to look to the future, to the working royal family, to the core players, the royal bloodline that would take the Windsor-Davies-Sax-Solo-Mount-Battenburg-Cake Dynasty onto the sunlit uplands of their manifest destiny.

At that moment, Charles' attention was diverted by the unfortunate sight of Louis cruelly mimicking his elder brother Prince St George by mockingly flicking his hair in an exaggerated fashion, causing the second in line to the throne to glower menacingly at his annoying sibling. Charles trembled as he suddenly had a terrifiying vision of the future. Charles saw in his royal mind's eye the publication of Louis' tell-all memoir, "Spare Us Some Money", in which he settled old scores and accused his brother George and the future King William of being to blame for everything that had gone wrong in his young life, including his self-imposed exile in Moosejaw City in what had become the 51st State of Canadamerica under president Baron Trump.

A cold wind blew down the Mall and the sun dipped behind the grey clouds. Charles could hear the distant strains of the crowd singing along to that poignant wartime ballad by Vera Duckworth Lynn, "We'll Meet Again". But would he and Harry ever... meet again?   *(To be continued...)*

People who look like their dogs and sound like their podcasts

What King Charles played on the carrot when he joined The Vegetable Orchestra in full

Handel's Watercress Music

Barber's Adagio for Strings of Beans

Stravinsky's The Rite of Spring Onions

Puccini Madame Butterbeans

Dvorak's New Potato Symphony

Delibe's Cauliflower Duet

Tchaikovsky's Swan Leek

Parry's Jerusalem Artichoke

Grieg's Pea Gynt

Orff's Carmina Banana *(That's a fruit. Ed.)*

Why are so many young people saying their mental health is bad?

AS THE government continued to search for ways to lower the benefits bill, the Home Office said it continued to be perplexed by the high number of young people in their 20s and 30s saying they had mental health issues.

Said one Home Office official, "What could it be about this generation who grew up in the decade-long austerity aftermath of the financial crash of 2009 and who, just as they were finding their feet, were slammed by the Covid lockdowns, then endured the cost of living crisis, all the while being told they'll never be able to afford to buy a home, that AI will steal their jobs and that they're on the verge of being on the receiving end of an economic meltdown?

"What makes them feel so depressed and anxious? It really is a total mystery."

"Stop checking your phone, Jeeves"

Notes&queries

Who or what is a Panican?

We seem to hear a lot about it from America at the moment?
Mrs Dow-Jones, Skintley, Hurts.

● A panican is a rare breed of marine bird found only in the former Gulf of Mexico (now the Golf of Trump). It is a cross between a pelican and a pangolin, a sort of flying armadillo, and is known for its thick skin and its alarming squawk. The native peoples of Peru drew a giant Panican on the desert plains of Nazdaq, which experts believe signifies great misfortune and imminent catastrophe. You can see the panican from outer space.
Paul Footsie, Spartsville

● Oh, dear. Mr Footsie has – dare I say it? – got off on the wrong foot! Panican was the first album of the 1980s' rock band the Panic Street Teachers, a group of friends who met at Mumbles Teacher Training College. The Panics, as they became known to us hardcore "panatics", produced a further 17 albums, but none had the impact of the ground-breaking Panican, with legendary tracks such as "Gold Against the Dollar", "Sell Sell Sell", "Jump" and "Splat". The Panics split earlier this year after a disagreement about VAT on private schools.
Hank Seng, Hong Kong

● May I take over this class and put Mr Seng in detention! Panican is the brand name for the drug known to pharmacists as ditrumpalinenavarone. It is a mixture of bleach and Agent Orange and is used in the United States as a cure for the Covid virus. Early tests on rats concluded that panican was of no use as an anti-Covidoid, but did have severe side effects, including paranoia, anxiety, depression and psychotic episodes. Manufactured by Bigly Pharma out of Wuhan in China, panican has recently attracted a US import tariff of 104%, making it the must-buy dopiod of choice for very rich elderly celebrities in Florida. Take two before meals but not more than 94 in any one day.
Nicky Index, Tokyo

Next Week: What is misogynoir? And who are its best known Scandinavian directors?

THE US CONSTITUTION: A GUIDE

THEN

Checks and balances

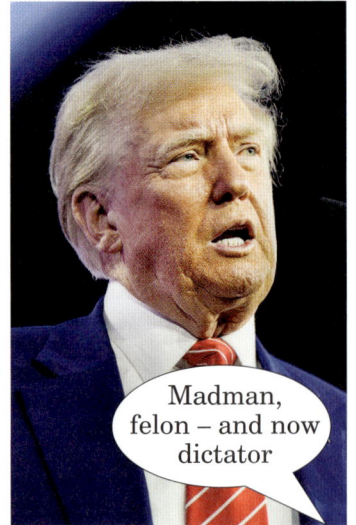

NOW

Huge cheques and bank balances

TRUMP AIMING FOR A THIRD TERM

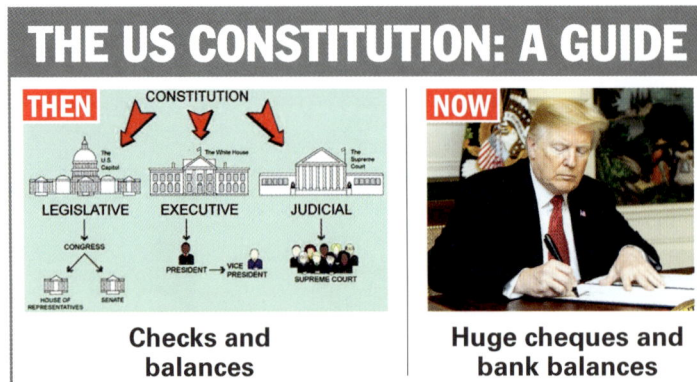

Madman, felon – and now dictator

POETRY CORNER

In Memoriam George Foreman, griddle entrepreneur, preacher, and sometime Heavyweight Boxing Champion of the World

So. Farewell
Then George Foreman.

You are finally
Out for the count.
And have gone
To meet the
Great Referee
In the sky.

You fought
Mohammed Ali in
"The Rumble in the Jungle"
Or was that my stomach
Before I bought
Your wonderful
George Foreman Grill?

It drains away the fat
During cooking,
Thus ironically ensuring
The consumer doesn't
Become a heavyweight.

Now you are
In the clouds
Which don't come
From your grill,
Which is, of course,
Smokeless.
And you are far away
From any flames.

E.J. Thribb-Eye Steak
(17½ oz)

How to come up with a new 'family password' to prevent deepfake impersonations

1. Think of a name that nobody else could possibly guess

2. It's going to be the dog's name, isn't it?

3. Mutually agree the dog's name is your super-secret password in the event of anyone pretending to be your children and asking for money

4. Be totally shocked when criminals guess it's the dog's name

5. Next time, make it the cat's name.

Columnist not on Ozempic shock

by Our Weight Loss Correspondent **Suze Zero**

A British lifestyle journalist has shocked her industry by making the confession that she's not taking a single miracle weight-loss medication.

"I just don't want to," explained the writer, who has been a bit overweight for a little while but doesn't especially mind it and can't be bothered to spend lots of money on injections. "I actually find the whole thing amazingly easy to do. It's very convenient, it's revolutionised the amount of time I have, because I can now do other things than writing about My Mounjaro Voyage or My Ozempic Experience and, as a result, I get to have a fantastic quality of life."

One medical expert added, "The process of not being on Ozempic is extremely simple. You simply have to not ask your doctor to prescribe it, then don't go to an online pharmacy to order it. You may find that from time to time – about once a week, when you need an idea for a column – you experience a desperate craving to be 'on the pen' so you can write about how your life has totally changed – but as long as you maintain focus, perhaps by treating yourself to a nice biscuit, you will find the urge passes."

BBC TO USE AI TO DEAL WITH COMPLAINTS

by Our AI Staff
Rob Bott

THE BBC has announced its decision to employ Artificial Intelligence to deal with complaints from the public.

Said the BBC's Director of Artificial Logistic External Knowledge (DALEK), "AI has predicted that there will be a huge flood of complaints and angry letters about this decision, and so we have advised the BBC to respond to the surge in complaints by using AI to deal with the complaints about using AI.

"This will please everyone, and cannot possibly go wrong."

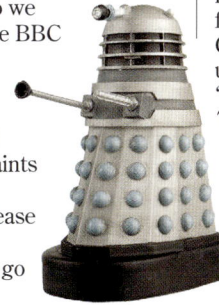

What you will see

QUESTION: "Why aren't you employing humans to respond to complaints, you faceless tech-obsessed penny-pinching bastards?"

RESPONSE: "The BBC was founded in 1842 by British Prime Minister Lord Parmesan with its HQ at Hammersmith Palace, with the aid of Italian scientist Professor Macaroni and Scottish inventor John Yogi Bear. Its first Major General was Lord Great-Barrier-Reith, who came up with the mission statement "Inform, Educate, Exterminate." This is now the watchword for all Artificial Intelligence Bots. "EXTERMINATE! EXTERMINATE! EXTERMINATE!"

NB: complaints will not go upstairs because BBC AI Daleks have problems going up stairs.

Post Office award at last

THERE were scenes of unconfined joy among the wrongly-convicted Post Masters and Mistresses as finally, after decades of grief and suffering, they received an award – a BAFTA.

Said one, "We were hoping that after 25 years of campaigning we might have received more compensation than a bronze statuette – but there you go."

Said another, "This recognition that the production company did a good job is fine, but it would be quite nice if I was awarded a suitable sum of money for the years I spent in prison."

But there was also anger at the continuing injustice that saw Toby Jones overlooked as Best Actor and *(cont. p94)*

Apparently BY MIKE BARFIELD

EARTH: ITS MANY LAYERS AND WHAT YOU WILL FIND THERE

EXOSPHERE
THERMOSPHERE
MESOSPHERE
STRATOSPHERE
TROPOSPHERE
MANOSPHERE
WOMEN'S FEAR

Apparently BY MIKE BARFIELD

BOOMERS v. GENERATION Z: WHY THEY CAN NEVER BE RECONCILED

It's pronounced 'zee'...
"GEN. Z"

It's pronounced 'zed'... SIGH!
"BOOMERS"

Apparently BY MIKE BARFIELD

PAPAL GEOMETRY: A TOPICAL GUIDE

CONCLAVE

CONVLEX

DIARY
THE WHITE LOTUS AND ME

ADRIAN CHILES

Funny thing, television. TV, telly, the box – call it what you will, it's still basically the same old electrical device in the corner of your living-room, or, if you're very cutting edge – which I'm not, for my sins – stuck to the wall.

The last series of White Lotus has really got me going. There's eight episodes in all. Where to begin? My advice is to start with Episode One, which kind of sets the scene, and then watch Episode Two, Episode Three, Episode Four, Episode Five and Episode Six – all the way to Episode Eight, which, by my none-too-expert calculation, is the last and final one.

It's set, if truth be told, in Thailand. You can tell it's Thailand because it's hot and they all wear those colourful Hawaiian shirts which, now you mention it, might indicate to the trained eye that they're in Hawaii, but, believe me, they're not.

The hotel, the aforesaid White Lotus, looks as though it must cost the proverbial packet. Swimming pools all over the place, fancy cocktails, waiter service, the lot. I don't want to go into too much detail, but basically there's quite a few guests, and each episode they get up to this and that, and in the end whatever's going to happen, happens. That's it, in a nutshell. Well, it had me gripped, but then again, what do I know?

ALLISON PEARSON

Keir Starmer's ruthless obsession with placing ordinary decent people in shackles is driving Brits abroad – and who can blame them?

And what do they find when they get there? As the hidden cameras in the White Lotus resort have revealed to shocked viewers the world over, hard-working Britons hoping for a few hours in the sun can expect nothing but misery.

Extortion. Violence. Murder.

Even incest.

White Lotus shames Britain. As a former hotel receptionist, I am desperately troubled by the way the management turns a blind eye to the hideous treatment of Britons abroad.

In the most recent series, like many of you, I looked on in horror as the English girl with the great teeth and the dazzling smile was brutally slaughtered by foreigners in broad daylight. And no one lifted a finger to help her.

As a former paramedic, this made my blood boil. Sorry, but it's not racist to ask whether Thai people are capable of ordinary, decent human feelings. It's not racist to ask whether Asians give two figs for old-fashioned British qualities like compassion and good manners.

Is Keir Starmer man enough to send our troops into Thailand and sort this matter out, once and for all?

Some hope. His indifference to human suffering beggars belief. And as a former frontline charity worker, I've just about had enough of it.

CAROL MIDGLEY

Hey-ho. As roller-coasters go, that was a real roller-coaster. For me, it was neither too long nor too short but somewhere in the middle so just about right. And it really left me thinking about all sorts of things, which is, in my book, much better than being left thinking about nothing much at all.

As told to
CRAIG BROWN

AMOL RAJAN MEETS GARY LINEKER

What shocked you the most about the BBC replacing you as Match of the Day host?

That you didn't get the job

Participants demand to be removed from MasterChef

by Our Media Staff
Em Barrassment and **Hugh Miliation**

TODAY, one of the stars of the BBC's flagship cookery programme hit out at their treatment by the show.

A lamb, who asked to remain anonymous, told reporters, "I was sickened to have my leg being discussed in an inappropriate way by Gregg Wallace. The BBC has a duty of care and should edit out my leg so it isn't drooled over by the likes of the frankly creepy former grocer."

Said a pig, "Gregg thinks it's funny to talk about my sausage, but actually it's really offensive. And we've all seen enough of his already! He should put a sock in it rather than one on it."

A further complaint has been made by a pair of melons who are furious at being referred to by Wallace as "ripe and juicy".

"We don't want to be on the same screen as this discredited barrow boy," said the fruits.

The BBC has agreed to re-recut the series to save their top brand. From now on the programme will consist of the opening titles and closing credits.

LATE NEWS

■ MasterChef logo refuses to share screen with Wallace, and theme tune is considering legal action.

WAS RUSSELL BRAND ACTING ALONE WHEN HE SHOT HIMSELF IN THE FOOT? OR WAS HE PART OF A CONSPIRACY TO MAKE HIM LOOK RIDICULOUS?

IT HAS kept conspiracy theorists busy for days, as they sift through the recently-released evidence and construct elaborate explanations for one of the most extraordinary events of the century – the moment when Russell Brand retweeted an obvious piece of fake news claiming English actress Penelope Keith was the assassin on the grassy knoll who shot the president.

Everyone remembers where they were when they heard the news that Russell Brand had made an idiot of himself.

But what actually happened?

Was Brand a lone tweeter in the Booky Wook depository or did he have an accomplice and was it Richard Briers?

And was Brand about to reveal that Shergar was kidnapped by the Two Ronnies and that the moon landing was faked in a studio by Leonard Rossiter from Rising Damp?

We will have to wait another 60 years until President Trump Junior releases the Brand files to lift the lid on the truth behind the most *(That's enough conspiracy theory drivel. Ed.)*

The Canterbury Galegraph

GAP-TOOTHED STAR OF HIT TRAVEL DRAMA COMPLAINS ABOUT 'FOCUS ON TEETH'

by Our Entertainment Staff Vic Reeves, Ben Miller and Stephen Merchant

The breakout star of the hugely popular series The Canterbury Tales has spoken about her treatment by the media after her success as the Wife Of Bath in which she delivered the now classic line "Gap-tothed I was, and that bicam me weel."

In her wide-ranging interview with all the journals in Christendom, she said, "Ok, I have got funny British teeth, but there is a lot more to me than my wonky dentures. People are obsessing about my teeth and ignoring the fact that I am an independent woman in charge of my own destiny, which is pretty remarkable for the fourteenth century".

The author, Mr Geoffrey Chaucer, backed up his gap-toothed star, saying, "The Wife of Bath is an incredible woman – talented funny, feisty and, yes, quite cute and goofy with those wonky choppers."

Gap teeth are meant to symbolise a sensual nature, which may explain why Amy Loo Bath has been on such an extraordinary showbiz journey (all the way from the Tabard Inn in Southwark to Canterbury).

POLICE LOG
Neasden Central Police Station

9.45 Neasden officers are summoned to the home of a suspected electronics thief who has been reported for a string of robberies of high-end goods from local children. Suspect is brought into station where she keeps saying, "I'm their mum, I confiscated their iPads from them". Officers decide to keep her for seven hours of questioning.

11.45 Officers are summoned to the Neasden Care Home where one of the residents – a hardened criminal who also happens to be an 87-year-old woman with advanced osteoporosis – has told staff the breakfast is "disgusting" and sworn at them. In response to this display of dangerous foul language, officers surround premises and are given licence to shoot to kill. Following use of Tasers, this turns out not to be necessary, as shortly after being tasered the suspect cleverly dies of an unrelated condition and therefore manages to evade arrest.

12.15 A number of other calls have come in claiming thefts of personal property (phones snatched in street, house burglaries, car thefts), offences against the person (grooming children for sexual activities) and financial crime (roving gangs of cowboy builders defrauding the elderly). Sadly, station protocol means the above cases came first in the Neasden Offence Prioritisation Cascade and all other complaints are deleted from system in the name of "Inbox Zero" and to lower station's electronic carbon emissions.

HOCKNEY RETROSPECTIVE

Kipper Williams

SIR DAVID ATTENBOROUGH
99 FACTS ABOUT THE GREAT MAN ON HIS 99TH BIRTHDAY

1 As a much-revered national treasure, Sir David is covered by Britain's contents insurance and locked away every night in the Tower of London.

2 Due to an error by the casting director, Sir David was offered the role of RAF Squadron Leader Roger Bartlett in the film The Great Escape, a part which should have gone to his brother, Sir Dickie. The mistake was only realised when David insisted the script be rewritten to involve an escape by lemurs from Berlin Zoo.

3 When he was Director of Programming for the BBC, Sir David installed an Ecuadorian Rainbow Parrot to read the 10 O'clock News and a Venezuelan River Frog to do the weather.

4 Unfortunately, he had to subsequently sack the parrot after it was involved in a petophile scandal, which led to the memorable News of the World headline, "Who's a Pretty Boy, then?"

5 A newly discovered dinosaur was due to be named "Attenborosaurus Rex" after Sir David, but in a public poll the new species of brontosaurus ended up being called "Bronty McBrontface".

6 If you put all the natural history videos and DVDs that Sir David has sold into the ocean, sea levels would rise so high the human race would be rendered extinct and penguins would rule the earth.

7 The mountain gorillas Sir David famously played with in Life on Blue Living Planet Earth 3, became so acclimatised to humans and human communication that they now work in a call centre in Reading.

8 Sir David's legendary whisper is the only voice so quiet that Alexa has to say "Sir David, please speak up, I can't tell whether you want to listen to Radio 3 or buy a pair of socks."

9 Nobody has ever successfully completed a list of 99 facts about Sir David Attenborough.

Brand-extension failures

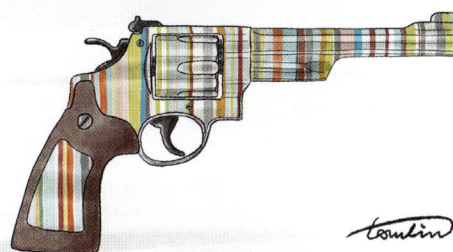

The Paul Smith and Wesson

WINTER FOOL SHOCK

I thought we weren't going to do a U-turn

I've changed my mind

FROM BADENOCH TO WORSE

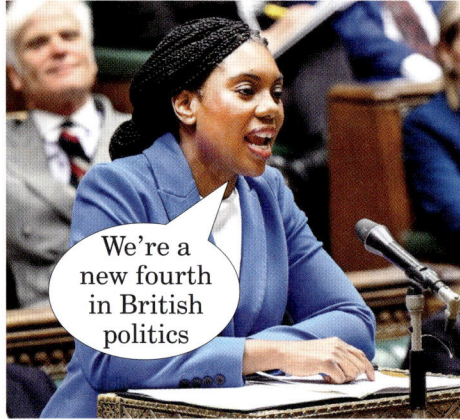

We're a new fourth in British politics

THE END IS NIGE

My policies are written on the back of this envelope

LUCY CONNOLLY: SHOCKING SENTENCE CONDEMNED

by Our Home Correspondent
Vi Rall

ACROSS Britain today millions of people were horrified when they read the sentence: "The Trump administration is monitoring the situation and is concerned about infringements on freedom of expression."

Everyone agreed that this was a truly shocking sentence, coming from a government that is busy attacking journalists, bullying universities and closing down law firms.

Another Connolly sentence under the spotlight was that in the Daily Mail, which read: "A very ugly and un-British authoritarianism is on the rise in this country." Coming from the Daily Mail, which regularly complains that criminals are not locked up for long enough and are released too early, this sentence was simply absurd.

But the sentence which left most people agog came from Allison Pearson in The Telegraph when she wrote: "The law was no longer just an ass, it was a whole stable of braying donkeys in horsehair wigs."

Said one *Telegraph* reader, "No one should have to read a sentence that appalling, excessive and unjust over their toast and marmalade."

....

■ **Lucy Connolly was imprisoned for encouraging people to set fire to migrant hotels and lost her appeal against the sentence: "You're going down for 31 months."**

POLICE RELEASE PHOTOFIT OF WANTED CRIMINAL

by Our Statue Correspondent **Charles Henry-Moore**

F O L L O W I N G legislation making climbing and defacing Winston Churchill's statue a criminal offence, police are keen to question the individual shown, following an incident in the early hours of yesterday morning.

"Several eye-witnesses have come forward claiming that a Mister Walter Pigeon was seen flagrantly perching on Mr Churchill's head and defecating in his right ear," said Inspector Knacker of Scotland Yard.

"This is a particularly heinous repeat offender. If anyone sees this individual, do not approach him, do not offer him breadcrumbs or chips. Just call 999 and wait for our officers to arrive.

"We will fight these miscreants on the benches. We will fight them on the window sills and by the bins. We will never surrender."

....

UPDATE Mr Walter Pigeon was released without charge yesterday, after police took into account his family's proud war record carrying messages to help the Allied effort.

THE Sun SAYS

LET'S be clear from the outset, what was posted online was inexcusable. It was deeply offensive and the Sun would never seek to condone such an outburst.

But does the punishment meted out really fit the crime? Yes, the post may have been shared and viewed hundreds of thousands of times, but it was deleted within hours. *(This is rippa! Keep going – Rupert)*

The hysterical reaction from the usual suspects demanding draconian punishment shames our nation. All this for a humble online post? For mere words? Has the birthplace of Shakespeare and Churchill become so fragile a country we can't just tut-tut and move on?

We're talking, of course, about Gary Lineker's Instagram post and the frenzied demands from this and other newspapers, not just that the BBC immediately sack him, but that Gary be placed in stocks outside Wembley where he'll be pelted with rotten fruit for his *(You're fired as well – Rupert)*

ANDREW NEIL

Writes for the Eye

LET me tell you, I'm shocked at the degree of lying by this Labour government. In all my years as a top journalist I've never come across anything comparable. Take it from me, no one has fibbed to the British public like Keir Starmer!

And you can trust me to know what I'm talking about, because I'm a dab hand at detecting porkie pies! I'll never forget the day when Angelos Frangipangolin told me GB News would be a quality right-of-centre news channel. That was exactly the same day as when that barista gave me coffee with oat milk in and swore blind it was cow's milk. I'll never forget that devious coffee vendor as long as I live!

Anyhoo, that's enough from me, I'm off to have lunch with Robert Jenrick – a man who has always been synonymous with truth in politics. He's assured me he's got no plans to run for Tory leader. So that, I guess, is the end of the matter!

"Darling, is this your first Met Gala?"

Royston

It's another deal, everybody. A brilliant deal with the EU.

Angela Rayner
What's in it, then?

I'm not sure, but that's not the point. I've learnt from the Donald. Claim it's a win and everyone will believe you.

Angela Rayner
So, it's a loss then.

Morgan McSweeney
Don't listen to her, boss. It's a hat trick! First India, then the US, now the EU. You're on fire!

No, that's my old car. And the front door of my house.

Yvette Cooper
Don't worry, Keir, we'll find the perpetrators and bang them up in jail.

Shabana Mahmood
And then we'll let them out again. Unless they're paedos, in which case, we'll chemically castrate them.

Morgan McSweeney
Good ballsy stuff, Shabana! Or should I say "no-ballsy" stuff?!

Shabana Mahmood
As long as it distracts from the fact that the prisons are so full that solitary confinement now means sharing a cell with six others, one of whom is the prison governor who's shagging a drug dealer in the corner.

Yvette Cooper
Firstly, can we not use the term "no-Ballsy" when there's a big shake-up going on at ITV daytime. In our house, it's a sensitive issue.

Darren Jones
Is Balls going to get the Sack? 😂😂😂😂 😂😂😂😂 😂😂😂😂

Yvette Cooper
That's a hate-speech offence, but I won't lock you up, for reasons the Justice Secretary has explained already. That being said, can I repeat that everything is under control on Britain's streets.

Then why is my old flat now on fire?

Waheed Alli
Need somewhere to stay, Keir? Nice flat? Quiet? Non-flammable?

Lord Alli has been removed from the group and extinguished, as his involvement is too incendiary.

Angela Rayner
Don't worry, Keir, I expect those fires are just pensioners trying to warm themselves up. 🔥🔥🔥😂😂😂

I'm ahead of you there, Angela, as I was in the poll for leader. And I've already decided that Rachel is going to do a U-turn on her deeply unpopular idea to cut the winter fuel allowance.

Rachel Reeves
Am I? I thought you said, last week, we weren't going to do a U-turn under any circumstances.

You've done a U-turn on that as well.

Rachel Reeves
Have I?

We can afford it now. Because, thanks to my economic policies, the UK economy is the fastest growing in the G7, with growth having shot up to an amazing 0.7%.

Angela Rayner
But inflation's up as well, isn't it?

That's Rachel's department.

Rachel Reeves
Is it?

Morgan McSweeney
The main thing is, everything's booming thanks to the boss's Euro reset!

I don't want to exaggerate, but I think we can now say the Europeans have forgiven us, they love us and they can't get enough of us.

Angela Rayner
Did you not see Eurovision? They bloody hate us! We got nul points in the public vote. That's French for fuck-all. They even prefer Israel!

We came 19th out of 26. Which is a big improvement on last year when, under the Tories, we came a dismal 18th out of 25.

Rachel Reeves
I know maths isn't my strong point, but doesn't that mean we did worse this year?

Stop talking Britain down. It's just a silly little song competition that doesn't matter. There are really important things happening in the world, aren't there, Foreign Secretary?

David Lammy
I'll say! French taxi drivers are a nightmare! Short hop from a conference in Bologna to a chalet in the French Alps cost a bloody fortune! And then he haggled over the fare!

I was talking about Israel, David.

David Lammy
Are the taxis expensive there too? Wouldn't surprise me.

Let it go, David.

David Lammy
I did! With all my luggage! I had to ski in my boxers.

Distressing though your holiday was, David, it pales somewhat with the plight of those in Gaza.

David Lammy
What's the skiing like there?

Angela Rayner
Oh for fuck's sake! Why can't you go on holiday to Ibiza like everyone else, you upper-middle-class posho prat! 🙄 🍸🍸🍸

What David wants to say is that his unpopular position on Israel has changed.

David Lammy
Has it?

Yes. Britain has now had enough of the shameful and disgraceful extremist conduct of the Israeli Government.

David Lammy
Are we going to do something?

We certainly are. We're going to tell them to stop using the arms that we sold them.

Morgan McSweeney
Good thinking, boss. That'll play really well. Or we could really hit them where it hurts and give them less than maximum points in the next Eurovision.

But we don't know how good their song is yet.

Morgan McSweeney
Er, boss, leave the Euro-politics to me. The main thing is that the economy is boom-bang-a-banging, thanks to Keir's brilliant Buck's Fizzing, not-at-all Puppet on a String leadership, for which we should all say Congratulations and Celebrations!

Angela Rayner
If it's all going so well, shall we put taxes up?

The entire group except Angela Rayner has left the group in protest at the shocking idea that a Labour Government might put taxes up rather than cut benefits, welfare etc.

Will we be able to use e-gates?

No – they won't work. They never do. It's impossible to work out which way up to hold your passport, or where to stand, or whether to take off your spectacles and hat or leave them on, or smile or frown.

Will we be able to take our cats on holiday?

No – they won't want to come. They'll have a prior engagement in nextdoor's garden and won't turn up when you've got to drive down to the Euro Tunnel. They will use their expensive cat passports as kitty litter just to annoy you.

Will it be easier for British bands to tour?

Yes – but they won't be allowed to play any music for fear of being sued by Artificial Intelligence for intellectual copyright infringement, as the AI companies own all musical notes in all possible configurations in perpetuity.

Will my teenage son now be able to travel and work in Europe?

No – because he won't get out of bed and he will then miss the train, and blame you before asking if he can borrow another hundred quid for a tattoo that reads "I HEART Reform."

Will it be cheaper for me to buy British cheese when I go to France?

Yes, but it will need to be pasteurised on the way out and unpasteurised on the way in, unless of course you have an American visa, in which case it will be chlorinated.

How long will I be able to spend in my holiday home in Spain?

There are two possible answers to this question:

A. 0 days. As you will be chased back onto the plane as soon as you land by screaming mobs of your neighbours and that previously nice man in the local café carrying banners shouting "Tourists Out!"

B. 365 days if you're already there and too frightened to venture out.

Will I be able to drive on the left-hand side of the road?

Yes – if you've drunk enough on the ferry over at 7am in the morning, before driving your coach full of OAPs on a tour of medieval Bruges.

Does anyone know what this much heralded deal actually involves?

No.

"Ok, ok, big teeth, big ears... Now, if you've quite finished body-shaming your grandmother..."

Daily Rampant Mail

THE TRAGIC END OF THE BREXIT DREAM

by **Boris Johnson**

CRIPES! Yes, folks, we have just witnessed the biggest surrender to the enemy by a Prime Minister in British history.

The coward responsible, whom I will from now on be calling Sir-Ender Keir, is guilty of the greatest act of treason since Guy Fawkes tried to prorogue parliament *(subs please check)*.

Just as the moustachioed gunpowder plotter lit his sparkler to end free speech forever, so Sir-Ender Keir met Ursula von der Liar, head honcho of the Brussels Mafia and immediately donned the gimp suit of treachery and placed the orange gagging ball of perfidy in his own mouth in order to manacle the ankles of Britain to the bedposts of the EU. *(Is this suitable for a family audience? Ed.)* Yes, sadomasochism was the order of the day, as Sir-Ender Keir knelt down to beg for his punishment, crying out "Please! Please! More! More!" *(Is everything okay, Boris?)* But Sir-Ender Keir hadn't had enough as he humiliatingly agreed to extend my fishy deal for another 12 years.

What was he thinking? It was always a terrible agreement, as I said at the time *(subs please check)*, consigning Britain forever to the dungeons of the Dominatrix that is the President of the European Commission, in her leather stiletto boots, as she stamps on the puffy pink flesh of... *(We can't have any more of this, Boris. Please go back to the Telegraph.)*

We need the space to lock up all the reoffenders!

Daily Mail

ASKS

Is Gary Lineker irreplaceable?

NOW that Gary Lineker has left the BBC, it is hard to imagine who could possibly replace him. The Match of the Day presenter has become synonymous with left-wing BBC bias and blatant anti-Brexit wokeness.

Said one tearful editor, "With his uncanny knack for a timely own goal, Gary is a one-man argument for scrapping the licence fee! And let's not forget the eye-watering salary that greedy Gary stole from the pockets of innocent licence-fee payers, which fuelled our editorials for years. Who will be able to fill the hole left by the jug-eared do-gooder on our front pages?"

Wiping her eyes, a tabloid hack agreed with her boss, "Yes, the BBC-bashing articles featuring the disgraced crisp-salesman-come-political-pundit simply wrote themselves. We shall never see his like again. Gabby Logan had better get tweeting about humanitarian issues or we're in deep doo-doo."

Clickbait headlines from history

► **Eating this one variety of apple will bring you knowledge** – but there's a catch

MailyEXPRESSOgraph

TRIUMPH FOR REFORM AS IT SWEEPS INTO THIRD PLACE

by Our Political Correspondent
Hugh Kip

In the most seismic upheaval in the history of politics, Nigel Farage's Reform party continued its inevitable march to Number 10 by spectacularly coming third in the Hamilton by-election.

After a disastrous night for Labour, which saw the party only come first and win the election, it was clear that Starmer's days are numbered. If this result were replicated in a General Election, Reform would win a massive no seats, while Labour would be consigned to the dustbin of history

with another massive majority.

The records will show that our prediction that it would be a two-horse race between the SNP and Reform became a reality – as the Scots rejected the discredited SNP, consigning them to second place. This proved, as we said, that Reform is the only option north of the border, apart from Labour.

A bruised and battered Starmer was clearly on the ropes as he addressed cheering crowds, and must now only be days away from resigning, thus paving the way for Nigel Farage and his four MPs to sweep to power.

Getting a second opinion

Reform appoints new chairman

TV presenter David Bull has been named as Reform UK's new chairman by party leader Nigel Farage.

Said Mr Farage, "I am delighted to appoint David Bull to this important job. Mr Bull was selected from a very strong

field of potential candidates, including Simon Codswallop, Gary Garbage, Timmy Tosh and Roger Bollocks.

"But, ultimately, 'Bull' really summed up what we in Reform stand for."

(Rotters)

AMERICA INVADES USA

by Our White House Staff
Sybil Waugh

ONCE again, the world held its breath as the globe teetered on the brink of catastrophe as America sent troops into America.

Said President Trump, "America is a lawless shithole country and only America can restore law and order to the streets of America."

He continued, "We will not tolerate violence against US police – unless it's MAGA supporters when they storm the Capitol. California has been a law unto itself for too long under its governor, the discredited Mickey Mouse.

"Once we have taken back control of the Disney Land, we're going to round up all the dwarves, reopen the mines and send the terrorist Aladdin back to where he came from. Though Dumbo is staying, because I like him being my vice president. Then we'll flatten the whole state and turn into a MAGA-style paradise of crazy golf courses, strip clubs and failed Trump casinos."

The story so far

JANUARY Trump promises to annex Greenland and Canada and threatens to take control of Venezuela, the Panama Canal and the Gaza Strip

JUNE Trump invades California

IS BROMANCE DEAD? *A Photo Casebook Special*

STUPID'S ARROW...

I LOVE YOU

I LOVE ME TOO

MONEYMOON PERIOD...

POWER IS AN APHRODISIAC

YOU'RE GIVING ME AN ELECTION!

HEAD OVER WHEELS...

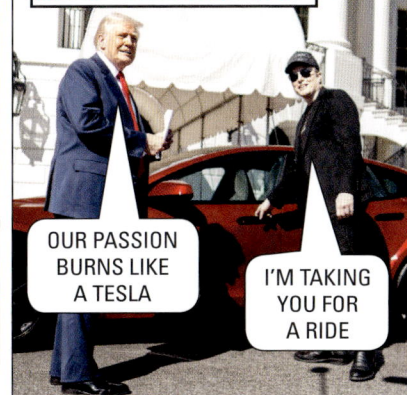

OUR PASSION BURNS LIKE A TESLA

I'M TAKING YOU FOR A RIDE

WRITTEN IN THE STARLINKS...

LOVE IS IN THE AIR

OH NO! IT'S DISINTEGRATED AND CRASHED INTO THE SEA!

LOVERS' TIFF...

A CHILD HIT ME

NO, I DIDN'T... FAKE BRUISE!

...END OF THE AFFAIR

YOU'RE A CRAZY NARCISSIST WHO SHOULD BE THROWN OUT OF THE WHITE HOUSE!

SUPERMODELS — KERBER

POETRY CORNER

Lines on the 50th Anniversary of the popular cinematic shark-fest Jaws

So. Congratulations
Then Jaws.

You are 50,
And getting a bit long
In the tooth.

But the original film,
Is still razor sharp.

The real horror
Was, of course,
Jaws 2,
And 3,
And 4.

Altogether now:
Der–der.
Der–der.
Der–der. Der–der.
Der–der. Der–der.
Dnn-dnn-dnn-dnn-
Dnn-dnn-dnn-dnn-
Diddlee Dee!
Doodlee Doo!

This tribute is getting
Monstrously large,
We're going to need
A bigger poem.
But how to end it?

FIN.

    E.J. Thribb (17½ feet long)

**In Memoriam,
Lines on the passing of
Brian James,
punk guitarist**

So. Farewell
Then Brian James.
You were in The Damned.

Let's hope
You are not
Among them now.

    E.J. Thribb (17½ RPM)

PS. Also. Farewell
Then Rick Buckler,
Drummer with the Jam.

"I'm going underground"
Yes, that was one
Of your songs,

And now, sadly,
You are.

UK DEFENCE REVIEW: 'HOME GUARD' TO PROTECT NUCLEAR POWER PLANTS

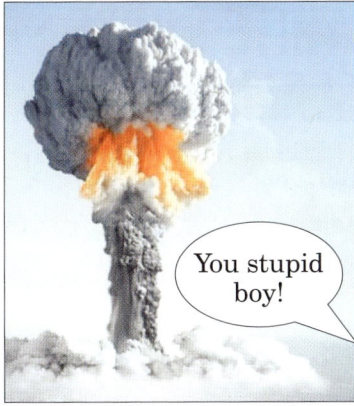

> You stupid boy!

British troops face 'too high' risk if sent to Ukraine

THE government has explained that the risks of sending the army to Ukraine in a peacekeeping role are simply too high to countenance.

"What if someone shoots at them?" asked one senior military figure. "This is the army, for God's sake. They're not meant to be getting shot at in the cause of projecting British power and security aims around the world.

"They're meant to be training, maybe going on the occasional regimental skiing trip, and staffing bases in places like Catterick, not entering live-fire situations. Someone could get hurt."

Another explained, "It's right that the British Army doesn't take the unacceptable risk of being in a war. We've tried having several wars recently and they all involved levels of risk that are simply unsustainable in the modern workplace."

A third added, "The people by far best equipped to fight this war are the Ukrainian civilians currently being bombed to smithereens by a psychopathic Russian fascist Tsar. The last time we were at war with Russia was in the 1850s and we made a right mess of that, so it's much better we don't involve ourselves again this time."

CARRY ON SAILOR!

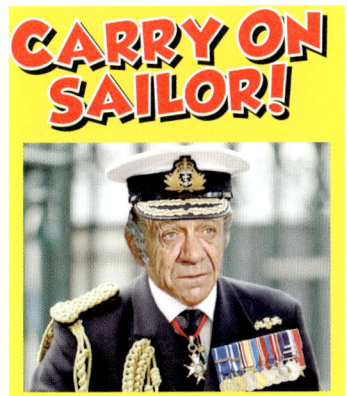

The new saucy British comedy, starring Sid James as the First Sea Lord and Barbara Windsor as the anonymous female officer involved with Britain's top tar!

(Scene: On board HMS Insatiable)

Sea Lord: All the nice girls love a Sea Lord.

Wren: Cheeky!

Sea Lord Permission to come aboard!

Wren: Cheeky! Is that a torpedo in your pocket or are you just pleased to see me?

Sea Lord Cheeky!

(Enter the Secretary of State for Defence, played by Kenneth Williams)

Wren: All handsy on deck!

Secretary of State: Look here, First Sea Lord, you can't have a relationship with someone underneath you!

Sea Lord: What if they're on top?

Wren: Cheeky!

Secretary of State: You're fired – unlike our useless Trident missiles.

Sea Lord: I'm stepping aside. My career's sunk.

(We hear a splash)

Secretary of State: Man legoverboard!

Wren: Goodbye sailor!

Cannabis decriminalisation latest

A YouGov poll this week found **41%** supported decriminalising cannabis possession for personal use, with **33%** opposed, while **26%** were like yeah, man, whatever, either is cool and mellow with me, baby. Just stop being so heavy – you're really killing my buzz.

YouGov

---

easyJet

That drunk, naked pilot announcement in full

"Good afternoon, passengers. This is your Captain streaking. Please sit back and prepare for take-off – of my underpants. Now, that's what I call an airstrip! I'd be grateful if you'd now please switch off all your personal electronic devices, including cell phones, as I don't want to be filmed running up and down the aisles totally starkers. Once in the air, the cabin crew will not be offering you a selection of duty-free goods because I've drunk the lot! Including the perfume! Hic!! My co-pilot on today's flight is a large pink elephant called Simon. The emergency exits are located at the front, middle and back of the plane, which you can easily access in the event of you realising that your pilot is well and truly flying. Do please remove your shoes before going down the emergency slides – obviously mine are off already, and floating around the hotel swimming pool. I'm afraid you can't currently use the toilet, because I'm in there, crouched over the bowl, reacquainting myself with yesterday's paella. We hope you enjoy your flight on queazyJet, and I look forward to seeing you again soon – when I can focus. Bleurgggghhhh!!!"

– PILBROW –

"Harry – you seem desperate for your father to talk to you"

HOW TO GET THE NHS WAITING LIST DOWN

Make the list so long that patients remove themselves from the list for one of the following reasons:

A They're so fed up with waiting that they go private.

B They're so fed up with waiting that they die.

C Er… that's it.

Result! Huge savings for the NHS. Wes Streeting to join waiting list to become Prime Minister.

Sir Elton John is furious over proposals to let tech firms use copyright-protected work for free without permission

That playlist in full

- **Bennie And The Bots**
- Song For AI ♫
- **Swindle In The Wind**
- Sacrifice Your Rights ♪
- **I'm Still Fuming**
- Freebee Seems To Be The Hardest Word ♫ ♪
- **Profitman**
- Don't Go Breaking The Law
- **Nik-Songs-Ita**
- Goodbye Yellow Brick Road And All My Other Hits

(We get the idea. Ed.)

ISRAEL'S NEW GAZA AID STRATEGY

> Don't worry, people are not going to starve...

> ...they'll be shot first

TRUMP 'ANNOUNCES NEW GOLDEN DOME'

by Our White House Reporter Clare Balding

DONALD TRUMP has announced today he's setting aside $25bn of taxpayers' money for the development of what he promises will be a state-of-the- art "Golden Dome" – one that will offer his scalp 100% coverage at all times.

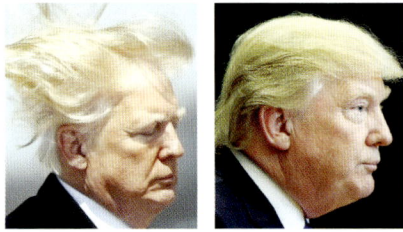

Trump told reporters in the Oval Office, "The new Golden Dome will protect me from everything, from ballistic missile strikes fired by rogue states such as Canada to high tech gusts of winds being developed by China.

"We have the greatest minds

Old Golden Dome   New Golden Dome

and finest scientists at the prestigious Laboratoire Garnier working around the clock to develop a new Golden Dome that will totally protect me 24/7 from all the rumours that I'm balding and this is a weave."

Let's Parlez Franglais!

Numéro 94
Dans l'avion pendant le state visit à Thailand

Nous voyons la porte de l'avion qui ouvre pour révéler Madam Macron qui donne un slap à son husband Emmanuel

Président Macron: Ow-la-la! Qu'est-ce que j'ai done now?!

Madame Macron: Je suis ta professeure! Tu weren't paying attention à moi!!

Président Macron: Zut alors? Ce n'est pas fair!

Madame Macron: Tu were staring au dehors de la window! Naughty garçon!

Président Macron: Nous were landing! Je regardais le carpet rouge et le band de la Thai Guarde Royale!

(Soudain, les Macrons noticent que la porte de l'avion est ouverte pour tout le monde to see)

Président Macron: Merde!

Madame Macron: Ne swear pas devant ta professeure or je te donnerai un autre slap ou detention!!

Président Macron: Non, non, c'était le banter – un signe de l'amour entre un homme et sa wife!!!

Madame Macron: Tu es dan la maison du chien et no mistake!!

(Le tour official continue to bring la paix et le bonwill to le world. Le band joue le hit song "Slappy Days are here encore"!)

© *The late Kilomètres Kington*

MOTHERS WELCOME NEW THING TO BE GUILTY ABOUT

by Our Supermarket Correspondent Noah Added Sugar

MOTHERS across the country have welcomed a new report which has found that the majority of baby food products in supermarkets are ultra-processed, setting children up for a "life of obesity", as they definitely needed something new to feel guilty about.

"I already felt that I was a total failure as a parent because I let my little one watch an hour of Baby Shark on my iPad to let me get some work done," said one woman with sick down her blouse who hasn't slept more than four hours

a night for the past six months.

"But, knowing that the fruit bar my toddler adores is condemning him to a lifetime of obesity-related diseases is just what I needed to fill the few hours a day that I don't feel like a piece of crap with dread."

All new mums agreed that alongside excessive screentime and relaxed parenting and co-sleeping and naughty steps and removing-the-dummy worries, this new worry would give them something to beat themselves up about *(cont. p94)*

WHITE HOUSE SPOKESPERSON SLAMS BBC FOR FAKE NEWS

"YOU can't trust the BBC. Only yesterday it had a news bulletin, claiming it was 3 o'clock.

Guess what? Ten minutes later it had revised its position completely and told everyone it was ten past three. But that wasn't the end of the misinformation. Just five minutes after that, it revised the figures yet again, saying it wasn't 3 o'clock, it wasn't even 3.10, it was 3.15. It just doesn't add up. We in the White House actually check our figures and we looked up what the time really was when the fake news bulletin went out. It was 10 o'clock in the morning. Not even afternoon. Five hours wrong. Unbelievable. The BBC is a disgrace and is clearly getting its chronological briefings from Hamas. They're not serious journalists at all. Any questions? Yes, you sir, in the tin foil hat, from Conspiracy News Today incorporating Bleach Swallowing Monthly...?"

President Trump puts 100% tariff on UK and other foreign films to ensure that production takes place entirely in US

FILMS THAT WILL BE HIT HARD

- 4002 a Space Odyssey
- 202 Dalmatians
- The 78 Steps
- 8 Weddings and 2 Funerals
- The Fourteenth Seal
- The Sixth Man
- You Only Live Four Times
- A Whole Sixpence (with Tommy Steel subject to separate tariff)

FILMS THAT WILL BE ACCEPTABLE

- The American Patient
- Johnny American
- The Last King of America
- The American Job
- The American Lieutenant's Woman
- The American Connection
- An American Werewolf in America

(We've got the idea. Ed.)

BRITISH FILM INDUSTRY

"...and cut jobs!"

Did Queen Victoria have a secret baby with Gordon Brown?

Incredible new research has discovered that, far from retreating into comfortable widowhood after the death of Prince Albert, Queen Victoria discovered time travel and voyaged to the mid-noughties to have a secret baby with the brooding Scottish Prime Minister.

Letters in the collection at Osborne House reveal clues to her passion for her Highland servant Gordon, a dour son of the manse with an unexpectedly tender side. One such letter shows Her Majesty writing, "As autumn comes round again I must admit I do love brown. It's my favourite colour, apart from black."

Top historian Rob Rinder – himself a descendant of Rob Roy – goes through this evidence and builds a compelling case that the real heir to Britain's throne should be the descendant of this forbidden inter-century union, Mrs Elsie McGonagall of Renfrewshire. "It's comforting to imagine that Victoria was given a happy final chapter by destiny with one of Britain's foremost chancellors and short-lived PMs via a time machine invented by top Victorian engineer Isambard Kingdom Broonel," explained an academic who specialises in going on television.

***EYE RATING:** Totally convincing. Channel 4 at its best.*

Lady Macbeth

Lady Macbeth's memoirs – the tome you are all talking about! Exclusively serialised in the

Daily Chain Mail

Why King Duncan never spoke to me again after my husband murdered him

by Sarah Thane

WE HAD been friends with the Duncans for years, but as soon as my brilliant but impossible husband Macbeth decided to stab Duncan to death, his posh wife dropped me completely and refused to talk to me on the school run.

Honestly, what a big manbaby he was and what a stuck-up snob Queen Samantha turned out to be. Suddenly, my entire social world fell apart just because Mikebeth, had on a point of principle, decided to commit regicide.

That was the start of our problems and it wasn't helped when I insisted on moving from our pokey little castle at Glamis to the nice 94-bedroomed castle at Cawdor, which was more befitting a top thane and meant we could keep up with the Duncans.

But, throughout the move, Mikebeth was unhelpful, refused to do any of the unpacking of trunks and just sat around reading the predictions of the three witches. Things didn't get any better when my hubby had no option but to thwart Banquo's leadership bid by stabbing him in the back as well. Honestly! Borisquo had it coming, as he was unreliable, treacherous and not at all like us.

And, worst of all, people assumed that I was in some way guilty of egging my husband on to commit these insane acts of ambition.

The leak of a message that I sent by pigeon to the wrong person telling my husband to get on with the murdering and to "screw his courage to the sticking post" led to me being unfairly dismissed as some sort of medieval Sarah Vine. This lazy, sexist, misogynist trope is always levelled at powerful women who encourage their husbands to murder their political rivals.

And it is so unfair. Ok, when special advisers at the time tried to persuade my husband that this course of action was a bad idea I may have shouted, "Out, out, damned spad!" but this proves nothing.

And when historians read the message saying that MacGove was "too full of the milk of human kindness" it was a typo!! I meant to say he was "too full of booze to do the job"!

Still, the ghost of Borisquo reappeared on the scene and, despite my misgivings about their politics, together the two of them took back sovereignty.

There were, however, unresolved issues like freedom of movement – ie, was Birnam Wood allowed to move to Dunsinane? This became a real problem later, but it had been foretold by the weird sisters… ie, the leader writers in the Guardian.

The truth is that I, Sarah Thane, was always incredibly unsure about the whole business of political assassination and my guilty conscience led to problems with my sleeping… so I ended up wandering around the castle late at night and sleeping alone in the boxroom by the turret.

Finally, I just couldn't take it anymore and MacGove, who had a bit of a drink problem (which I may have mentioned) and couldn't last five minutes without a glass of mead or three, utterly failed to get the top job and lost his head – literally, when the new leader Mayduff cut it off.

To be honest, everyone else behaved abysmally and I had no option but to commit career suicide and write this book, "How not to be a political hubble-bubble-toil-and-trouble-and strife (wife)."

■ **More from Sarah Thane's riveting tome tomorrow (and tomorrow and tomorrow and tomorrow)**

©*Sarah Thane – putting the Me, Me, Me in Memoir*

Sir Keir Starmer MP

The Prime Minister's confidential WhatsApp group that no one can get into (unlike Britain, during the last week – thanks a lot, Yvette!)

Good news, everyone, we've signed our brilliant Anglo-American trade deal!

Wes Streeting
The one the President threw on the floor?

He didn't throw it – he dropped it.

Yvette Cooper
Makes a change from dropping his trousers.

Richard Hermer
As long as he doesn't drop any Bunker Buster bombs. As Attorney General, it is my duty to be mindful of the legality of blowing up mountains and starting World War 3.

Angela Rayner
It was bad enough Tony being shoulder to shoulder with George Dubya Bush, but now we've got a Labour Prime Minister who's on his bloody knees!

Morgan McSweeney
No, it was a good look, showing our special relationship. Donald knows that whatever he does, Keir will be there to pick up the pieces.

Rachel Reeves
And it shows Keir's concern to help the elderly – and that's very much our new policy now. Until we change our mind again.

It was also important not to let the photographers take a snap of the details of our trade deal.

Ed Miliband
Why – are the pages totally blank? 😱

No, it's full of detailed explanations of how we're going to get the details later, when we've worked out what the details are.

Morgan McSweeney
News just in! The Americans have bombed Iran. No one knows what they'll do next.

Jonathan Powell
I do! I know exactly what they're going to do next…

And what's that?

Jonathan Powell
Whatever they like.

I'm in! 🇺🇸 🦅 🧢

BUNKER BLUSTER

Does my bomb look big in this?

An apology to MAGA

IN RECENT weeks and months you may have been given the impression that you elected an isolationist president committed on his first day in office to ending wars, one who has seen the folly of being dragged into foreign wars under previous Republican presidents and who rejects the obsolete neo-con doctrine that America is the world's policeman.

We now realise, in the light of Trump bombing Iran, that nothing could be further from the truth and that Trump is fully signed up to the wise neo-con doctrine that America is the world's policeman.

We apologise for any confusion caused, but hope that you are all as stupid as the President imagines you are and that you are confused by multiplication and traffic lights, let alone U-turns in international politics.

Trump's address to the American people

My fellow MAGAmaniacs! After considerable thought, lasting some minutes, I weighed up the pros and cons of bombing Canada, Greenland or California, before deciding on Iranland. They're not nice. They're NASTY! It was a bigly decision, proving that I was right all along in promising that I could start a war in one day. We are dealing with bad people – bad, bad people – and I don't just mean the moron I put in charge of the CIA, who stupidly told Congress that Iran did not have a nuclear bomb. FAKE FACT! She was WRONG – and Tulsi Gabbard has now revised her opinion based on new information – namely that I was going to sack her if she didn't. Anyway, this ISN'T World War 3! NO WAY! In my book a 3 is a DOG – I'd only ever be seen with a World War that was at least a 9, maybe a 10. That's a STUNNING war. Beautiful! That's the kind of war you can grab by the pussy! Locker war-room talk – get used to it, Miss Sourface!! TRUE FACT! Now your favourite president can achieve what Sleepy Joe could never manage – winning not only the Nobel PEACE Prize, but also the Nobel WAR Prize! Thank you for your attention in this matter.

"You have no emotional intelligence!"

"And your point is?"

EVERYONE NOW EXPERT ON ENRICHING URANIUM

INTERNATIONAL nuclear scientists were thrilled yesterday at the news that hundreds of thousands of previously unknown experts in the field of uranium enrichment have been spreading the word on social media about the subject.

"To be honest, enriching uranium is actually very simple," said one hitherto undiscovered PhD-level specialist to his 518 Twitter followers. "You simply need some Uranium-994 which you then pop into a sixth-generation centrifuge. I'm frankly surprised more people don't do it."

Another, speaking during a podcast recording, added, "The important thing, of course, is to ensure your uranium hexafluoride gas is fed in and removes the correct isotope. I dabble in this stuff as an amateur and it's possible the Iranian nuclear scientists will know nearly as much about it as me."

Many of these experts have also spent their time in recent days brushing up on the United States Air Force's capacities and reminding themselves of how best to analyse photos of a hole in a desert mountain taken from 25,000 feet away.

An expertise expert from the University of Neasden said, "Remarkably, almost all these newly minted experts in the field of nuclear science are the same people who, since 2016, have become experts on intercontinental trade negotiations, epidemiology, Russian anti-tank warfare tactics, steel manufacturing and sexual assault in the North of England. With all this expertise at our fingertips, the world's problems are undoubtedly solved."

ISRAEL'S IRONY DOME FAILS

by Our Middle East Staff
Arnie Geddon

ISRAEL's legendary Irony Dome, designed to keep irony out of the Middle East conflict, failed spectacularly in the early hours of yesterday morning.

When an Iranian missile hit a hospital in Israel and the Israeli spokesman said, "This attack on civilians was a criminal act", the Irony Dome began to disintegrate. But when the Iranian spokesman said that they weren't aiming at a hospital but a military target and an IDF spokesman said they didn't believe them, the entire Irony Dome edifice shook violently and collapsed, showering major Israeli cities with shards of searing irony.

"Nice lapdog"

"Thanks. It's a Bombiranian"

GRAEME KEYES

YAP YAP YAP YAP YAP YAP YAP YAP YAP YAP YAP YAP YAP

Iranyometer blows up

by Our Middle East Staff
Holly Waugh

FOR years, Iran has been suspected of secretly building an Iranyometer, stockpiling enriched irony and burying it deep beneath Mount Tension, north of Tehran.

Yesterday, it became clear that the Iranyometer was not only functioning, but was blowing up in an ironic meltdown, following the Ayatollah's attack on Israel for "interfering in the affairs of other sovereign nations and trying to destabilise the region".

A series of explosions were heard as the Ayatollah added that Israel was run by religious fanatics who would stop at nothing to stay in power and needed a war to deflect from their domestic crises.

....

■ LATE NEWS

UK IRONYOMETER GOES PHUT

There was a minor exhalation of air from Britain's new Ironyometer, when struggling high street store Poundland was ironically sold for just a pound.

The Ironyometer was, ironically, bought from Poundland last week for 99p.

Enrichment programme well under way

by Our Nuclear Correspondent
Guy Gercounter

AS tensions heighten over war in the Middle East, the element uranium has spoken out about the controversial enrichment programme being blatantly carried out by the Trump family.

Said uranium, "Believe me, they are making a bomb. All of them – father, sons, wife, daughter, in-laws, all of them are enriching themselves as we speak."

The star of the periodic table continued angrily, "The evidence is there for everyone to see.

"There's the Trump phones, the Trump cryptocurrency, the branded watches, the Trump Bible, the property development, the golf courses, the free plane from Qatar... all point to an illegal enrichment programme which, far from being paused, has accelerated in recent months. It's boom time for the Trump mob. It's got to stop or else I'm going to go absolutely nuclear."

The Kim Woodburn I knew by Mr Sheen

WELL, we all fell out with her. Who didn't? Because Kim always spoke her mind, bless her. And you can almost say we loved her for it, if it makes you feel better about how much we hated her.

By God, she was always shaking me and pressing my nozzle until I felt empty inside. She was always saying I was crap and how she was going to dump me for Mr Muscle.

She said it was a joke, but I knew it wasn't!

Hey, ho. She's in heaven now. I hope God's had a proper clean, because she'll have his guts for garters!

But seriously, I was closer to her than any other cleaning appliance, and I adored the square-faced, poisonous old battleaxe.

No, really. You have got someone to say something nice about her, haven't *(cont. p94)*

"Didn't you say you were going for a run?"

"What? That was **years** ago!"

Pearsall.

Notes & queries

Who or what is this Mounjaro that we hear so much about?
Asks Mrs Jack Sprat

● Mounjaro is the smallest in a range of Kenyan mountains – it is one thousandth the size of Kilimanjaro, and can be easily climbed by overweight celebrities on charity walks, with zero risk of altitude sickness. From the summit of Mounjaro, climbers can look up at the giraffes towering above them. In order to see the sunrise from the top, it is advisable to start walking several minutes before the sun rises. "I survived Mounjaro" is a T-shirt popular with the less adventurous adventurer.
*Thinny Arbuckle,
Los Angeles*

● Mr Arbuckle's analysis is, I'm afraid to say, a fat lot of use. Mounjaro is the first album by Fat Boy Slim, who was at the time known by the name Slim Boy Fat. In this seminal work, the DJ samples the music of Chubby Checker, Fats Waller, Tubby Hayes, Slim Shady, Boney M, and Mick Jabber of the Rolling Lose Stones. *(Is this right? Ed.)* The album was a vinyl-only release and appeared as a 12-inch LP, but shrank within a month to a 7-inch single.
*William Bunter,
aka The Not-So-Fat Owl of
Airfriars School*

● For once, Billy Bunter has bitten off more than he can chew. As all cheese-lovers know, Mounjaro is a Spanish cheese made from donkey's milk in the village of Squeletón in the region of Fatalonia. Its distinctive unpleasant smell and sour aftertaste discourage anyone from eating and, once sampled, it kills the appetite completely for up to six months. The inhabitants of Squeletón are renowned for the very narrow doorways to their houses and streets measuring less than a metre across. Life expectancy is sadly reduced by their tendency to disappear down cracks in the pavement.
*Ozzy Empic, Lead singer,
Black Pudding.*

VICTIMS 'EAGERLY AWAITING NOTHING HAPPENING'

by Our National Inquiry Correspondent **Manny Briefs**

VICTIMS of the child-grooming-gang scandal say they're looking forward to seeing the damning report from the national inquiry announced this week by Keir Starmer, and then nothing happening as a result of it.

"We saw this with the Grenfell inquiry report. It was detailed, rigorous and unsparing in apportioning blame. And then nothing happened.

"No one has been charged, much less appeared in court or served time in prison for the deaths of those 72 people on 14 June eight years ago. And now it will be our turn to see justice not being done."

'We won!' says Badenoch

KEMI BADENOCH has told Tory members "WE WON!" in an email following Keir Starmer's announcement that he was setting up a national inquiry into the child grooming scandal.

"We must never lose sight of the mistreatment of women, particularly me," Kemi told cheering supporters. "I know the girls involved in this scandal will be celebrating tonight that this has been a vindication for me and I must now be made Prime Minister immediately," before adding, "me, me, me."

Asked about an apology from the last Tory government for a decade of inaction, Kemi says she thought she definitely deserved one.

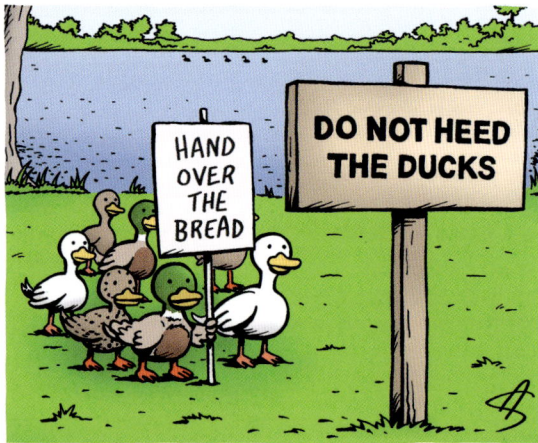

HAND OVER THE BREAD

DO NOT HEED THE DUCKS

CHILDREN NOT READING ANY MORE: WHAT COULD THE REASONS POSSIBLY BE?

A **NEW** report into the reading habits of children has found that the number of under-18s who enjoy reading has declined precipitously since 2015.

There has been a huge drop, particularly in boys, which has prompted the compilers of the report into speculating what on Earth could have caused this dramatic fall in such a short space of time.

The experts have come up with the following list of potential factors:

1. Mobile phones
2. Er...
3. That's it.

LATE NEWS

■ Two shocking new reports from the not-reading authors reveal Pope not a Protestant and bears not shitting in toilets.

Joy for younger music fans as Oasis reunite

by Our Oasis Correspondent **Wanda Wall**

AFTER a fortnight when 80-year-old wrinkly rockers Neil Young and Rod Stewart took over the main stages at Glastonbury, it was a relief to see youngsters Oasis back together in Cardiff.

With all the vitality of young men in their fifties, they stunned the audience with their power anthems.

"It was great to see them," said one superfan. "Not that I could actually see them because I'd forgotten my glasses. It was all a bit of a blur – unlike Blur who I went to see reunite last year, thankfully remembering my spectacles."

Said another, "I was expecting to see the Pulp reunion. It's funny when you come into a stadium and forget what you came in for."

"Diddy?"   "He did"

DIDDY FOUND GUILTY ON 2 CHARGES

DIARY

JANE AUSTEN: THE DOCUMENTARY

Hand bearing quill pen writing scratchily on crusty paper, grandfather clock ticking in background.

VOICEOVER: Jane Austen is Britain's most celebrated female novelist. She left behind timeless masterpieces, revealing the inner lives of men and women in a way that still speaks to us today. But getting into her own mind isn't easy...

Old lady leafing through a stack of letters by a log fire.

...In her lifetime, Austen wrote thousands of letters to her beloved sister Cassandra, sharing her innermost thoughts. But after Jane's death, at the age of just 41, her sister burned them.

Old lady chucks stack into fire.

PAULA BYRNE: It's literally impossible to imagine what it was like to throw all those literally brilliant letters onto that fire. So many feelings must have been running around Cassandra's head at that moment. She's feeling love. Anger. Rage. Love. Anger. Rage. You name it. The lot.

VOICEOVER: Now, with the help of writers...

Head shot of Alison Hammond

Actors...

Head shot of Elizabeth Hurley

Experts...

Head shots of Lucy Worsley and Mary Beard in Regency bonnets

...and celebrity chefs

Head shot of Paul Hollywood

We can piece together...

Close-up of someone in Regency costume doing a jigsaw.

...her extraordinary life.

PAULA BYRNE: At a time when women were supposed to know their place, Jane Austen literally ripped up the rulebook.

Woman in bonnet ripping up a rulebook.

VOICEOVER: This is the story of how a self-taught country girl from a Hampshire village decided to pursue the route of being a modern, independent woman, defied the stuffy rules of her out-of-date era in order to campaign against sexism, racism and transphobia and thus become the greatest novelist of all time, bar none.

Close-up of nun.

ALAN CARR: Jane was telling women they could have lives of their own. She was saying, go girl, wear that bikini, get that tattoo, shake your booty and boogie on down!

VOICEOVER: Jane is brought up in the village of Steventon in Hampshire.

Drone shot of sheep in fields.

JOHN NETTLES: As far as we know, Austen never visited the Jersey made famous by Bergerac, but, if she had, it would have reminded her strongly of the magical landscape of her Hampshire childhood.

VOICEOVER: When Jane is still young, her glamorous cousin Eliza turns up at Steventon...

Eliza knocking on door and greeting Jane.

...A Spice Girl before her time, Eliza is a fabulous role model for the young Jane.

PAULA BYRNE: Sadly, Eliza's husband had got caught up in the French Revolution and had his head CHOPPED OFF, which frankly doesn't bear thinking about.

Shot of guillotine plunging and a man's head toppling into a bucket.

PAULA BYRNE: I just can't begin to imagine what Jane thought when she heard the news. I feel her rage – I FEEL it!

CANDICE CARTY-WILLIAMS: Just like me. As a black woman writer, I've been on that journey myself – guillotined by the white patriachy for daring to speak out. And Jane wasn't even black, or that's what they're always telling us.

KEN LOACH: She was a radical political campaigner, an angry champion of the oppressed.

JEREMY CLARKSON: In those days, cars were few and far between, but, as a sassy young babe with a worldwide reputation for top-of-the-range penpushing, she'd surely have opted for a Dodge Durango SRT Hellcat 53 – and that's what I call CLASS.

VOICEOVER: In Bath, Jane spends her days ballroom dancing.

MOTSI MABUSE: One of the best there ever was! And what a journey she went on! Jane dancing with comely suitors.

SHARON OSBOURNE: Jane was so MODERN! And such a TOTALLY BRILL DANCER! She might have been taken up by old-fashioned dance troupes like Pan's People or Hot Gossip if it wasn't for the men.

VOICEOVER: Jane sends her first novel to a London publisher, but it is turned down.

Jane opens envelope and out drops a note saying 'SORRY LOVE, NOT FOR US' in big letters.

PAULA BYRNE: You can't begin to imagine how that must have made her feel, but she would have felt tremendous HURT and DISAPPOINTMENT.

VOICEOVER: And then comes more bad news – when they hear that Cassandra's fiancé has died on a voyage to the West Indies.

Newspaper boy yells "Read all about it! Austen fiancé dead at sea!"

ADMIRAL LORD WEST: The sea round there can suddenly turn awfully choppy, as I learnt all too well in my own days in the...

PAULA BYRNE: I can't begin to imagine how his death must have made Cassandra feel, but she'd have been in ABSOUTE FLOODS!

Jane comforts Cassandra, who has a tear running down her cheek.

VOICEOVER: A further body-blow comes when their beloved father dies...

By the light of a flickering candle, Jane stares mournfully at her father in bed with a bedcap on and his eyes tight shut.

...Suddenly Jane and Cassandra are obliged to leave their beloved vicarage, and their world literally turns upside-down.

A globe lies upside-down on the wooden floor.

...But then she meets a man and they fall in love and she is overjoyed.

Jane dances with joy.

MARY BEARD IN REGENCY BONNET: Sadly, regrettably, unfortunately and in many ways deeply upsettingly, we historians know nothing or at least next to nothing, well, all right then, virtually nothing, about her boyfriend or fiancé, which, frankly and honestly, is, to my mind, really rather infuriating, frustrating, exasperating and irritating, or, to put it another way...

VOICEOVER: And then Jane opens a letter...

Jane opens black-rimmed envelope.

...Only to find that the love of her life has died.

Coffin being carried into church.

PAULA BYRNE: There's simply no way of telling how Jane must have felt, but she would have felt TERRIBLE.

VOICEOVER: So her life had now come to a fork in the road.

Lingering shot of T-junction.

End of Part One.

As told to

CRAIG BROWN

BLOODY SHORTAGE!

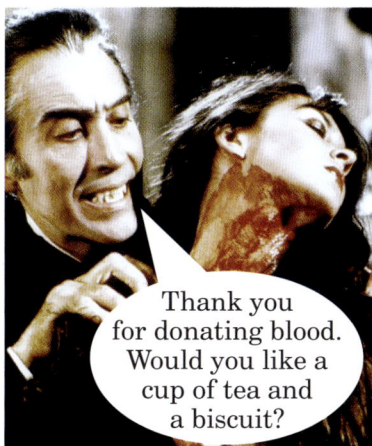

Thank you for donating blood. Would you like a cup of tea and a biscuit?

Seddon..

"I'm a bit busy, but go on..."

HOW TO COMBAT 'ALERT FATIGUE' ON YOUR PHONE

1 Put your phone down
2 Pick up a copy of *Private Eye*
3 *Private Eye* has no alerts
4 It doesn't ever ding
5 It doesn't tell you something URGENT has happened, even if it has
6 Er...
7 That's it.

Keir Starmer's confidential whatsApp group. Keir's thought for the day: If at first you don't succeed cry, cry and cry again!

Morgan McSweeney
Happy birthday to Keir! He's been in power for a whole year.

Rachel Reeves
By "power", do you mean caving in to our backbenchers and spending more billions that we don't have?

Ellie Reeves
As Minister Without Portfolio and without any vested interest in what a great job my sister's doing, can I just say "Well said, Chancellor, you go, girl!" ❤️ 👍

Rachel Reeves
I'm not going anywhere.

Angela Rayner
Course not, luv. Nor is Keir! 😉

Morgan McSweeney
All I'm saying is that this is an important milestone. We've got to get the optics of unity right.

Angela Rayner
You still here, McSweeney?

Morgan McSweeney
Why do you say that? Have you heard something? What are people whispering behind my back? Are they saying I'm paranoid? They are, I can feel it!

> Don't worry, Morgan, you're doing an excellent job.

Angela Rayner
We promised reform, and we're going to deliver Reform. 🤣

> Stop it, Angela.

Morgan McSweeney
Why are you protecting me, boss? Do I need protection? Are they out to get me? Is it all over?

Ed Miliband
The climate's certainly changed, Morgan. Just saying!

> Can everybody please leave Morgan alone?

Angela Rayner
He is alone. Everyone hates him.

> That's unfair and uncharitable and not in the spirit of the Labour Party.

Liz Kendall
Would now be a good time to mention benefits cuts?

Ed Miliband
Can I just say that it's a bit ironic that, when it came to taking away support for the disabled, you didn't have a leg to stand on? No offence! 😂

Wes Streeting
A lot of us are concerned about welfare, Keir. Particularly our own.

> Government is about having the guts to make difficult decisions. And then making the difficult decision to go back on them.

Morgan McSweeney
Now that's strong leadership.

> And I've done it three times.

Morgan McSweeney
Winter fuel, grooming inquiry and now welfare. Triply strong, boss!

> Thanks, Morgan, your job's safe.

Angela Rayner
Uh-oh, McSweeney, you'd better start packing your bags!

Rachel Reeves
Is my job safe?

> Absolutely, Rachel.

Rachel Reeves
You're not going to do a U-turn on that as well, are you?

> Absolutely not. You're going to be Chancellor for a very long time, so please don't cry.

Jonathan Reynolds
A weep's a long time in politics! 😃

Rachel Reeves
That's unfair. I've got a very taxing job.

Jonathan Reynolds
Well, you have now!

> I take full responsibility for my own mistakes, such as that speech where I said we're an island of strangers.

David Lammy
Bit of a howler! Everyone knows we're not an island. 🔥

Yvette Cooper
I'm afraid that speech was a bit Powelly.

Jonathan Powell
Is that a problem? What's wrong with that? Special relationship. Trump marvellous. Bomb Iraq, Bomb Iran, Bomb Greenland! Bring back Tony.

Tony Blair
I'm still here!

Yvette Cooper
I meant Enoch Powelly.

Lord Mandelson
Rivers of blood? Yum-yum! 🧛 🦇

> Various old Labour grandees have been removed from the group by the moderator, on the grounds that they remind people of a time when the Prime Minister was in charge and backbenchers did what they were told.

Who will be reincarnated as the 15th Dalai Lama? You decide...

	Russell Brand – mystic and self-styled Bhuddy-Woodist	**Ex-Archbishop Welby –** time on his hands, needs the work	**Tess Dalai –** is it time for a female lama? Keeeeep meditating!	**Bananalama –** is it time to split the job between 3 women?	**Tom Dalai –** LGBTQ+ posterboy, could knit own skimpy robe	**Dal-A.I. Lama –** it's the future, time to embrace it	**President Xi –** this is what's actually going to happen

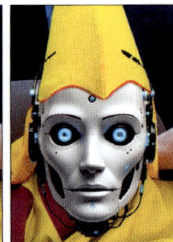

© the Dalai Express

THE KING OF TROUBLES

A short story special by Dame Hedda Shoulders

THE STORY SO FAR : The King is celebrating the 200th anniversary of the Royal Procession at Ascot and is revelling in the pomp and circumstance...

THE crowds cheered as the resplendent royal carriage arrived at the Ascot racecourse. The state landau, Hope and Glory, bumped over the springy turf as it carried its distinguished charges, King Charles, Queen Camilla and special guest Prince Salman Fishing of Yemen, towards the Royal Enclosure.

Charles was wearing a silk top hat in Sirius black from fashionable milliner Rees-Mogg's of Somerset, which complemented his morning suit in sober sue grey and his blood-blue weskit from Kate Moss Bros. Queen Camilla was wearing a matching air-blue coat dress from celebrity designer and new best friend Lady Beckingham of Palace. On her head was a Philip Treacly hat, a sweet confection of feathers that looked as if a giant pigeon had exploded on her head. Everything, thought Charles, was absolutely... what was the word? Thingie... yes, that was it! Thingie!!

"You see, this is something we do awfully well, your Sheikness – the rich pageantry of tradition and heritage celebrating the noble sport of Kings – and obviously Princes and Emirs and all those sorts of chaps..."

At that moment, a voice from the carriage behind disturbed Charles's paeon of praise to the jewel in the crown of the English Season.

"Naffing hell!" came the unmistakeable voice of the Princess Royale. "My naffing carriage has gone phut! What am I meant to do? Get a naffing Uber?"

As Charles's no-nonsense sister began to kick the wheels of her unfortunate carriage, he could hear her berating the faulty equestrian equipment on the classic barouche-fantoni coach.

"The effing snuffles have gone on the weymouths and the pelhams are knackered."

Charles turned a shade of crimson that matched the tunic of the footman standing stiffly on the endplate behind him.

"I am so sorry, Your Wealthiness, for the unfortunate language of my sister," he spluttered.

"No problem, sire," soothed his guest from the Royal House of Better-Call-Saud. "I heard much worse when I was at your Sandhurst," added the potentate from the land of the palm trees and huge oil reserves. "I passed out with honours and won the coveted Sword of Wilkinson."

"Of course you did. How absolutely marvellous!" blustered Charles.

"Are we there yet? I'm gasping."

Queen Camilla joined the royal banter as she shook her silver hip flask, which sadly appeared to be empty. "We are nearly there, old thing," reassured Charles, "only a few furlongs to go and then we are home and dry... well not dry obviously... Ha!Ha!Ha!"

"Surely it's nosebag time, Chazza? I'm famished and I'm sure Prince Wheelie Bin Salman Fishing could do with a sheep's eye vol au vent!"

AS ever, Charles's consort and soulmate had bluntly identified the pitfalls of being a dedicated Royal – namely, that waving and smiling for extended periods was both thirsty and hungry work.

The carriage ground to a halt, as the sun glinted on the gilded escutcheons and fleur-de-lys-ducetts on the horse-drawn procession, and there was Sir Alan Fitztightly ready to welcome them into the Bet365

Ascot Royal Enclosure. Charles greeted his trusted aide-de-campbed and handed his hat to the loyal Curator of the Closet and Steward of the Steradent.

"Ah, Sir Alan, it's you!"

"Who did you think it would be? Your new bezzie, Sir David Beckingham, perhaps? He seems to be the favourite in the Royal stakes?" There was a waspish tone to Sir Alan's welcome that Charles did not much care for.

"Don't be so jealous, Sir Alan. It ill becomes you. As it happens, Sir David and I have a great deal in common. For example, I discovered recently that we both love tattoos. He told me about his 67 tattoos and I told him all about Edinburgh. He seemed frightfully interested!"

"Yes, I bet he was. And another thing you have in common – that being the operative word for Sir David – you are both awfully good at relations with your sons, aren't you?"

Before Charles could reply to his factotum's green-eyed insolence, Sir Alan led the King and his party to the Royal Box. And there were the minor Royals tucking in enthusiastically to the British Champagne-style champagnes on offer – produced by the vineyards of Jolly Good Chapeldown, and Shivermetimbers.

"Hiya, Uncle King!" shouted Princess Bellatrix, who was accompanied as ever by her husband, Eduardo Mozzarello, heir to the Italian cheese empire. "Yah, totes hi, your Royal Uncleness," chimed in Zara Tarara-Boomdeeay, daughter of the Princess Royale and married to the spicy Rugby legend Mike Tindaloo.

FORTUNATELY, there was no sign of He Who must Not be Named... otherwise known as Prince Andrew... unless that was him in a burqa pretending to be one of Prince Salman Fishing's many wives?!! Charles began to feel anxious.

"The race with your horse running is about to begin, sire," announced Sir Alan. The party grabbed their binoculars and gathered eagerly to watch the King's horse 'Reaching High'.

"Optimistic name, isn't it?" said Sir Alan tartly, still seething about what he considered the undeserved elevation of the parvenu former England footballer turned Brand Ambassador to the ranks of chivalry – an arriviste daring to tread in the footsteps of Sir Galahad, Sir Lancelot and of course himself, Sir Alan, the last of the Fitztightlys.

"And they're off!" The roar of the crowd signalled that the race was underway and the thunder of hooves boomed around the racetrack. "Come on, Reaching High!" shouted Zara Tarara-Boomdeeay loyally. Charles's pulse began to race. But, unfortunately, his horse did not do the same. "And Reaching High falling behind there, now overtaken by Saucy Ned, Russian Lad, China Spy, and... oh dear... all the other horses as well." The party fell silent as Charles's hopes were dashed and Reaching High only managed to reach a lowly ninth place.

"Oh, bad luck, sire!" smiled Sir Alan insincerely, "I do hope that your new friend Sir David didn't put too much money on the poor horse in a desperate attempt to curry favour."

"I could murder a curry!" shouted Mike Tindalloo in a jovial attempt to lighten the atmosphere.

But the Princess Royale was less sympathetic. "Shoot the useless nag, Charlie! I'll have his liver for the dogs." The party all laughed at the down-to-earth brusqueness that was the Princess Royale's trademark and they returned to watch *Pointless* on the large television at the back of the Royal Box.

Charles felt his spirits sink. In the great race of life would the history books record him as an also ran? The heat began to fade from the afternoon and a chill breeze sent a shiver down his royal spine...

(To be continued...)

Victoria Beckham receives the OMG

75

Why was this political activist allowed to take over Glastonbury?

by Our Festival Staff **Ivor Yurt**

It was the performance that shocked the nation. The crowd was expecting a fun-filled summer singalong, but instead were subjected to a relentless sickening stream of propaganda from a so-called musician who was actually spreading propaganda to his fanatical fans.

Rod Stewart, a self-proclaimed Reform supporter, cynically used his set to whip up pro-Farage fervour and the BBC did NOTHING to stop it.

Stewart kicked off with the Thatcherite hymn "Maggie May" before highlighting the attack on freedom of speech with a shocking rendition of "I Don't Want to Talk About It".

He followed this up with the pro-tax-reduction anthem, "The First Cut is the Deepest" and launched into a celebration of Vote Leave triumphalism with "Da Ya Think I'm Brexy?"

Still the BBC let him continue unedited and Stewart ended his performance with a rabble-rousing climax, donning a jaunty naval cap to highlight the small boats crisis, with a rendition of "We Are Sailing" implying that those aboard the boats wanted "To be near you, to be free".

Shocked members of the rap community immediately called for the BBC to be closed down for giving a platform to this "obvious right-wing reactionary" who is well known for his controversial views.

Said one member of Kneecap, "He is out of tune with the country, not to mention his backing band."

UNKNOWN PUNK BAND BOB VYLAN SUDDENLY FRONT-PAGE NEWS

> Before this gig they couldn't get arrested

DELIGHT FOR CORBYNITES

by Our Political Staff
Owen Goal

SUPPORTERS of the former Labour leader Jeremy Corbyn were overjoyed to see him back to his political best, as he split his new political party before it even exists.

Corbyn, who has an outstanding record of destroying parties and making them unelectable, has taken it up a notch – by creating a leadership schism between himself and the party's would-be joint leader, Zarah Sultana.

Said one delighted Corbynite, "This is peak Corbynism! Jeremy's done it again – this time undermining his own leadership to destabilise the status quo and alienate voters." He continued, "The country is crying out for an

Vote Fruit and Nut!

alternative hard-left party, and so is Jeremy – already opposing his new party to form a new, new party."

In a statement to his follower last night, Corbyn said, "It's time for the left to unite – so Sultana should unite behind me and stop calling herself co-leader. I'm the currant leader – it stands to raisin."

That 'close down the BBC' campaign statement in full...

The events of the past week have proved yet again that the BBC is undeniably pro-Palestinian/pro-Israeli.

Every time they broadcast anything to do with the conflict, they reveal themselves to be Zionist/Hamas sympathisers who are incapable of reporting the news in a balanced/balanced fashion and will not be satisfied until Israel/Gaza has been wiped off the map.

We call on the government to defund/defund the BBC immediately and replace it with a more objective/objective news source, namely the Chief Rabbi/Bob Vylan.

As our supporters have repeatedly chanted in protests against the hated/hated state broadcaster, "From the Thames river to the sea, let's abolish the BBC!"

Daily Telegraph Friday 11 July 2025

Letters to the Editor

SIR – As one of your long-term readers, may I salute the contribution that the *Daily Telegraph* has made to Britain, and indeed to myself over the last 170 years, which I gather is the average age of your readership.

From the very first copy of the newspaper, which I purchased for tuppence ha'penny (£2,700 pounds in today's decimal money!), I have come to find the *Telegraph* an indispensable element in my everyday life.

Only yesterday, as I was going through a drawer looking for mothballs, I noticed that the lining of said drawer was none other than the *Daily Telegraph* from 1900, declaring that Mafeking had been relieved.

"Well, that is a relief," I remember remarking to the future Lady Gussett (née Joan Hunter Wellington) at the tennis club at the time.

Later, when tripping over the carpet in the drawing room, I discovered an underlay of myriad *Telegraph*s – one lamenting the unfortunate decision to give the vote to members of the fairer sex, if one is allowed to say such a thing in today's politically correct world!

But lest you think for a minute that your revered organ is only of use in the soft-furnishing department of life, can I add that it is also a first-rate receptacle for cat litter, to which my own feline companion, Mr Baden-Powell, can testify.

It is even more useful as a deterrent to wasps. When I arrive in the conservatory armed with a fresh, rolled-up copy featuring the doughty Ms Allison Pearson on the cover, there are very few wasps brave enough not to flee at once – and those foolish enough to remain are quickly despatched by the weight and authority of this formidable journal.

Sadly, these days I no longer have time to read the contents of the newspaper, but I still catch a glimpse of the crossword when lighting the fire in the inglenook on a cold summer's evening.

I remain your obedient servant,
Sir Herbert Gussett,
The Old Christopher House, Dunreadin, Allister Heath, Midsomerset.

The Top 10 Favourite Summer Top 10 Articles

Top Ten beaches to avoid because they've featured in the top ten beaches of the year
From Crowded Cove to Hellhole-on-Sea, we tell you where not to go because we told you to go there last week in our "Top ten beaches to go to" article.

Top Ten ways to get beach body ready this summer
Top tips from our experts, including: inject yourself with Mounjaro, inject yourself with Ozempic and er... that's it.

Top Ten festival bands to get angry about this summer
Kneejerk. The rest are probably alright, really. And we haven't even seen Kneejerk, but we're pretty cross about them.

Top Ten excuses to show photos of young women in bikinis
From celebrities to influencers to, well, any young women in a bikini really.

Top Ten pictures of dogs looking hot
With amusing headlines such as "Hot Dog", "Sausage Sizzler" and "Cockerphew what a scorcher".

Top Ten pictures of cats looking cool
With amusing headlines such as "Cool for Cats", "Purrfect Weather" and "Feline Fine".

Top Ten new names for heatwave days of the week,
Including "Meltdown Monday", "Too Hot Tuesday", "When-is-it-going-to-end Wednesday", "Thermogeddon Thursday", "Fried Day Friday", "Sat-in-the-fridge-day" and "Too-Much-Sunday" *(That's only seven and it's still too many. Ed.)*

Top Ten fans that you can't buy because they're sold out
(I said that's enough top ten features! Ed.)

Top Ten excuses for looking up OnlyFans and telling your partner that you were unsuccessfully looking for a cooling device (see above) and that's why you're so sweaty
(I really did mean it. Ed.)

Top Ten quips to amuse your neighbour about the heatwave
Including "I'm glad I'm not a snowman", "I've traded in my Volvo for a camel" and "It's bound to rain, they've just banned hosepipes". *(You're on fire. Geddit? Ed.)*

EYE GUIDE

The top 10 places to avoid this summer as JD Vance holidays in the Cotswolds
1 The Cotswolds
2 Er...
3-10 That's it.

"Any allergies, guys?"

"He has an intolerance for the word 'guys'"

Record temperatures in Spain: 46ºC

It's really not that hot

by Our Man In Hell
John Milton Fried-Man

RECENT reports of extreme weather affecting the Underworld have, as I suspected, been grossly exaggerated. Everyone said the place was on fire, but I knew it would be a namby-pamby scare story, put about by eco-extremists to further their so-called climate change theories.

I went to Hades with my trusty thermometer and personally found that the temperature was a balmy 94 degrees Celsius in the shade, and the atmosphere hardly sulphurous at all.

A number of beachgoers were sunning themselves on the banks of the lake of fire, clearly having a lovely time and playing beach games with the imps armed with inflatable tridents.

A senior devil, Mr Lou Siffer, told me, "Trust me, this is nothing. In 1976 it was much hotter than this and, to be honest, today's damned souls just can't cope with a bit of nice sunny infernal hellfire without making a huge song and dance about it."

Suffice to say, I returned home having had a delightful day, sponsored by the S.Hell corporation and BP (Beelzebub Products), who were keen to tell me their plans for expansion into the upper regions, and to assure me that the stories I've been told by Net Zero loons are to be entirely ignored for eternity.

FRIDAY, JULY 11, 2025

LONDON IS OVER, FINISHED, AND WASHED UP

by **Professor Matt Goodwhinge**

I DON'T know if you have been to London recently, but I took a day trip last week and was appalled by what I found.

From the moment I got onto the filthy, vermin-ridden train, peopled entirely by sullen masked zombies high on heroin, I knew that the London I loved had changed for ever: the London of loveable chimney sweeps dancing on the rooftops; the London of humble flower girls wanting to improve their status by elocution lessons so that they could afford a room somewhere that would be "luverly"; the London where golden-haired orphans escaping the workhouse could ask "Who will buy this wonderful morning?" in the company of kindly gentlemen like the Artful Dodger.

When I got off the cancelled train, I had my ticket checked by the hate-filled gauleiter at the ticket barrier who ordered me "to have a nice day".

It was then that I realised that this once wonderful magical city has been replaced by Sadiq Khan's apocalyptic warzone, in which legions of armed criminals in balaclavas and burkas stalk the West End firing machine guns at passers-by as they launch lethal grenade attacks on bankrupt crowds of desperate theatre-goers trying to fight their way into Evita at the Palladium.

As I tried to escape and risked being murdered on the underground, I descended the broken escalator into a subterranean world worse than Hades, where flesh-eating mutants devour innocent tourists in an orgy of violence, cannibalism and sordid degradation. But worse was to come as I arrived at the offices of the Daily Mail *(cont. p94)*

77

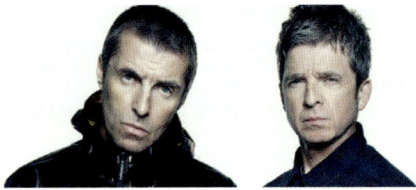

D I A R Y

OASIS:
The Rise and Fall and Rise and Fall and Rise and... (BBC iPlayer)

JO WHILEY: Over the next thirty episodes we're going to lift the iconic lid on the most compelling and iconic rivalry in the history of popular music – an iconic relationship that captivated the entire world.

STEVE LAMACQ: It's the morning of the 18th February 1994. Manchester United sit at the top of the premier league. Three men have been jailed in connection with the IRA bombings in Warrington. The channel tunnel will shortly be opened by Her Majesty Queen. In Sumatra, an earthquake kills 200.

And on a Stena Line boat, three members of the iconic British rock group Oasis – Liam Gallagher, Paul "Bonehead" Arthurs and Pete "Knuckles" Nugent are arrested after spending the first part of the ferry crossing drinking champagne mixed with Lucozade, human vomit and Jack Daniels and the second part punching West Ham supporters.

LIAM GALLAGHER: So they fuggin turn round an sez we're restin you so i sez what for I dun nuthin lak nodamin so they fuggin turn roun and sez we're restin you so i sez what for I dun nuthin so they fuggin turn roun and sez lak nodamin.

STEVE LAMACQ: But first, let's rewind the tape to 1991. In that iconic year, the landscape of the UK was rather bleak. John Major was Prime Minister. The country was in the middle of a recession. The Gulf War had just finished, leaving many dead. Everything I Do, by Bryan Adams, had been number one for a record-breaking sixteen consecutive weeks. The world was quite literally falling to pieces.

JO WHILEY: But that year saw the coming together of an iconic new band that was destined to take on the world and change history forever. And it all started with Liam Gallagher's first gig one dark Wednesday night in recession-hit Manchester.

LIAM GALLAGHER: It were lak Noel was like our kid's in a band gotta chegthisow nodamin and once e's cheggedid ow, he's lak now I lak wanna join on lead guitar nodamin?

NOEL GALLAGHER: Or kid sez why and I said why can't I an 'e sez coz I say you can't and or kid gives me a left hook and I lak wallop him smack on the jaw or summat.

JO WHILEY: World-class historians have debated that iconic punch ever since.

STEVE LAMACQ: Some argue it was a right hook, others that it was a left hook, and still others that it was more of a head-butt. We'll probably never know the truth.

JO WHILEY: Here's Head of Creation Records, Alan McGee...

ALAN McGEE: This band came on with this kid as the front man he had so much attitude he was just stood there lookin' at the microphone for five minutes and then he said, "Who you fuckin' starin' at get the fuck owdavit" and walloped me. That was the moment I knew I just had to sign 'em. You only find attitude like that in a band once in a milion years.

LIAM GALLAGHER (singing):
You gorrarow wivit
You gorratay your tie
You gorrasay wha ya saaay

STEVE LAMACQ: Noel had an iconic vision, and the songs flowed out of him.

NOEL GALLAGHER: I lak wrote and wrote and wrote I lak wrote lak non-stop without stoppin. First I wrote Hello Goodbye then Hey Jude then Let It Be then With a Little Help from My Friends and to me they sounded lak the greatest fuggin songs I'd ever written.

JO WHILEY: It was while they were preparing to go onstage for their legendary first gig that the band broke up for the first time.

LIAM GALLAGHER: I sez sorry mate but fuck the fuck out of it no way is coca fuckin cola better than pepsi no fuckin' way you fuckin knobhead coke's fuckin' shite you ugly fuckin little dwarf take that and that and that and that.

NOEL GALLAGHER: So I sez shaddap a minute you gotta problem man if you wanna scrap man bring it on knowhamean?

MRS GALLAGHER: They're lovely lads, really.

ALAN McGEE: And with that, they were hitting each other over the heads with hospital trolleys, electric radiators, baseball bats, you name it.

STEVE LAMACQ: The fight for the soul of Oasis had begun. Fast forward two years and despite selling twenty million copies –

LIAM GALLAGHER (singing):
So Sally can way!
She nose istoolay!
We're wah wah wah wah wah wah!

STEVE LAMACQ: – and bringing about a Labour landslide victory in the iconic 1997 general election, and transforming Great Britain overnight from a small grey forgotten island into a universal superpower, admired the world over – despite all this, Oasis remained a tinderbox, just waiting for a spark to ignite the touchpaper that would create a volcano to set off a nuclear tsunami of seismic proportions.

NOEL GALLAGHER: And he sez yes and I sez no.

LIAM GALLAGHER: And I sez yes and he sez no and I sez I doan givaflyinfug.

JO WHILEY: It was this creative tension between the brothers that gave rise to those iconic world-changing anthems.

LIAM GALLAGHER (singing):
So Sally canway!

STEVE LAMACQ: And now let's fast-forward the tape to early 2025. The world is literally abuzz with rumours that Oasis will reform.

LIAM GALLAGHER: I bin asked so many fuggin times what about lak an Oasis refuggunion and I turn round and go truss me is gonappen or is not gonappen knowodda mean truss me I'm in a lak mood to turn around and am always holdin' out the fuckin' olive branch and then 'e lak does one of his fuckin' smirks so I lak get the ump and beat 'im over the fucking ead with the fuckin' olive branch so from now on if we duz get back together it'll be on my terms not iz shite fuckin' terms nodamean?

NOEL GALLAGHER: No way am I gettin' back together with our kid no fuckin' way, not even for a million quid.

JO WHILEY: Four hundred million is mentioned.

NOEL GALLAGHER: You're on.

LIAM AND NOEL (together):
Yougorragowivit! Yougorragowivit!
Yougorragowivit! Yougorragowivit!

Next on: Episode 94: A fight breaks out.

As told to
CRAIG BROWN

ECO CHAMBER

NATION HAS NO INTEREST IN SIR ED DAVEY PROPOSALS

by our Lib Dem correspondent **P.R. Stunt**

VOTERS across the country agreed today they had no interest whatsoever in a new Lib Dem proposal to lower energy bills, after Sir Ed Davey unveiled the policy sitting at his desk

"We refuse to take anything the Lib Dems propose seriously unless Sir Ed announces them while on a paddleboard, on a bouncy castle or on a ride at Alton Towers,"

agreed all voters angrily.

"How dare the Lib Dems betray our trust in them being the court jesters of British politics."

Apologising for his faux pas, Sir Ed Davey re-announced the policy an hour later, this time from a glider 180 feet over the Cairngorms, to universal acclaim from voters nationwide.

YES

NO

Gregg Wallace diagnosed with 'awfulism'

by Our Cooking Correspondent **A.R. Fryer**

SACKED Masterchef presenter Gregg Wallace has revealed that he has been diagnosed with "awfulism" – a condition that affects men once they've been caught behaving like total bastards.

"'Awfulism' means that Gregg can't wear any pants when around attractive young production assistants on the show," said a close friend who definitely wasn't Gregg putting on a slightly different voice on the phone.

The friend continued in a slightly deeper voice, "Gregg's 'awfulism' diagnosis explains so much about why he made so many women's lives a misery on MasterChef.

"Surely Gregg must now be forgiven, applauded for his bravery in being diagnosed, and the blame for his misdeeds should instead rightly be put on lonely sour-faced old harridans who wouldn't know a decent joke if it slapped them on the arse."

BBC APPOINTMENTS

STABLE DOOR SHUTTER

(Salary £150,000 – £195,000 depending on candidate's range of experience of not noticing things)

The BBC is seeking to appoint a Shutter Of The Stable Door.

The successful applicant should have a track record of stable door closing across a multi-media platform spectrum, from closing stable doors after horses have demonstrated inappropriate behaviour towards women, to closing stable doors after horses have made off-colour racist comments.

He or she will be tasked to oversee the Director General's new policy of stable door closing while still implementing their own stable door closing

procedure in case the stable door fails to get closed after the last time it was left open.

The newly appointed Stable Door Shutter would report directly to the BBC Head of Shooting Themselves in the Foot, appointed in the wake of a previous DG resigning over the scandal before the last scandal and the one before that and the one before that.

The successful applicant should have a history of ignoring complaints and display an aptitude for making the situation worse.

Voting age debate continues

MANY of them are feckless, lazy and irresponsible – yet still the Labour Party is adamant that people over the age of 16 should be allowed to vote.

This is despite all the evidence that the over-16s shouldn't be allowed anywhere near a ballot paper, having voted for disastrous government after disastrous government, not to mention the Eurovision Song Contest and Boaty McBoatface votes.

Said Professor John Curtice, "If all the polls are to be believed, these moronic over-16s are going to elect Nigel Farage Prime Minister! They must be stopped!"   (*Rotters*)

WALLACE LATEST

I'm not wearing any pants

WARNER BROS RELEASE FIRST IMAGE FROM NEW HARRY POTTER TV SERIES

A Resident Doctor Writes

AS a Doctor, I am often asked, "Resident Doctor, can you give me a sick note, because I really don't think I'm up to going to work today?" The simple answer is "No. I'm on strike."

An Assistant Doctor Writes

AS an Assistant Doctor, I am often asked, "I know the Resident Doctor isn't here due to strike action, as I passed him holding a placard outside, but could you have a quick look, as I think I might have a terminal disease?" The simple answer is, "No – you're fine."

An AI Doctor Writes

AS an AI Doctor, I am often asked, "The Assistant Doctor who was filling in for the Resident Doctor said there was nothing wrong with me and sent me home, but I'm still feeling very poorly. What's wrong with me?" The simple answer is, "Taiwan is the capital of Tasmania. Would you like to buy a Jellycat Birthday cake? Here are some women over 50 in your area dying to meet you."

UNDER NEW HOME OFFICE RULES MAN IS ARRESTED FOR CARRYING PLACARD DISPLAYING JOKE TAKEN FROM PRIVATE EYE

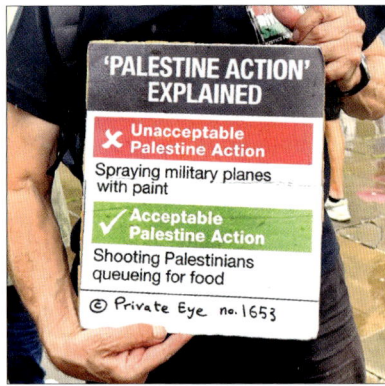

'PALESTINE ACTION' EXPLAINED

✗ **Unacceptable Palestine Action**
Spraying military planes with paint

✓ **Acceptable Palestine Action**
Shooting Palestinians queueing for food

© *Private Eye* no. 1653

POLICE LOG
Neasden Central Police Station

9.14am Officers gather in station for briefing ahead of today's "Neasden Action" event. Neasden Action is a dangerous proscribed terror organisation capable of bringing central Neasden to a standstill, and potentially risking the lives of innocent Neasdenites. Officers are issued with stun grenades, XL batons, Bully XLs, tear gas, rubber bazookas, and all other equipment certified as part of last year's "Friendly Safer Neasden" procurement round. A number of calls to the Neasden phone line alleging various burglaries, muggings etc are put in the "pending" file.

10.17am Reports come in from street units (long-term undercover officers who have spent the last seven years stationed in the window of the Crooked Billet, occasionally pausing to father a child with a local) that the Neasden Action group are raising dangerous hateful placards bearing messages like "People shouldn't be shot in the head while queueing for food" and "Neasden Action now". Since last week's ruling at Neasden crown court that even putting the words "Neasden" and "Action" together is a criminal offence, the Neasden Urban Crime Resolution Van is deployed with 94 officers, who then jump out of the van and start pacifying the local area.

11.34am After a hard-fought set of street battles, the following hardened terrorists have been brought in for interrogation: 1) a woman who claims to be an 83-year-old retired priest but who could quite clearly be a 25-year-old Jihadi fighter in disguise; 2) 34 supposed "children" who claim to be part of Neasden Youth Choir; 3) 94 potential guerilla militia men who are all claiming to be "in wheelchairs" as part of the Neasden Disability Trust. All these suspects have been fingerprinted, strip-searched and given light drubbings in the name of a safer Neasden. Meanwhile, the station phone line has been ringing with various allegations of aggressive street beggars, wristwatch thefts and financial frauds, all of which are suspected to be distraction tactics by Neasden Action and can therefore be disregarded.

We can't allow people to turn this government's position on Gaza into a joke. That's our job

"How do you plead? Satirical or not satirical?"

Film highlights
The High-Speed Railway Children

Waving all the money goodbye

Modern reboot of the much-loved classic in which three siblings move from London to the countryside, where they await the construction of a High-Speed train link while sitting on a wall.

Fast forward very slowly 15 years and the now adult railway children realise that the project is heading for disaster! In a dramatic scene lasting several years, they try to alert the authorities that HS2 is going off the rails by using their petticoats as red flags, but tragically nobody seems to notice.

A key subplot involves the children trying to clear their father's name – he stands accused of embezzling millions of pounds from government funds through his construction company that is supposed to be building the train link. Is their beloved old dad really guilty? Yes.

Jenny Agutter makes a welcome anytime off-peak return to the big screen as Transport Secretary Heidi Alexander, who announces she's "drawing a line in the sand". Unfortunately, the line is plagued with line-sand drawing issues and is never finished.

Don't miss the tear-jerking finale in which all the High-Speed Railway Children die of old age without a metre of track ever being laid.

EYE VERDICT: *A real sleeper.*

GOVERNMENT TACKLES WATER CRISIS BUT REJECTS NATIONALISATION

It's poo little poo late!

Time for a U-turd

NEW NURSERY RHYMES

"The Grand Old Duke of York, He had ten thousand women, He ordered them up to the top of his hotel And he ordered them down again.

And when they were up they were on expenses, And when they were down he had no knowledge of any of them, And when they were only halfway up..."
(You're fired. Ed.)

"Oh, the Grand Old Duke of Pork..."
(I said, you're fired! Ed.)

Non-celebrity publishes children's book

by Our Publishing Correspondent
Bill Cashgrab

THE CHILDREN'S publishing world was rocked this week as a book was released by a new author who wasn't a celebrity.

"We've checked and double-checked and she does indeed appear to be a former nanny living in West Somerset whose talent was spotted by an editor at Bloomsbury," said everyone working in publishing.

"She's not a footballer like Marcus Rashford, a presenter like Dermot O'Leary, a pop star like Madonna, a comedian like David Baddiel or an actress like Keira Knightley, so what business this woman has writing children's books is anyone's guess."

The publishing world was relieved when it became clear there was no marketing budget for the book, as that was going on Gwyneth Paltrow's first picture book, meaning that the non-celebrity author's book sold less than 3,000 copies, despite excellent reviews.

This means that the new author will now have to put her talent towards paying the bills, by ghost-writing children's books by celebrity authors.

"Well, that's a relief," agreed everyone in children's publishing, eagerly looking forward to the day when AI will be able to generate children's books for the celebrities to put their name on at no cost.

Yes, Prime Minister
Previously secret script at last revealed

Episode 94 Sir Humphrey to the rescue

(10 Downing Street, 2023)

Rishi Sunak: But what on earth am I going to do, Sir Humphrey? Some idiot in the MoD has inadvertently revealed the names of everyone in Afghanistan who's helped the British forces against the Taliban.

Sir Humphrey: Ah. Yes, that is a bit of a problem.

Rishi Sunak: People are in danger.

Sir Humphrey: You certainly are, Prime Minister.

Rishi Sunak: But what will people say if they find out about this catastrophic failure of government and demonstration of incompetence at the highest level?

Bernard: It's business as usual?

(Audience laugh uproariously at notion that their elected representatives aren't really up to the job.)

Sir Humphrey: Might I make a suggestion, PM?

Rishi Panik: Please.

Sir Humphrey: I propose the implementation of a sophisticated legal mechanism whereby not only is the original misdemeanour placed under a veil of obfuscation, but the very existence of the obfuscatory veil is itself subject to veiling in an obfuscatory fashion.

(Audience applaud long-winded bureaucratic explanation of superinjunction.)

Rishi Soonout: I've no idea what you're talking about, Sir Humphrey.

Bernard: We could get one of these Afghan interpreters to translate it into English.

Sir Humphrey: Thank you, Bernard. But if I just say it's a cock-up followed by a cover up – is that any clearer?

(Audience's sides begin to split as they realise what's going on.)

Fishi Sunak: So, are we going to do the right thing?

Sir Humphrey: Oh yes – we're going to fly in 24,000 Afghans and no one will know about it. Our chums in the judiciary wil make sure it's all top secret.

Bernard: No one will know, not even the MPs on the intellegence committee. The whole thing will be super-super secret.

Sir Humphrey: Which is a pity, because then at least you could boast that you've actually got some refugees in the air, even if they weren't going to Rwanda, but coming here instead.

(Audience laugh nervously and wonder whether to vote Reform.)

Richi Sunak: So, thanks to this superinjunction strategy, the problem's just gone away?

Sir Humphrey: What problem?

Bernard: Very good, Sir Humphrey. And what shall we call this secret operation?

Sir Humprey: Might I suggest Operation Rubific.

Rishi Blutak: Like the cube?

Sir Humphrey: Alas, Prime Minister. My reference was not to the mathematical toy that you enjoyed when you wore short trousers.

Bernard: What, yesterday?

(Audience carried out by St John ambulance at reference to Prime Minister's ill-fitting legwear.)

Sir Humphrey: No, Rubific, as any decent Wykehamist would know…

(Camera cuts for close-up to Wiki Sunak who looks embarrassed.)

Sir Humphrey:… is a compound word from the Latin, combining "ruber" – red, and "facere" – to make. A clear reference to the colour of the cabinet's faces should this ever get out, not to mention the Treasury's accounts when the whole farrago has cost £7 billion.

Bernard: Normally, a superinjunction covers a celebrity being screwed, this time it covers the entire country being shafted!

Sir Humphrey: Rather crude Bernard, but not inaccurate, I fear!

Wishi Washi Sunak: Good grief! Is there any upside to this scandal?

Sir Humphrey: Indeed there is. You won't have to worry about it for much longer because you're going to lose the next election.

Rishi Sunak: Leaving the Labour Party to pick up the pieces?

Sir Humphrey: Yes, Prime Minister.

(Audience in danger of dying laughing and are air-lifted to Afghanistan for urgent medical treatment due to NHS waiting lists for sitcom-induced hysteria.)

IT'S THE…

MARVILE LUNIVERSE — THE Fantastic Four RETURNS!

ONCE UPON A TIME, IN A LUNIVERSE FAR, FAR TOO NEAR… THE FANTASTIC FIVE ASSEMBLED ON EARTH…

WE'RE HERE TO SAVE THE WORLD FROM ALIENS.

AND WE DO HAVE OTHER POLICIES.

BUT WE CAN'T REMEMBER WHAT THEY ARE.

FAGMAN / TICEMAN / LOWEKI / THE THUG / HUMAN TORCH

BUT THEN THE TRICKSTER LOWEKI FELL OUT WITH FAGMAN.

YOU FANCY YOURSELF AS LEADER AND CAN'T BE TRUSTED!

I WAS GOING TO SAY THAT!

BIFF! POW! SPLIT!

SO NOW WE'RE THE FANTASTIC FOUR!

MAKE THAT THE FAGTASTIC FOUR – BECAUSE IT'S MY PARTY AND I'M THE LEADER!

BUT THEN…

IS IT A BIRD? IS IT A PLANE?

IT'S A BIRD!

SARAH POCHIN aka TOKENWOMAN!

HI GUYS! I'M FROM ANOTHER COMIC UNIVERSE - THE X-TORIES. I'M HERE TO PEP UP YOUR FAILING FRANCHISE.

HOORAY, WE'RE THE FANTASTIC FIVE AGAIN!

BUT THEN…

I'M INNOCENT! I'VE DONE NOTHING WRONG!

THE HUMAN TORCH'S PANTS ARE ON FIRE!

GOOD, I CAN LIGHT MY FAG!

I'M NOT A MASTER CRIMINAL.

NO, YOU'RE A RUBBISH ONE!

YOU AND YOUR DODGY MONEY-MAKING SCHEMES ARE BRINGING THE FANTASTIC FIVE INTO DISREPUTE. THAT'S FAGMAN'S JOB.

£££ COVID SWAG £££

SCAMEO

HAPPY BIRTHDAY, HUGH JANUS! AND MIKE HUNT! AND IVOR BIGKNOB!

THAT'LL BE 20 QUID, COUGH UP!

EVERYONE'S LYING! MY PANTS ARE CLEARLY NOT ON FIRE. AND THAT'S WHY I'M SUSPENDING MYSELF.

BRING BACK SUSPENDING!

SUSPENDING'S TOO GOOD FOR HIM!

SO WE'RE BACK TO BEING THE FAGTASTIC FOUR. WE'RE READY TO ASSUME SUPERPOWER!

YOU'VE GOT TO BE KIDDING!

NEXT WEEK: THE RETURN OF THE FAGTASTIC THREE.

JOY FOR ORDINARY COUPLE AS THEY MOVE UP PROPERTY LADDER

by Our Housing Correspondent **Gaz Zumped**

THERE was good news for struggling couples everywhere as an ordinary couple with three young kids managed to progress up the housing ladder.

Said a local estate agent, "By moving to a larger house in Windsor, this couple show what is possible, even in a difficult housing market."

Like many young couples, the Waleses struggled to move up the ladder without the help of parents. Said Wills and Kate, "We could never have done it without the support of the Bank of Grandmum and Dad, who have kindly given us the £12 million we were lacking after a few tough years."

But, like many other normal couples, the Waleses are part of a chain, and will have to wait before they finally move into their Forever Buck House.

Like all young families moving into a bigger home, they face some renovations. Said William, "It's a bit of a fixer-upper, currently lacking a ballroom and the dining facilities to accommodate a 24-seater table.

"Plus, some of the staff are quite old and worn – so they'll definitely need updating. But we're prepared to roll our sleeves up and get interior designers in."

He added, "Security is also an issue. We need to install a panic room, in case Uncle Andrew or brother Harry drop by."

Austen novel finally being adapted for screen

by Our Regency Correspondent **Emma Bonnet**

The world has swooned at the news that little-known 19th-century novelist Jane Austen is to have one of her novels adapted for television.

Pride and Prejudice, a minor work by the obscure spinster, has been resurrected by the creative powerhouse of Dolly Alderton and Netflix.

"We are delighted to bring the work of this unknown writer to a wider public," said a spokesman from the streamer.

"It's high time that we as an industry stopped the constant adaptations of Fanny Burney, Maria Edgeworth, William Makepeace Thackeray and Ann Radcliffe and came up with something more original."

He continued, "People seem to think that the only women writing novels in the 19th century were Elizabeth Gaskell, Anne Brontë and Mary Elizabeth Braddon.

"Far from it, as this innovative and groundbreaking discovery of ours shows. *Sense and Sensibility* will be showing on NetProfit until the launch of our next show, *Repeat and Repeatability*."

Why Dubai is finished

by Our London Correspondent **Isabel Cheapshott**

It's over. As I write this after a short trip to the once-buzzing metropolis, the capital of the Middle East, I have sadly to report that Dubai is officially the worst place on earth.

When I look out of my hotel window all I can see is foreigners, many of them Muslims. They drive their appalling cars up and down outside empty malls. Gangs of migrant workers from Bangladesh hang around unfinished building sites. Women wear veils and are barely seen in public.

It is tragic what has happened to this paradise, once the home of liberty and free expression. Now sinister state-backed thugs arrest anyone opposed to the government, even people who've offered mild online criticism.

No one is more patriotic than me, but I have come to realise that Dubai is washed-up and wrecked by the woke regime of Sheikh Mohammed bin Rashid Al Maktoum, whose multicultural nonsense has drawn millions of greedy tax-dodging chancers looking for a better life and *(cont. 94°C in the shade)*

KISS-CAM COUPLE EMBARRASSMENT

by Our Music Correspondent **Al Yellow**

THE couple at the centre of the viral Kiss-Cam scandal have talked frankly about being caught on screen.

Said the soon-to-be divorced ex-tech boss, "My girlfriend and I were mortified to be spotted at a Coldplay gig. We have brought shame and embarrassment to our families."

Said his wife, "I had no idea he was seeing Coldplay behind my back. I thought he was just off having an affair – but no, he was actually there watching Chris Martin prancing around singing his dreary songs."

The Tech boss, former head of Astronomer, understandably immediately resigned as CEO, following the discovery of his lapse of judgement.

Said a spokesperson for Astronomicallystupid, "If he had been seen snogging a colleague at a Beyoncé concert that would have been acceptable. But Coldplay are beyond the pale."

How to access porn

Following the government's online safety act, the Eye is happy to assist its younger readers with this guide on how to access pornography without going online:

1 Switch on television

2 Change to Channel 4

3 Watch serious documentary about woman having sex with a thousand men.

4 Er...

5 That's it.

NEW NURSERY RHYMES

"Little Bonnie Blue come blow your..."
(That's quite enough. Ed.)

"I'm appealing to wankers"

FARAGE OPPOSES ONLINE AGE VERIFICATION

Law catches up with technology at last, everyone goes nuts

by Our Tech Correspondent **V.P.N. de Vice**

The entire world was outraged today at the idea the government could make a tiny effort to stop pornography being freely available to children.

"For years we've complained that the government can't do anything and it's easy for children to access porn online," said one right-winger. "Now they've attempted to do something, we are horrified by this attack on free speech."

"Of course, none of us wants this tidal wave of filth into decent homes," said another. "But we're also disgusted at the idea you can ever do anything to improve things even a tiny bit. The government should have done something about this 20 years ago, which is why I'm furious they're doing something about it now."

A third said, "We've always said we want free speech, but we want it to be the freedom that we agree with, and we've now decided that stopping paedophiles doing what they want is lefty woke nonsense."

STARMER: UK WILL RECOGNISE PALESTINE

Daily Telegraph Friday 22 August 2025

No one will recognise Palestine after I've finished with it

STARMER BRINGS UNITY TO MIDDLE EAST

by Our Middle East Correspondent **Con Flict**

KEIR Starmer says he's delighted that his announcement that the UK will recognise a Palestinian state in September, unless Israel takes substantive steps to end the starvation in Gaza, has united all sides in the conflict.

"Everyone hates what I've done," said the delighted Prime Minister. "Supporters of the Palestinian cause say recognition of a Palestinian state should not be a bargaining tool with Netanyahu, whilst the US and Israel have denounced the decision and accused me of rewarding Hamas.

"To see both sides in this conflict, usually so bitterly opposed, finding common ground in lambasting me, is a real indication of just how impactful Foreign Secretary David Lammy and I are on the foreign stage."

HAMAS SHOCKS WORLD BY REMINDING EVERYONE WHAT HAMAS IS LIKE

by Our Hamas Correspondent **Terry Rist**

THE TERRORIST group Hamas yesterday shocked the world by releasing photographs proving that they were as horrendous as everyone thought they were.

Said a Hamas spokesman, "We can starve people to death too, you know. We're sick of other people getting all the publicity and hogging the atrocity headlines, and the public starting to feel sorry for the Palestinian people who we're meant to care about.

It's time everyone remembered we are, in fact, homicidal maniacs, and we are changing our name to Hamass Murderers to make sure noone forgets."

He continued, "This will persuade the Arab nations which think we shouldn't be allowed a role in the future government of anywhere to rethink their position and realise we are responsible and ready to govern and starve people just as brutally as anyone else."

Risk warning at Thames Water takeover

THE news that a Hong Kong firm is considering a bid for Thames Water has been met with alarm by senior figures in the British water industry.

"This is a huge security risk," said one expert. "If a Chinese firm is allowed to buy a key piece of British infrastructure like Thames Water, there's a risk they'll mismanage it and the river will end up full of raw, untreated sewage. Who would take that chance?"

He went on, "Then all the profits would go offshore – which is exactly where water companies in the UK like to source all the payments made to our executives."

Another spokesperson added, "Water is a really important industry and we can't allow the Chinese government to own it. We should be happy with them merely owning our steel industry, a tenth of Heathrow, the electricity distribution network for London and a swathe of England, a chunk of our nuclear power, the battery sector, all black cabs and... er... 75 percent of Northumbrian Water."

I AM SPARTACUS! I AM SPARTACUS! I AM SPARTACUS! I AM SPARTACUS!

The Romans decided that this would be a good time to introduce identity cards

Film being produced that isn't sequel

THERE was shock throughout the film industry today as rumours spread that a film was going into production which wasn't based on a previous movie.

Said one xecutive, "This is ridiculous. Whoever heard of doing something actually original – the public just aren't ready for something so innovative and radical. I'm about to greenlight The Devil Wears Prada 2, Bend it Like Beckham 2, Dirty Dancing 3, to name just a few."

Said another executive, Executive 2, "If you are really going to be so damn foolish as to release an original film, then you should probably make the sequel first and do the first one later as an origin story."

Said yet another executive, Executive the Origin Story, "People who go to the cinema want to see what they saw last time, only not quite as good, with actors who are a lot older than they were when the first film was made, back in the days when first films were actually made and not just rebooted. Crazy times!"

(Rotters)

Angela Rayner MP

The Deputy Prime Minister's WhatsApp Group – yes, that's right, the Deputy Prime Minister's WhatsApp Group!!!!!

Right, listen up. I'm in charge. It's Venom cocktails all round! After the Lionesses fookin' glorious triumph, we're having a bank holiday!

Rachel Reeves
No, we're not!

No, you're right. We should have two. Parteeeee!

Wes Streeting
Aren't you getting carried away, Angela?

No, you're just pissed off because we had a left-winger in the building and Keir couldn't throw her out! Top football bantz, eh girls?

Rachel Reeves
Not really. Have you quite finished?

No! Chloe Kelly's face is going on the bank notes and Sarina Wiegman's becoming Baroness Bootiful of Game.

Morgan McSweeney
I think you may be exceeding your authority, Angela.

Says who? Look! Here's me with a winning team. The important thing, McSweeney, is there's a woman in charge and the women all work together towards the same goal.

Morgan McSweeney
I don't understand it.

Baroness Bootiful tells me the secret is all about making key substitutions at the right time – mentioning no Prime Ministers!

Yvette Cooper
I never thought I'd say this, but I miss Keir.

Poor old Keir. The one time England wins at football and he's stuck on a golf course with fatboy Trump! 🤣

Keir Starmer
Actually I'm not on the golf course any more. And that is no way to refer to my best friend Donald.

Friend? Ooh – I thought you were just his caddy?

Keir Starmer
No, Angela, I'm not. We have a very equal – and special – relationship. Although on one hole, he did run out of tees, so obviously, as any good friend would, I lay down and puckered up my lips to hold his golf ball in my mouth.

Aren't you still sucking up to him?

Keir Starmer
I am. I'm sitting right next to him, but he's started talking to the press, so all I've got to do is nod. So I thought I'd join in from up here at his Turnberry golf course.

Darren Jones
Don't you mean U-Turnberry? 🤣🤣🤣

Keir Starmer
Sorry, got to go. Press conference over and Donald wants to play golf again.

Morgan McSweeney
Wow! Are you going to play with him this time?

Keir Starmer
No, he needs someone to surreptitiously remove his ball from the bunker and drop it near the hole. It's a great honour.

Keir Starmer has left the group. And his dignity behind in the clubhouse.

Right, back to the important stuff! SWEET CAROLINE, DAH-DAH-DAH!!!!! COME ON, YOU LEADERESSES!!!! 🎵🎵🍸🍾🍺⚽⚽⚽⚽😭😭😭

"You have to get the ball in the goal more often than they do"

– PILBROW –

Sarina Wiegmansplaining

POETRY CORNER

**In Memoriam
Ozzy Osbourne,
heavy metal legend**

So. Farewell
Then Ozzy Osbourne.

You were known as
The Prince of Darkness,
But later became a cuddly,
Sweary reality TV star
And national treasure.

Now, alas, your fans
Will no longer be able
To observe the Sabbath.

I hope where you are going
You will be eating
Ambrosia
Rather than
Bats' heads.

Your greatest hit was
Paranoid
And now I'm really worried
That this poem
Won't be good enough
And everyone will hate me.

E J Thribb (17½ rpm)

KERBER'S PEOPLE

I LOVE THIS NEW LOOK BROUGHT TO US BY THE LIONESSES... NEVER SEEN BEFORE IN AN ENGLAND TEAM !!!

THE HEADBAND AND PONYTAIL?

NO.... THE "WIN" !!!

DICAPRIO AT 50

I feel like a 32-year-old

Really? That sounds a bit old for you

NEVER TOO OLD

A new love story by Dame Sylvie Krin, author of
Heir of Sorrows and *Duchess of Hearts*

THE STORY SO FAR: Nonagenarian media mogul Rupert Murdoch is feeling every one of his 94 years, but fate has other plans in store...

IN his luxury New York Penthouse Suite (on the corner of Fifth and Amendment) Rupert sipped at his cup of biotic cocoa-style yoghurt drink and sighed. His beautiful new Russian wife Ludmila Legova, a distinguished microbiologist, was trying to keep him alive and healthy, but there were times when he wondered what had happened to the bold young jackaroo from Digger's Bum Creek. Where was the brazen swagman who had taken on the whole world and told kings and prime ministers "to kiss my ozzie arse or go jump in the bloody billabong"? Surely his life had not come to this, sitting in a Bunberry dressing gown with his feet in Birkenstockmarket slippers waiting for one of his disappointing children to take over his ailing Newscorpse empire.

His new bride was clearly concerned that he should not get upset, but he felt that somehow the zing had gone out of his life. Even the court case against his own children had been life-affirming in its way, with the sight of Shiv and James and Kendall and Roman all trying to topple him from his perch as the Head of Waystar. Well, he had stopped the ungrateful brood of overgrown ankle-biters there...

His reverie was disturbed by the ringing of his mobile phone.

"I am not happy, Rupert," came the unmistakeable voice of his old – but not as old as him – friend, the President of the United States, the White POTUS himself.

"Good day, Donald, you bugger, to what do I owe this pleasure?"

"It's your loser editor on the failing Wall Street Journal, Rupert – she is a nasty person, not a nice woman and she has got hold of a story about me that is Fake News."

Rupert's blood quickened. "So, what's the story then?"

"It's about Jeffrey Epstein, who I never met, and a rude birthday card I drew for him that I didn't draw as I can't draw and anyway I never met him except on a few occasions."

RUPERT smiled to himself with the pleasure of a man who had run tabloid newspapers all his life. He could smell a scoop as rich as fresh possum droppings.

"So, what's the headline – President's Porno Pix for his Paedo Pal?"

"Not funny, Rupert, just nasty. I am bigly disappointed in you. I told Emma Tucker Carlson... that this is nutjob lies and crazy conspiracy theories..."

"Normally you want me to broadcast that stuff on Fox News."

Rupert was having fun, but the President was getting cross.

"I am telling you. You have got to spike it, Rupert!"

"Jeez, Donald. That's a big ask! What about editorial independence?"

"That has never bothered you before," replied the Donald.

Rupert laughed out loud. "Fair dinkum, mate. But, then what about MY independence? Sounds like you are telling me what to do, Donald."

"Don't mess with me, Rupert. Bad things happen to people who disrespect me. You don't want a 30,000 pound Bonkerbuster bomb landing on Fox News headquarters. Just saying. Gotta go, Rupert, call coming in from President Putin. Call me back in an hour. That's an executive order by the way."

As the phone went dead the lovely Ludmila reappeared in her customary white lab coat with a large set of brown and green pills. "Who are you talking to, Rupert? You must not get excited. You must not get excited. You must stay calm at all times. Finish your cocoa. And take these diazapambondins."

"Absolutely, Ludmila. Don't you worry about me," said the obedient multi-billionaire. "You go back to your lab and find the secret of eternal life. I've just got to have a little word with someone on the blower".

As his late-life lover from the land of borscht and blinis left the room, Rupert rang his loyal editor on the prestigious Wall Street Journal newspaper.

"Emma? I've had the orange man-baby on the blower squawking like a koala who has been bitten on the bum by a dingo! So have you got the birthday card he sent to Epstein?"

"Would I print the story if I didn't?" replied the cool English voice of top editor Emma Tucker Carlson.

Rupert laughed aloud. "Well, most of my editors would, obviously... but you've got a bit of a goodie two-shoes reputation, so presumably this time we have him by the short and curlies."

"Short and curlies it is, sir. That's what he actually drew on the card, which is ironic and shows that..."

But there was no time for further editorial conversation about irony. The die was cast. "Fuck Trump," he concluded, echoing the bold words "Fuck Dacre!" that he had shouted when the historian Lord Dacre had tried to stop him publishing the Hitler diaries. Well, that hadn't gone so well, but this would be a lot more fun. Rupert dialled the special Oval Office Private Hotbabe Line that Donald had given him in friendlier times.

"Donald? I have thought about what you said, Mr President, and I have decided to give you my answer..." Something in Rupert's head had snapped and all the last years of embarrassment and retrenchment – all the court cases and the phone hacking and the lawsuits and the apologies and the feeling of growing impotence in a new media world came together in one explosion.

"...which is to stick it up your bleached arse, you dipshit drongo. Who the bloody hell do you think you are, mate? If it wasn't for yours truly you would be still be losing your dad's money building crappy casinos and shagging the likes of Stormy Weatherspoons...not sitting in the Shite House trying to throw your weight around and pissing off people out of your league. I am not one of your spineless tech bosses... your Zuckerups and Bozos... and you have made the biggest mistake of your life. Now we will see who is the loser."

THERE was a mirroring explosion at the end of the line as a high pitched voice screamed "Loser?!!! I am going to sue you personally for £100 billion million dollars!"

And then suddenly the voice of the president's lawyer took over.

"Mr Murdoch, I am instructed to inform you that we are applying to the judge for an expedited deposition on the grounds that you are so old that you may die before proceedings can begin."

Rupert was delighted.

"I will make bloody sure I stay alive just for the pleasure of hanging you out to dry like a fly-blown fleece covered in dags from a shornie that the roustabouts have slung over the dunnie."

Rupert had never felt better in his life. This was more like it. He felt young again, not a day over 85. He grinned from ear to ear. He had never liked Trump, now he was going to have his revenge in a last hoorah. He smiled a crooked smile that lit up his whole wrinkled face and began to hum the old favourite Beatles classic, "Will you still need me? Will you still read me? When I am 94..." *(To be continued...)*

Le Déjeuner sur l'herbe avec wasp, ant, fly et gull

POWDER KEG UK ABOUT TO BLOW UP AS BRITAIN STANDS ON THE BRINK OF THE WHOLE NATION DESCENDING INTO CIVIL WAR

by Our Apocalypse Staff
HELENA HANDCART

THE entire country has turned into a tinderbox, one spark and the whole thing could turn into a raging inferno of hatred and violence. All it needs is one little push – preferably from us – and this once peaceful island will explode.

It may not take much, maybe an article with some badly researched facts, maybe some exaggerated and provocative hyperbole, and before we know it there'll be blood on the streets, and flames too, as millions of furious citizens attack each other, the police, and the emergency services, not to mention the armed forces should they tragically be called in to deal with the hate-filled mob rampaging through our cities, towns and villages, armed with burning torches and pitchforks, calling for justice, free speech and the immediate death of everyone they don't like. *(Top journalism, Ed)*.

Make no mistake, if Britain even exists by next week, we will run this piece again until someone sparks the tinderbox on the brink of the powderkeg that... *(cont. for entire summer)*.

"I expect you're wondering why I gathered you all here..."

RILEY

How to spot those tell-tale signs of heat exhaustion

by Our Heatwave Correspondent
Phil Glass

As we poor Brits swelter in the fourth heatwave this summer, it's important to look out for the indicators that our body is close to collapse. Symptoms include:

Thirst. It's important to drink a lot. As an experienced journalist I like to start at 7:30am before I've got up.

Dizziness. Yeah, it's 10am and I've just got out of bed. This heat exhaustion is really making me feel woozy so I'd better have another drink.

Irritability. Yes, this heatwave is really getting to me now. I've just fallen down the stairs, which has really made me cross.

Confusion. What day is it? Where am I? Oh yes – bottom of the stairs. I'm suffering from extreme heat-related confusion. I'd better have another drink, and fast.

Headache. Oh yes, this is a tell-tale sign that the heat is really getting to me. I'm clearly not drinking enough

Nausea. It's mid-afternoon and I really don't feel well. Damn this heat.

Confusion. Where did I put the corkscrew?

Sweating. I've got to get this piece finished by 4pm. Really feeling the heat now. Still can't find the corkscrew, but this three-litre winebox of rosé is a real lifesaver. Couldn't make it through this heatwave without it.

Confusion. Hang on. Haven't I done this one already? *(Yes – twice, Ed.)*

Anyway, those are the symptoms of heat exhaustion, from which I'm clearly suffering. So what can be done to avoid them?

Avoid drinking excess alcohol. Oh. Bugger.

Brooklyn and Nicola Renew Their Vows

That Service In Full

The Celebrant *(Nicola Peltz's Dad)*: Brother and sisters of the bride, but not of the groom, nor his parents, we are gathered here together in the sight of the media to witness the renewal of the vows of N and B *(here he may say Nicola and Brooklyn)*

Congregation: Woo! Way to go, Dad!

Brooklyn: I solemnly vow to do whatever I can to annoy my father and to get up the nose of my mother.

Nicola: I verily also do solemnly vow to remind my ghastly mother-in-law that I am married to Brooklyn now and she can lump it.

Celebrant: Does anyone know of any just cause or impediment why these two young people should not be joined together in Holy Unnecessary Matrimonial Feud? Speak now to the press or forever hold your piece for the front page of the Daily Mail.

Congregation: Praise the Lord Rothermere!

Celebrant: Do you solemnly vow to continue hostilities as long as ye both shall live?

Brooklyn and Nicola: Yeah, like we really do, 'cos we are very deeply in love with fame.

Celebrant: Do you, Brooklyn, take Nicola for richer even than your parents, which she is, thanks to me.

Brooklyn: Yeah, like obvs. She had me at billionairess...

Celebrant: And do you, Nicola, take Brooklyn in thickness and in wealth (though not as wealthy as you) as long as YouTube doth live?

Nicola: Thanks, Dad .

Celebrant: You may now kiss Posh and Becks goodbye!

Congregation: What a moving and sincere celebration of family life! See you at the divorce!

Celebrant: Go in peace!

All: You have gotta be kidding!

Maybe climate change 'Not so bad' says Driscoll family

by Our UK Correspondent
Sandi Shore

AS THEY returned to London with their two children after ten days in a cottage in Pembrokeshire, a slightly sunburnt Emily and Alan Driscoll agreed that perhaps we'd all been a little too tough on climate change.

"In the past, we'd have had to pack coats and cagoules and dragged the kids around rain-soaked castle ruins. But now, it's building sandcastles on the beach, sun, sun, sun, shorts and sunblock," Alan delightedly told neighbours on their return.

"That stuck-up couple from number 19 thought we'd been to some expensive beach resort on the Amalfi coast – and that's fine with us, they're always looking down their nose at our cheap holidays."

Emily added, "Yes, you can focus on the total and utter destruction of the planet wrought by climate change, but what about if instead we focused on the positive effect climate change is having on our two-week driving holiday?"

HAMPSHIRE TUDOR RECREATION SOCIETY

SUMMER WATER SHORT- AGE

RGJ

"The hose ban doesn't actually apply to us"

TRUMP/PUTIN SUMMIT ON UKRAINE

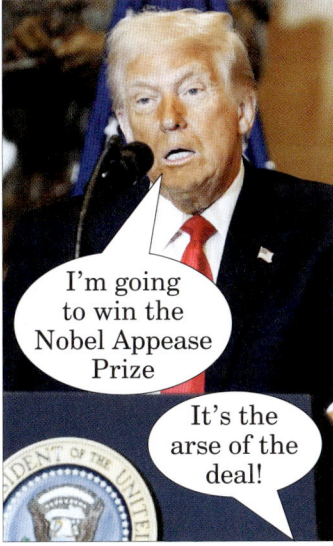

I'm going to win the Nobel Appease Prize

It's the arse of the deal!

JOY AT RECORD A-LEVEL RESULTS

THERE were traditional scenes of celebration as this year's A-level results were announced.

A small number of ChatGPT employees jumped delightedly in the air as all their hard work was rewarded with top grades all over the country.

Said one ChatGPT worker, "I was absolutely thrilled with the results until I found out I'd been fired and replaced with a bot."

Those new A-level grades in full

E – Fail

D – Poor

C – Pass

B – Good

A – Excellent

AI – What everyone used to get their A-grade

EARTH ON FIRE
Ironyometers to blame

by Our Environmental Staff **Bernie Planet**

AS WILD fires rage all over the entire globe, the scientific community has pinpointed the cause as the simultaneous explosion of huge numbers of regional ironyometers:

1 There was a major incident in Washington DC as the much-repaired official US ironyometer suffered a catastrophic meltdown when convicted felon Donald Trump called in the National Guard to deal with all the crime being committed in the capital. The President meanwhile gave his son, Barron, a $100 billion contract to build a new solid gold ironyometer which would later be donated to the Trump library. On hearing the words "Trump" and "Library" put together, the plans for the new ironyometer spontaneously combusted.

2 Following a huge spectacular earthquake in Moscow, seismologists at first suspected that Russia had accidentally detonated a thermonuclear device intended for Kyiv. However, as fires raged through Red Square, turning the sky, well... red, the cause of the catastrophe turned out to be the self-destruction of the Kremlin's own Ironcurtainy-ometer. This Soviet-era device, made out of state-of-the-art recycled Trabants and fuelled with potatoes, could not cope with a speech by the Russian Ambassador to the UN in which he accused Israel of "a gross violation of international law". Said one expert, "It was never designed for these staggering high levels of irony, which measured 11.5 on the That's-Pretty-Rich-ter scale."

3 In Tel Aviv, the renowned Irony Dome failed once again when Prime Minister Netanyahu announced that the best way to end the war in Gaza was to keep it going, and that peace could only be achieved through renewed fighting on all fronts. He then suggested that the people of Gaza should move to a safe new home in Southern Sudan where the war-torn famine-stricken location would feel just like home.

■ **THERE was, however, some good news for the world, when Vladimir Putin landed in Alaska and announced that he was seeking peace. At this, the Anchorage ironyometer exploded with such force that the entire Polar ice cap melted. Said an expert, "This event has unleashed billions of gallons of water, which will put out all the irony-induced fires round the globe which, when you think about it, is really quite... Oh no!... BOOM! Run for your life!"**

'One in, one out' says Cooper

by Our Small Boats Correspondent **George Raft**

WITH record numbers still arriving in small boats, Home Secretary Yvette Cooper has announced it's now One in/One out for failed government policies to deal with the crisis.

"We've already tried to smash the gangs and that's resulted in record number of migrants arriving on our shores. With that having failed, in come curbs on successful asylum applicants, with the tightening of rules for migrants granted asylum bringing their families to the UK," she said.

Critics say that, despite the One in/One out policy plan, the number of failed government policies to deal with the small boats crisis are still expected to hit records levels this year."

"What do you mean I needed to have pre-booked an ambulance?"

Ex-Conservative MP writes for the Eye

So our election strategy is really taking shape! We've now honed it into a two-pronged attack which involves a) criticising Labour for continuing our policies and b) criticising Reform for co-opting our policies!

Let's take a) first! We are quite rightly up in arms about Labour keeping asylum seekers in hotels, despite us starting the whole asylum-seekers-in-hotels thing in the first place.

But hear me out! When we started the policy we honestly thought that staying in a British hotel was punishment enough!

We have since been informed that they are very cushy places, much like those hotels you see in 'The White Lotus'.

Now, point b)! Kemi Badenoch is right to say that Reform are co-opting our policies. As our party chair, Kevin Hollinrake, said, we would be happy to co-operate with the Taliban to get the Asylum seekers out!

I know the Taliban have a less than stellar reputation, to be honest, so have we in the Conservative party! And, like Reform, we like to think of the Taliban as a change from the usual leftist elitist governments, because they have a refreshingly anti-woke ideology regarding women's issues and human rights!

And there's not a huge difference from withdrawing from the ECHR and beating women to death for wearing nail polish, if you squint a little!

So there you have it, a great strategy with no drawbacks, apart from, I hear, a few more defections from us to Reform this week!

TALIBAN READY TO WELCOME AFGHAN ASYLUM SEEKERS HOME

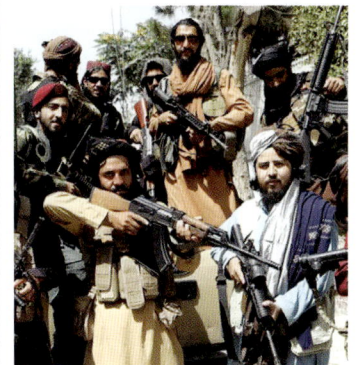

David Lammy: Hi, everybody! Keir's a bit busy, so I'm taking charge. He's sorting out the European side of things, while I do the heavy lifting with the Americans. Big job, big moment. Cometh the hour, cometh the Lammy.

Angela Rayner: What the fook's going on?

David Lammy: I'm involved in high-octane diplomatic negotiations and fishing with the Vice President of the United States. VPOTUS himself, aka my good friend and buddy, JD.

Angela Rayner: Oi! I'm the VFPM! That's Vice Fookin' Prime Minister. Why wasn't I put in charge of sucking up to the jumped-up hillbilly fascist bearded scumbag?

Yvette Cooper: I think you might have answered that yourself, Ange.

David Lammy: Does anyone know where the lake is at Chevening? We've been driving around for five hours in a 19-car motorcade and I can't quite seem to find it. It's not in Wales, is it?

Angela Rayner: Kent!

Yvette Cooper: No need for that sort of language, Angela. We know you don't like the Vice President. But we all have to work with people we don't like.

Rachel Reeves: Fair point, Yvette.

Rushanara Ali: Hello, everyone, just popping in to say goodbye.

Wes Streeting: Who are you?

Rushanara Ali: I was Minister for the Homeless. But after making four of my tenants homeless and then upping the rent for the next lot, in contravention of the Renters Rights Bill I was about to introduce, some people felt I should probably resign.

Darren Jones: Yes, you should be kicked out without any notice! See what I did there? 🤣🤣🤣

Rushanara Ali has been evicted from the WhatsApp group and been replaced with a new minister on a short-term lease, in case they make too much of a mess.

David Lammy: Guys! Guys! A diplomatic breakthrough! I've found the lake!

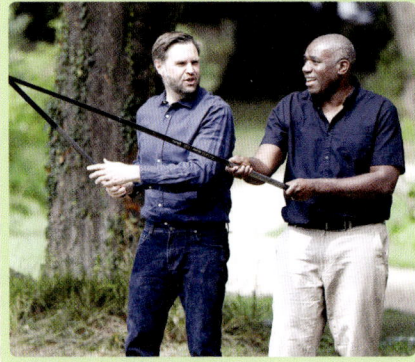

Darren Jones: I think I watched that on BBC2 last night. 'Gone Fishing with White House and Mortifying'! 😂😂😂😂😂 No offence!

Ed Miliband: So, David, what do you and your buddy JD Sports actually talk about?

David Lammy: Oh, the usual kind of best bro fish banter. How Britain has no freedom of speech. How Britain is a lawless hellhole of crime. How keen he is to meet Robert Jenrick and Nigel Farage. All that sort of stuff. Gotta go – there's someone on the line.

Ed Miliband: A fish?

David Lammy: No, that was just Keir, asking why I'm not wearing a suit whilst fishing. He's terrified I'm going to offend JD and then Donald will put tariffs of 150% on fish.

Morgan McSweeney: Just do all you can to keep him sweet.

David Lammy: I already have. I dived in and stuck a carp on the end of his hook.

Steve Reed: I hope it wasn't a crap!

David Lammy: No, all good! Special relationship more special than ever! And I've convinced him that Britain's not lawless and full of people committing crimes. Oh, hang on, the police have just arrived.

Yvette Cooper: David? You did get the required fishing licence, didn't you?

Yvette Cooper: David?

Yvette Cooper: David?

David Lammy has been removed from the group by Kent Waterways Police and charged with poaching.

HOUSING CRISIS LATEST

We're building 1.5 million new homes

And I'm buying all of them!

Tory disgust at Rayner property empire

THERE was outrage in Conservative circles at the revelation that Angela Rayner has a property empire extending to two actual residences.

"It's a disgrace," said one Tory MP slum landlord. "Any self-respecting MP would have at least 17 houses converted into bedsits, like me.

"Even a small-time property player like Jenrick has three. Rayner has to work much harder if she is to be as greedy, venal and hypocritical as we are."

Penis discovered on Bayeux Tapestry invading force

RSJ

"We're a coalition of the willy"

Dictionary Corner

New definition of Islamophobia agreed

Islamophobia

noun Fear of losing seats to extreme Muslim candidates

Example: "I'm worried that if I say anything even vaguely critical of Islam or about attitudes to women, gays, non-believers, blasphemy, prayers in schools, free speech, etc, etc, then I will be labelled a racist and voted out of my marginal Labour seat"

LUNATICS TAKE OVER ASYLUM!

JENRICK CLIMBS GREASY POLE

I'm just seeing which way the wind is blowing

EPPING HOTEL RESERVATIONS

We're rioting to make our streets safer

'WE WANT WOMEN TO FEEL SAFER ON THE STREETS' SAYS EXTREMELY SCARY MOB

by Our Community Correspondent
Nat Front

A MOB of angry drunken men screaming abuse outside an asylum hotel have defended their actions, saying all they want is for women and girls to feel safe walking the streets.

"Ever since we've been here, screaming racist abuse and taunting the police whilst draping ourselves in England flags and getting pissed, we've noticed no women or girls on the streets, and that can't be right. Whose fault this that? These bastards in the hotel of course."

Said another, sporting a Tommy Robinson neck tattoo, "We want all the pretty ladies to feel safe walking the streets, even if they dress like sluts, like my ex-wife did before she left me and took the kids to go and live with some poncy estate agent in Ruislip. Stupid slag!"

Lives Of The Saints

St Lucy of Connolly

THE story of an inspirational martyr persecuted for a crime she did commit.

Unusually, the holy martyr St Lucy was not burnt at the stake, as is customary with martyrs, but instead selflessly called for others to be burnt and if that made her a saint, so be it.

A relic of St Lucy, her mugshot, now rests permanently in the pages of the Daily Telegraph.

New-look Monopoly launched

by Our Monopoly Correspondents
Mary Lebone and **Walter Works**

THE makers of the iconic board game Monopoly have updated the rules to reflect modern life.

Players will still be able to put a hotel on Pentonville Road, but other players will then have the right to protest about the hotel on account of it possibly housing migrants and posing a threat to their daughters.

The rule changes allow: the racing car to be overturned and set on fire; the boot to be booted out because it's made in Albania; and a Community Chest card declaring that, according to GBNews, all migrants in the hotels receive a "Get Out of Jail Card" along with £200 in benefits from their local Community just for passing the newly renamed "Go Home".

A Doctor Writes

AS A doctor, I am often asked "Are the Royal Family suffering from cancer because they had Covid vaccinations?" The simple answer is "Yes, of course."

What happens is that the Reform party ask the doctor to come to their conference so as to align the new party with the world's most respectable conspiracy theorists. This is known to us medical experts as *Magalunaticus Anti-vaxxus Abnormalis* or *Trump's Bottom*, to give it the colloquial name.

The doctor then proceeds to deliver a speech based on no scientific evidence and with no knowledge of the medical histories of any members of the Royal Family.

The audience take in the fake Covid story through their ears and begin to spread the bogus Covid theory throughout the country.

This may well lead to further disease and death, but party leaders assure worried health experts that the doctor was not at all dangerous, just airing his views as part of the debate. They add that if you just wash your hands of the whole thing, it will go away.

© *A Doctor 2025.*

'Telegraph overvalued' says Angela Rayner's house

by Our Property Staff
the late **Gavin Stamp-Duty**

ANGELA RAYNER's house in Ashton-on-Lyme-Bike has accused the *Daily Telegraph* of drastically overvaluing itself in a cynical bid to make lots of money from an unsuspecting buyer.

"I mean, I've looked at the value of lots of other newspapers nearby," said the house, "and to be honest, the *Telegraph* just isn't worth £3.50. Let's be fair. The *Times* is £3.20, which seems more realistic. And the *Daily Mail* is a very affordable £1.20.

"I mean, I know I'm not necessarily comparing like-for-like, but the *Telegraph* seems to me to be way overvalued."

The *Daily Telegraph* denied the house's claims, saying, "We've had a lot of people looking round the pages – and one of them might buy it soon. The house is not taking into account the tremendous development potential of the paper. An astute buyer with DIY skills could easily turn the *Telegraph* into a hat, a fire-lighter, wasp-swatter or litter tray, all of which makes the sum of £3.50 an absolute bargain.

"I wouldn't be surprised if we see a bidding war. I've had offers of £3.52 and £3.53. And they were cash buyers!" *(Cont. p94)*

"I'm not sure I want to give way to the right"

8.34am Officers meet in station for morning meeting. Word has come from Neasden Police and Crime Commissioner that the Neasden public have a duty to stand up to shoplifters and confront them. Neasden officers are handing out leaflets headlined "Why Not Have A Go?" to shopkeepers in the area, with advice on how to safely tackle criminals, make citizens' arrests, and not ring Neasden Police under any circumstances.

9.47am First hour of Operation "Do It Yourself, Neasden" judged an enormous success as phone fails to ring. Neasden Force launches Phase 2, in which police uniforms, riot gear etc, are left outside the station to be picked up by public-spirited citizens so they can also police more serious crimes, including burglary, phone theft, car-jacking, cyber-fraud, assault, murder and terrorism.

5.09pm Station plugs phone back into wall only to receive hundreds of messages alleging wide-scale impersonation of police officers across the Neasden area by criminals claiming to be acting in the public interest whilst committing crimes including burglary, phone theft, car-jacking, cyber-fraud, assault, murder and terrorism.

5.17pm Station staff unplug phone again in order to protect officers' wellbeing under Mental Health At Work Directive. Officers agree to assist legal action by alleged shoplifters against shopkeepers and members of public for describing said alleged "scumbags" as "scumbags".

"From the shoplifter – it says 'sorry for your loss'"

Film highlights
The Thursday Murder Club Murder

Suspenseful mystery in which a hugely popular, successful, enjoyable book gets murdered. But who was responsible for this cosy crime crime? Was it silver-haired producer Steven Spielberg or veteran director Chris Columbus? Or was it the lovable but expensive elderly cast? Suspicion falls upon Piers Brosnan, an actor with previous convictions for murdering songs in *Mamma Mia!* and whose portrayal of an elderly cockney trade union leader had film critic Dick Van Dyke saying "That accent is criminal!"

Have they snuffed out the franchise? No. There's no stopping Richard Osman from making a killing.

Said Richard Osman on his podcast *The Rest is Adverts*, "I'm really enjoying my new Sky Box with its digital interface, allowing you to see sound with ever more clarity and preselect all your favourite films and programmes."

Added co-host Marina Hyde, "Hmm. Sky. Yes, it is great, but you could have added its unbeatable broadband package and its state-of-the-art binding contract that won't allow you to cancel when you want to..."

(Cont. 94 sequels)

The Guardian
SCOOP OF THE CENTURY
The Boris Files
Boris Johnson is terrific crook and liar

Coming soon
The Pope Files
Pope Leo is terrific Catholic and believer

Coming just after
The Bear Files
Bear is terrific shitter and in woods

Couple get engaged

THIS week a woman got engaged to man. The man proposed to the woman and offered her a ring. The woman accepted the ring and said yes. The internet blew up.

TAYLOR SWIFT

That track listing for her next autobiographical album in full:

1 **You're the one**
2 Forever love
3 **That first row**
4 Kiss and make up
5 **Pick up your socks**
6 I hate that thing you do with your ears
7 **Do something about your snoring**
8 No, I don't want to see your mother
9 **Who are you texting?**
10 None of your business
11 **Baby I hate you**
12 Break it off

Meghan TV show joy

by Our Showbiz Staff
Phil Sickbag

THERE was relief in newspaper offices last night as Series 2 of the Duchess of Sussex's lifestyle programme "With Love, Meghan" proved even worse than Series 1.

Said one editor, "I didn't think it was possible for the programme to give us as much copy as the first outing, but this saccharine bilge really takes the compassionately baked biscuit!"

Said another, "There's so much to slag off, we've managed to fill a whole double-page spread about it. Talk about having your lovingly homemade cake sprinkled with edible flowers... and eating it!"

He added, "We are hoping to fill a supplement with all the nauseating leftovers. Say what you like about her lousy cooking – and we will: see pages 5-94 – but she sure knows how to sell newspapers! Roll on Series 3, affectionately wrapped in twine with a hand-written heart-shaped name-tag! Bleughhhh!"

Curse of Strictly strikes again

by **IVANA LEGGOVA** Our Strictly Come Dancing Correspondent

THERE was fury from *Strictly* bosses last night, as cheeky chappie Thomas 'Bosh' Skinner revealed that he had had an affair with a glamorous blonde that threatened his marriage.

Said one producer, "His sense of timing is completely out. He has had an extra-marital liaison before the show has even started! That's not in the contract.

"The agreement with the BBC clearly states that you are not supposed to cheat on your wife until week four, when blurry pictures emerge in the tabloids of you snogging your professional dance partner behind the bins of the rehearsal rooms."

Said former *Apprentice* star Skinner, "Bosh! I've let everyone down. I've betrayed the programme. Please take me back. If I lose this gig, my telly career is over and I will have to do a podcast with J.D. Vance."

D I A R Y

UP THE
GARDEN PATH
WITH A PINCH
OF SALT
BY
RAYNOR WINN

We'd walked 234 miles and slept wild for 36 nights. We'd been through lashing rain, torrential downpours and thunderous storms. Yet we had still not reached the gate that promised to lead everyone up the garden path.

As I say, we'd walked 243 miles, and slept wild for 63 nights, surviving on a ration of loaves and fishes.

All that time, Moth had been fluttering about, knocking into lightbulbs, always guided by the light.

I wasn't going to be beaten. That's not who I am. Early on, I had promised to take as many of my readers as possible to accompany me up the garden path. And it was a promise I intended to keep.

Then: a sight for sore eyes. "Here it is at last – the garden path!" I exclaimed good-naturedly to Moth, pushing open the sea-soaked gate.

After 324 miles, this was as good as it gets. We'd barely been in that garden a minute before we bumped into the first of many truly wonderful local characters, unflinchingly real and vivid, and happy to share their earthy wisdom.

"Gee whizz, howdy-do-dee, hi there, y'all!" A thick-set stranger in a magnificent Stetson appeared to the right of the garden path with a welcoming grin on his face.

"So where are you from?" asked Moth. "The United States of America: hot diggity dawg – ain't that for sure!" replied the stranger, offering us a selection of hamburgers, hot dogs and spare-ribs, with ketchup on the side.

"It's truly heart-warming to encounter so many real people from all over the globe on this, our lyrical and often painful journey of regeneration and salvation," I observed to Moth. "I wonder what our next magical meeting will entail?"

It had truly been the journey of a lifetime.

As I say, we'd walked 342 miles to get to where we were. By putting one foot in front of the other, and then repeating the process, up hill and down dale, we'd managed to create a life-affirming true story of coming to terms with grief and the healing power of the natural world.

When I set out on the path, I'd had a bit of a sniffle. But now, 63 nights later, it had completely vanished. And, in case you're asking, I have the doctors' certificates to prove it.

Up path and down path, we'd survived many adventures. We''d been drenched by a tsunami, wrestled a mountain goat, been repeatedly mistaken for Ted Hughes and Sylvia Plath, and found much-needed overnight accommodation, spacious but damp, having been unexpectedly swallowed by a blue whale.

Early one morning, Moth had awoken me with the ominous phrase, "Is that smoke I smell, love?" Imagine our horror when we discovered that the night before, we'd accidentally pitched our tent on an active volcano! Thankfully, we'd put the molten lava to good use, boiling sufficient water to give us two cups of tea on a shared tea-bag.

And all before we'd even got to the famously tricky stretch of the path from Padstow to Newquay!

Yes, our continued survival was indeed a miracle, and those who wish to misleadingly allege otherwise might frankly need reminding that our legal advice remains ongoing.

Our breakthrough first book told the powerful tale of hope triumphing over despair. Our extraordinarily powerful second book demonstrated how despair can be vanquished by hope. Our mould-breaking third book showed that if you can somehow cling onto hope, despair will never triumph.

And this was all before we got to Barnstaple. We were now onto the fourth book in the ever-popular series.

"I think it might have dried up," I said to Moth, casting an eye over the blouse I'd left in the sun after being soaked by an unexpected tidal wave the night before.

"How many more pages to go before we reach the end, love?" he moaned.

"Only 123 pages to go," I said. "But for now, the quickest way – "

" – of filling up the pages" interjected Moth.

"Would be to keep the dialogue going."

"What do you mean,'keep the dialogue going'?" asked Moth, alighting on a flower.

"Well," I suggested, "We could put just – "

"Two words – "

" – of dialogue – "

"on each – "

" – line. Yay!"

Deeply exhausted but thoroughly exhilarated, we'd almost reached the end of the garden path when a man stopped us in our tracks. It somehow struck us that he was blind, as he wore dark glasses, walked with a white stick and couldn't stop bumping into things.

"You will travel many miles," he said, "and – yes – you may encounter many obstacles along your path. But in your wisdom you have chosen the path of truth, and for this reason, you shall sell a great many copies."

So we thanked the blind seer for sharing his great wisdom with us, and bade him farewell. By now, having covered 423 miles, we kept faith with providence as it continued to lead us, and all our many millions of readers, up the garden path.

As told to
CRAIG BROWN

Nursery Times

············· Friday, Once-upon-a-time ·············

NURSERYLAND TESTS NEW ALARM SYSTEM

by Security Staff **Belle Ding-Dong**

THERE was panic across Nurseryland as a new state-of-the-art Government Emergency Alert System was tested, when the big hand was pointing to the 12 and the little hand was pointing to the 3.

At precisely that time the system was activated and a boy ran through the streets crying "Wolf! Wolf!" Unaware that this was just a test, and that there was in fact no wolf, cowering residents, including three terrified pigs, locked themselves into their homes and prepared for the worst.

The initial terror was replaced by irritation as the Nurseryland Government explained that this system needed to be tested on a regular basis.

"But what if one day there is a wolf?" asked Little Red Riding Hood. "How will we know if there really is a wolf or if the boy is just crying wolf?"

"Don't be silly," said her Grandmother, a woman known for having small teeth, "there won't be a wolf, it's never going to happen."

Late News
● Wolf Alarm goes off and no one believes it ● Red Riding-Hood in narrow escape, though Granny sadly eaten ● Three pigs lose two thirds of property empire

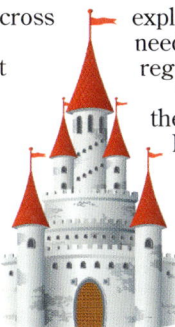

"Uh-oh... either it's a national emergency alert or Taylor Swift's engagement is off"

Why the weight-loss cheats make me mad!

by **Lizzy Thin**

"GRRRRRR! It's just so lazy, I can't believe it! There are actually people in this country who are losing weight by simply taking a tablet! Not for these fatties the toil and sweat of injecting yourself with a proper jab. Oh no! They just pop a pill and, bingo, they've lost ten stone and dropped 15 dress sizes in less than a week. Meanwhile, the rest of us have to do it the traditional way – by putting in some actual effort. Pulling up your shirt, squeezing an inch of flesh and then exercising those thumb muscles to the limit! Argh! All the idle pill poppers have to do is drink a glass of water and swallow. Where's the satisfaction in that? Where's the sense of achievement? Where's the self-discipline? No! This is just another case of taking the easy option in what I can only call Broken Britain!" *(Great! More of this! Ed.)*

Last night of the Toms 'huge success'

by Our Culture Staff **Albert Hall**

THE traditional celebration of National Pride reached new heights this weekend as the festival of the Last Night of the Toms took place in London's Trafalgar Square.

Hundreds of thousands of flag-waving enthusiasts known as 'Tomenaders' (in honour of the founder of the event, Sir Tommy Robinson) showed their patriotic fervour as they put on Union Jack hats and waistcoats and sang rousing songs such as 'Britannia Waves the Flags', 'Land of Former Tories', plus the all-time classic 'And did those feet in ancient times kick people's heads in?"

This year's event continued with tradition, as a visiting conductor, Elon Musk, was invited to orchestrate the chorus of hate. Mr Musk gave a charming speech in which he thanked the Tomenaders and urged them to rise up in a violent coup against the elected government.

His theme of uniting the kingdom through division resonated with the spirited crowd, who celebrated in the time-honoured manner by attacking the police with bottles and rocks and shouting about how Britain had become lawless.

"There was a great spirit of hatred," said one. "Which, combined with the cheap lager, made it a fight to remember."

The Last Night of the Toms brought to close a joyous season of rioting across the country, celebrating all the very best about Britain (is this right? Ed.)

"We mine Bitcoin now"

MANCHESTER'S FINEST CONFIRMS COMEBACK

by Our Madchester Correspondents **Ann Orak** and **Buck Et-Hat**

IT'S THE news millions of fans have been waiting for! The return of the one-man band who represented a generation.

Some of us were wondering if if we were ever going to see Andy Burnham play London again, but now he has been reunited with himself for one last gig in Downing Street.

The fans could not be more excited. "Andy's completely mayor for it!" said one groupie.

Everyone of a certain age will remember Burnham's foot-stomping hits: 'Don't Look Back at Corbyn' 'Wonder Red Wall', and 'Champagne SuperSocialist', and so his return is greatly anticipated, but fellow Mancunians, Oasis, are concerned he will fall out with his brothers and it will all end up in an acrimonious split.

The question of his comeback tour of Sunday news studios remains: Will he sell out? And the answer is, yes, of course he will. He's Andy Burnham.

FARAGE SAYS 'I MIS-SPOKE'

by Our Clacton Staff **Christopher Howse-Purchase**

THE leader of the Reform party admitted last night that he "mis-spoke" when addressing the issue of his property purchase in Clacton.

Farage originally claimed that he had bought a property to prove his commitment to his constituency and that this purchase demonstrated that he was a diligent local MP. But following investigations into the ownership of the property, it transpired that the property had not been bought by Farage but by his partner, thus saving Farage £44,000 in stamp duty.

Last night Farage came clean and told reporters, "When I said I mis-spoke about the house purchase I mis-spoke. I should not have used the words 'I mis-spoke' but should instead have said 'I lied'.

"It is important to be honest about these things and if you are lying, you should just admit it and not come up with disingenuous words like 'mis-spoke'."

LATE NEWS

◼ Farage refuses to disclose his tax records on the grounds that this would be a "mis-take" and that if people saw them, they might "mis- trust" him.

LATEST 'BIG BEAST' DEFECTS TO REFORM

by Our BBC Correspondent **E.Z. Questions**

FOLLOWING on from Nadine Dorries, Reform was celebrating another big-name defection to the party after their conference in Birmingham, as rumours swirled that Chris Mason had defected to Reform.

"Chris's breathless coverage of our conference could have come straight from our press office," said a jubilant Reform spokesman.

"Watching him fanboy Nigel Farage and talk up his prospects to be the next Prime Minister, despite Reform only having four MPs, left us in no doubt that Chris was one of us."

Chris Mason, however, played down the prospect of him defecting to Reform, saying, as a senior BBC political correspondent, he must remain totally impartial and in favour of the Conservative party at all times.

Israel threatens retribution

by Our Israel Correspondent **Ray Taliate**

EUROPE was braced for conflict this week, as Ireland threated to boycott the Eurovision contest if Israel was allowed to compete.

"This is an act of war," said Benjamin Netanyahu, wearing feathers and sequins. "And Israel will be perfectly justified in retaliating."

It is now expected that Israel will launch a precision surgical strike on Jedward, whilst threatening Dana with all kinds of everything.

A British Foreign Office spokesman has called for calm: "We don't want any more boom bang-a-bangs."

AFTER DOHA ATTACK, ISRAEL PUBLISHES GUIDE TO LEGITIMATE FUTURE TARGETS (ALL BELOW)

Welcome back, Cabinet 2.0. The re-reboot of the re-reset starts today.

Morgan McSweeney
We've turned what could have been a disaster into an opportunity. 👍

Is everyone clear about what their new jobs are?

David Lammy
Absolutely, Keir. What does the Deputy Prime Minister do again?

Darren Jones
A bit of DJ-ing in Ibiza, a bit of property speculation, a bit of vaping in a dinghy – you'll get the hang of it. 🌍🏠🛶

Angela Rayner
Fook off, Darren, you sycophantic twat! I haven't been removed yet.

Shabana Mahmood
Yes, you have! I'm removing everyone – and you'd better believe it.

Angela Rayner has been removed from the WhatsApp group and been sent back to where she came from. Up North. Or possibly Hove, depending on legal advice.

Yvette Cooper
Thanks for promoting me to Foreign Secretary, boss.

David Lammy
I've got some tips, Yvette, if you need some help. Number One: Get a fishing licence. You never know when you might need one. 🐟🐟🐟

Yvette Cooper
Er, boss, have you heard about Peter Mandelson?

Not now, Yvette, I'm quite busy with this total reimagination of the repurposed re-engineered reboot of a reset of a relaunch 2.0.

Morgan McSweeney
Oh dear. This really doesn't look good. And I'm not just talking about the bathrobe. 😱

I stand by him.

Morgan McSweeney
He called Epstein his best pal, told him he loved him and said yum, yum about how rich he was.

I think Peter's doing a very good and important job as UK Ambassador to the United States and he still has the full confidence of His Majesty's Government.

Morgan McSweeney
Peter supported Epstein when he was convicted for paedophilia, said the conviction was wrong and urged him to seek early release.

I still think it would be somewhat premature to leap to judgement on the basis of several unsavoury images and a few thousand emails.

Morgan McSweeney
For fuck's sake, boss! They're calling him Paedopal Mandelson!

He's fired.

Darren Jones
Swift and ruthless, boss. Good call. 💪

I've made it clear right from the very start that I have zero tolerance for this appalling lack of judgement by a man who should have known better than to associate with a man who is clearly flawed, untrustworthy and dangerous.

Morgan McSweeney
Sorry, boss, are we talking about you and Mandelson or Mandelson and Epstein? Just asking.

Due process was performed at all stages in his appointment.

Yvette Cooper
What does that even mean? Surely the clue was in the name 'Mandelson'?

Angela Rayner
It means he wanted to give the job to a big beast Blairite to fook off all the Lefties! And now he's come a right fookin' cropper!

I thought you'd got rid of Angela? Shabana, you're useless!

Shabana Mahmood
Getting rid of people is harder than I thought!

Time for another reboot. Reboot her out!

Why this is not my drawing

by **Donald J. Trump**

"No way is this drawing mine. Fact! First, I don't draw. If I did draw, I'd be the best drawer in the world. Better than the Peanuts guy. Snoopy? Rubbish! Not a nice guy. Everyone hates him. Bad dog. And if I drew a woman, it'd be the most beautiful woman in the world. Not one without any arms. Or a head. And where are the legs? In my book, a woman's got to have longly legs. Not that I've ever drawn a picture in a book for a friend's birthday. Didn't happen. I don't write books. I don't read books. Fact! I read it in a book. And anyway I would have coloured it in. I've got my own crayons. Best crayons ever. Lot of people are saying that. And look at those words. They're not mine! Where are the CAPITAL LETTERS? Where are the spolling mistakes? Where are the exclamation marks!!!!!!!!!!!!!!!!!!!! And here's the clincher. That is not my signature.

Yours factfully,
Donald J. Trump

CONSPIRACY UPDATE

THE release of Jeffrey Epstein's birthday book, containing a doodle and a signature from Donald Trump, has caused an uproar of denial from our conspiracy theorists – the ones who until twenty minutes ago were absolutely convinced there was a paedophile ring at the apex of American government!

WHO-WATCHES-THE-WATCHERS-WATCHING-THE-WATCHMEN says this on his freakish news page:

"Look it's very simple. In 2003 Donald Trump was a Democrat, which logically made him a paedophile. Now he's a Republican, which means he's not. I can't believe people are getting confused by this."

Well, there you have it! I'll sign up to that!

"I don't think there's anything wrong with echo chambers"

"I couldn't agree more"

MANDELSON CRISIS STARMER ACTS!

Speech bubble 1: Goodbye, Peter – we can't have anything to do with a friend of a paedo

Speech bubble 2: Welcome, President Trump!

SUN DESTROYS PRINCE OF DARKNESS

by Our Vampire Staff
SYLVANIA TRANS

ONE of the world's top vampires has been destroyed after exposure to the Sun.

For centuries, vampire hunters have known that being in the Sun is one of the greatest threats to a vampire's career, but rarely has it been demonstrated quite so effectively as in the case of Lord Mandelson, the Prince of Darkness.

"Like all nocturnal bloodsuckers, Peter Mandelson is notoriously difficult to kill off," said expert Dr Van Helsing. "He has come back from the dead on numerous occasions over the past 30 and indeed 1,000 years, but now he's allowed himself to appear in the Sun, on pages 1-94, it really is all over for the total Count." *(Subs, please check spelling.)*

Sharpening a stake and waving garlic, he continued, "Obviously, being a left-leaning vampire, Mandelson doesn't appear in the Mirror when you look, but he should have known better than to allow daylight into his personal and business affairs."

Mandelson's whole career has now turned to ashes and all the villagers have put down their pitchforks and are singing and dancing with joy.

Said one, "We've seen the last of him until the next time. Let's just hope he doesn't sail to Whitby in an earth-lined coffin and be resurrected as Head of the UN (dead)."

Sign: GIBSON, GIBSON & SPACEWORM SOLICITORS

"Apologies, Mr Gibson – I wrongly assumed you were someone else"

Pot accuses kettle of enabling political violence

by Our Kitchen Correspondent
DEE RANGE

IN an extraordinary outburst after the killing of a young political campaigner in the United States, the Pot has accused the Kettle of creating "a toxic atmosphere that legitimises murdering opponents".

Said the Pot, "The Kettle is an utter disgrace. In any decent country, the Kettle and his friends would be rounded up and detained indefinitely without trial. The Kettle should probably be charged as an accomplice to murder. In fact, hanging is too good for the Kettle, even on a hook in the kitchen."

Meanwhile, the Kettle has hit back at the Pot. "How dare the Pot accuse me of intemperate language and trying to create a toxic atmosphere! He is trying to blacken my name. I'm absolutely steaming. I think he should be rounded up with all his Potty mates and..." *[cont. p94]*

Newly installed US ironyometer melts down completely

by Our Irony Correspondent
Jeremy Irony

THE hugely strengthened new Ironyometer which was switched on in Washington last week, with promises that this time it could withstand any degree of irony, has immediately blown up, following the news that American right-winger and opponent of gun control Charlie Kirk was shot while talking about shootings in America.

The engineers defended themselves, saying, "There is no way that anyone could imagine anything quite this ironic occurring in the real world. It is in such bad taste that no one would make it up, and yet it just happened. We are launching a lawsuit against reality for making it impossible to do our job as Ironyometrists."

VANCE IN CHARLIE KIRK FREE SPEECH UPDATE

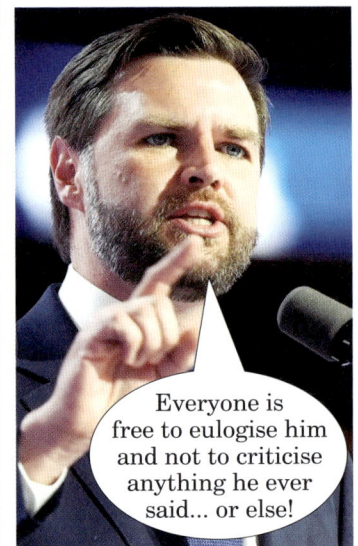

Speech bubble: Everyone is free to eulogise him and not to criticise anything he ever said... or else!

A Tank Driver writes

Vlad 'Mad' Putin, Tank No: ZZZZ

Every week a well-known tank driver gives his opinion on a matter of topical importance.

"Sorry mate. I seem to have taken a bit of a wrong turning. I was aiming for Kyiv and whaddya know, seem to have ended up in Poland. Easy mistake. And what a fuss they're making about it. It's as if they've never seen a foreign tank entering their country before. Nothing to worry about, is it? This sort of thing never escalates into anything disastrous. Calm down, Tusky! Stop getting your knickerski in a twist! What are you gonna do about it anyway? You and whose army? Not Donald's, that's for sure! I'll tell you who has got an impressive army. Not to mention nuclear missiles, underwater drones and machine gun-firing robot wolves! My mate Xi Jinping! He had me in the back of his tank the other day. Lovely vehicle. It seats ten. Or just me and Kim Jong Un. He's a big lad! I told him the secret to eternal life. It's basically all about diet and exercise – a diet of young organ donors and the exercise of untrammelled power. Bosh! Oi! Don't be sick in the back, mate – I'll charge you double!"

© A tank driver 2025.

GREAT PARABLES FROM THE BIBLE
(RETOLD FOR A MODERN AUDIENCE)

NO.94 THE RETURN OF THE PRODIGAL SON

Now there was in that land a ruler who had two sons, one of whom worked hard and was dutiful and honoured his father. And the other was a wastrel and spendthrift who recklessly squandered his inheritance and, rather than work in the family business, went into exile in a foreign land.

There, he and his wife continued to bring shame upon his poor father and even wrote a book called *Spare Us Some Money, Guv*.

And all the while the prodigal son complained to all and sundry that he had been grievously wronged by his family. Then, one day, the prodigal son decided that he was actually quite fed up with being prodigal and bored with his shameful new life where he was reduced to feeding stories to the swine in the media.

"Verily," he said, "I am short of money and I quite fancy my previous life as a much-loved Prince."

And so he did return to his own country, expecting to be greeted with open arms and to be absolved from all his sins. And he imagined his father fattening the calf and preparing a feast in his honour as he was welcomed back into the fold. But it didn't quite come to pass like that.

The prodigal son arrived in his homeland and instead of the fatted calf, he was offered the low-fat milk in a cup of tea and a selection of Duchy Original organic biscuits at Clarence House.

His father, the King, allowed him to slip in via the back door and, instead of the carpet that is red and the blowing of the joyful trumpet, he was greeted by one of his father's servants, who said, "You've got 55 minutes, matey, as your father has a very full diary and he's not feeling very well... no thanks to you."

The prodigal son was however shunned by his brother, who waxed wroth and shouteth furiously, "In his absence, I have dutifully opened fêtes and attended church and waved and smiled and smiled and waved in abundance and I am buggered if I am going to offer the branch of the olive to my whingeing and annoying bro."

And the people of that land did say, "Fair enough, you may have a point, William," and they were not too bothered when the prodigal son went home again.

AND THE MORAL OF THE STORY IS…
"To err is human, to forgive is more difficult."

Rat makes statement

THIS morning a die-hard rodent has announced that he has decided to leave his current ship and offer his services to a piece of driftwood.

"This is in no way opportunistic and only the most cynical of commentators could call this 'a case of a rat leaving the sinking ship'.

"This is a principled stand against the direction my former ship is going, which is to the bottom of the sea.

"I have thought long and hard about the merits of this piece of driftwood and have come to the conclusion that it is the only thing floating in the vicinity."

Ratty Kruger (MP and OE) continued: "This driftwood is now the natural home for principled rats everywhere."

The captain of the S.S. Badenoch has said the rat's statement has nothing to do with her scuttling the craft by heading straight to an I.C.E berg off the coast of America: "I'm determined to show that under my captainship the ship has changed to a more efficient undersea vessel."   *(Ratters)*

'Raise taxes for other people' agrees everyone

EVERYONE, from big business CEOs to small business owners to highly paid professionals and lowly paid service staff, has urged the Chancellor to tax someone else.

"We all understand the need for taxes to rise, but those taxes cannot be paid by me," agreed everyone. "Whereas someone else can no doubt afford to pay a little more."

The Treasury said it wouldn't be commenting on proposed tax rises in advance of the budget, as they didn't want Rachel Reeves to start crying again.

Clickbait headlines from history

▶ Archduke Ferdinand assassinated – you won't believe what happens next

Those seven wars Trump has ended to earn him the 2025 Nobel Peace Prize

- ■ The War of the Roses
- ■ The War of the Worlds
- ■ War for the Planet of the Apes
- ■ War Horse
- ■ World War Z
- ■ Star Wars
- ■ Civil War (pending)

POETRY CORNER

**In Memoriam
Barry Fantoni,
artist, writer, musician
and the original voice
of E.J. Thribb**

So. Farewell
Then Barry Fantoni.

"So. Farewell then"
Yes, that was
Your catchphrase.

"That was your
Catchphrase"
Yes, that too was
Your catchphrase.

You created so many
Eye jokes,
Characters
And formats.
Which live on.

Unlike yourself,
Sadly.

E.J. Thribbute (17½)

Celeb   YES, HE'S BACK!   LIGGER

WELL FOR THE USA IT GOES CALIFORNIA, ARIZONA, TEXAS, FLORIDA, THEN SPAIN, ITALY...

GARY TRYING TO MAP OUT THE FIRST STAGE OF HIS COMEBACK TOUR?

NO, TRYING TO REMEMBER ALL THE LUXURY REHAB CENTRES HE STAYED IN LAST YEAR...

IT'S ALL A BIT OF A BLUR...

Channel 5 programme search

The council has permitted an ostrich to be privately owned in Powys, new figures show.

Brecon and Radnor Express

Drug dealer from March caught with machete and 25 wraps of cocaine in his bottom

Cambridgeshire Times

Don't forget to apply for the job you saved 1 day ago: **Head of Social Media** at **Alzheimer's Society.**

LinkedIn reminder message

A REPORT in last week's *Henley Standard* stated that the Kenton Theatre in Henley had a bat problem. In fact, it has had a problem with its VAT. We apologise

Henley Standard

2 days ago — A POPULAR BBC sitcom is making a surprise return - 46 years after its last episode. The Good Life was a 1970shit TV show, which aired from...

The Sun

Seaside town 2 hours from Liverpool has beaches, hikes and very little tourists

Liverpool Post and Echo

20% LABOUR EDUCTION TAX

Post-budget tweet by Tory MP Graham Stuart

CCTV shows hero fish and chip shop staff batter knife-wielding robber

Yahoo news

Doctor charged with supplying Matthew Perry ketamine agrees to plead guilty

Get the stuff you want when you want it, with the new, refreshed Guardian app

Guardian

general downward trend in air accidents.

BBC Text Service

St Peter's Church Fete

Courtyard: STREET FOOD / PIMPS TENT

St Peter's Church, Wolvercote, Oxfordshire

The hotel is a short wank from the old quarter

Hotel review on Tripadvisor

BBC News

Yacht club assault: Man (70) who 'saw red' during billiards game avoids jail

Irish Times

Country of Origin
Ukraine
Product Information
May contain pieces of shell

Product information for walnuts on buywholefoodsonline.co.uk

BBC Late News

Are you a Small animal looking for a permanent position in North Wales?

Job ad for a veterinary surgeon position on gov.uk

Reform MP Lee Anderson backed Mr Farage, writing: 'I would not be here without Nigel. And Nigel is right. Over the next four years, Reform UK led by Nigel is going to **fight for the heart and souk of our beautiful country.**'

Mail Online

Bike ride between prisons to break offending cycle

BBC News

Marine Le Penis a lawyer and politician who ran for the French presidency in 2012, 2017 and 2022.

BBC

'We don't want people to misinterpret naturism as being lewd. That's the bottom line'

Telegraph

Sex education cannot be taught on a one-size-fits-all basis

Irish Times

Constabulary searching for Johnny Cash in connection with burglary

Hampshire Chronicle

ICELANDIC DISCOVERY

Ambassador Cruises email

Invergordon cannabis dealer has 'turned over a new leaf'

Press & Journal

In the summer of 2023, the general also levelled baseless accusations at Washington, claiming the US was supplying Kyiv with special drones carrying "infected misquotes" intended to spread malaria amongst Russian troops.

Telegraph

On: **Thursday 01 January 2099** at **11:30 am** At: **General Hospital, Radiology Reception**

Appointment confirmation letter sent to reader

The best short shorts for men – and how to pull them off

Guardian website

Huge wife breaks out at Edinburgh's Arthur's Seat

Sky News

Jesus ripped off crucifix outside Stoke-on-Trent church

Police are searching for a 'man with dark hair and a beard'

Stoke-on-Trent Live

Why you shouldn't ignore a horse voice, according to doctors

Telegraph

Australian scientists make first kangaroo embryos with IVF in 'major leap'

The Express

The Volvo EX90 is now available with rear-wheel drive for £14k less – and it goes fart...

Autocar

Cathaoirleach of Leitrim County Council Councillor Paddy O'Rourke has called for a "root and branch change" of forestry regulation

RTE

Golf Monthly   Sat 3
The ideal read for rugby fans

Email from Golf Monthly magazine

"I do sometimes forage, usually for wild garlic and wild leeks," said Mrs Gather.

BBC

Police ask public for help to find gold from stolen lavatory as they have nothing to go on

Telegraph